SAUDI ARABIA
A Case Study in Development

In the Name of Allah, the
Compassionate, the Merciful

بسم الله الرحمن الرحيم

*To the memory and the soul of the leader of
the Arab and Islamic* Ummah :
   *To the rejuvenator of the scientific, social
and industrial Renaissance and Unifier of
the Islamic* Ummah

الى روح حبيب الامة العربية وباعث النهضة
العلمية والاجتماعية والصناعية وجامع شمل
الامة الاسلامية

*AL-IMAM FAISAL IBN ABDUL
AZIZ AL-SAUD*

الامام فيصل بن عبد العزيز آل سعود

May God Rest his soul peacefully in Heaven.

تغمده الله برحمته واجزل له المثوبة والأجر

F.A.F.

SAUDI ARABIA

A Case Study in Development

Completely Revised and Updated Edition

Fouad Al-Farsy

KPI

London and New York

First published in 1982.
This edition, completely revised and updated,
published in 1986
by Kegan Paul International
11 New Fetter Lane, London EC4P 4EE,
and reprinted in 1987 and 1988.

Distributed by
Associated Book Publishers (UK) Ltd
11 New Fetter Lane, London EC4P 4EE

Routledge, Chapman & Hall Inc.
29 West 35th Street
New York, NY 10001, USA

Produced by Worts-Power Associates

Set in Ehrhardt
by Inforum Ltd, Portsmouth
and printed in Great Britain
by Redwood Burn Ltd.

ISBN 07103–0128–6

Contents

Military Institutions in Saudi Arabia
Ministry of Planning
Polycommunality and Manpower

Introduction
The Constitution: The Holy *Quran*
The Saudi Council of Ministers (*Majlis Al-Wuzara*)
The Cabinet
Institute of Public Administration, Riyadh

Introduction
United Nations Development Program (UNDP) – Riyadh
Center for Training and Applied Research in
    Community Development, Ad-Dir'iyah
The First Five Year Plan 1970–1975
    (1390–1395 AH)
The Second Five Year Plan 1975–1980
    (1395–1400 AH)
The Third Five Year Plan 1980–1985
    (1400–1405 AH)
The Strategy of the Fourth Five Year Plan
    1985–1990 (1405–1410 AH)
University Education
Higher Education
Note on Industrial Development
SABIC
Saudi Arabian Aid to the Developing World

Introduction
Synopsis of Journal Content
Synopsis of Books
SAGE Series
Social Science Research Council Committee
    on Comparative Politics (SSRC-CCP)
    (Princeton Series)
American Society for Public Administration –
    Comparative Administration Group (ASPA-CAG)
    (Duke Series)

Foreword

THIS NEWLY revised fourth edition of Dr Fouad Al-Farsy's significant study continues to be of increasing importance. Several reasons for this were developed in my Foreword to the second edition in 1982. In the intervening years since the book's first appearance in 1978, some circumstances have changed. These changes, however, in no way diminish the importance and relevance of this new edition.

The appendix in the earlier editions demonstrated incontrovertibly that Saudi Arabia was given virtually no attention in journals or books dealing with political development. It was partially to fill the lacuna that Dr. Al-Farsy undertook this study. In the near decade since, there have been only slight changes in these circumstances. Several books on Saudi Arabia have appeared, though they have not all been of scholarly quality. The works by David Holden and Richard Johns, Willard Beling, Ragaei el-Mallakh, and broader works on Islam by James Piscatori and by John Esposito certainly merit the attention of meticulous scholars. They provide a more panoramic intellectual context which did not exist in 1978 and into which the Al-Farsy volume fits comfortably.

Some thirty or forty journals and quasi-popular magazines are now being published, though they did not exist a decade ago. Many of these lack scholarly merit, but some such as the *Journal of Muslim Minority Affairs*, *American–Arab Affairs*, *Journal of South Asian and Middle Eastern Studies*, *American Journal of Islamic Studies*, *Journal of Arab Affairs*, and *Arabia* are of a high quality.

In the broader global political context in which Saudi Arabia is a pivotal country, many entities have evolved which seek to put the Kingdom, as well as Arabs generally, into a perspective of balance and understanding. I refer especially to the National Council on U.S.–Arab Relations, the American–Arab Anti-Discrimination Committee, the American–Arab Affairs Council, and the Council for the Advancement of Arab–British Understanding, to name but a few. Organizations which existed before 1978, such as the Muslim World League, and Americans for Middle East Understanding, continue their work invigorated by the somewhat more receptive context in which they now function. Finally, new books have appeared which take the offensive in placing the Arab and Islamic world in a context which refutes the stereotypes of an earlier period and which exposes the massive campaigns of disinformation generated in the United States in anti-Arab terms horrendous in their viciousness and distortion. Outstanding in this group are the books by George Ball, Paul Findley,

Michael Saba, Edmund Ghareeb, Edward Said, Noam Chomsky, Michael Jansen, Dov Yermiya, Geoffrey Aronson, C. Mayhew and Michael Adams.

This felicitous change in the intellectual environment of Arab affairs makes my earlier reference to the state of scholarship as "revealing an aridity comparable to the *Rub' al-Kahli'* somewhat less applicable than it was a decade ago. Nevertheless, analysis of the developmental experience of Saudi Arabia still has not entered into the mainstream of western scholarship. In that important respect, there is no change. And in that respect, this fourth edition by Dr. Al-Farsy still stands alone.

The reasons for the uniqueness of Saudi Arabia as a developing country to which I allude in my Foreword to the 1982 edition remain equally valid today. The galvanic impulse of the Kingdom has demonstrably aided in the recovery of Islamic identity throughout the world. The unique equation of political participation and institutionalization remains very important. Western observers fail to understand that the Kingdom has functional equivalents to political parties and legislators. These equivalents are the representative composition of the Council of Ministers, the *majlis* operating at all levels of society, and emerging interest groups such as chambers of commerce. The gradual evolution of these forms into formalized consultative entities will be of continuing interest. The cultural homogeneity of Saudi Arabia remains a critical characteristic. The problem of expatriate manpower which appears to disturb that homogeneity has not yet been resolved. The dominant position of Saudi Arabia as guardian of Holy Makkah and Medina continues unchanged.

This fourth edition, with its new analysis of the Fourth National Plan and its revised charts, is essential to an understanding of the institutional base of government which Saudi Arabia has constructed since 1932 and, at a more accelerated pace, since the 1970s. It remains a distinctive and unique contribution to our understanding of development theory and practice and of the Saudi Arabian experience in particular.

Ralph Braibanti
James B. Duke Professor of Political Science
Director, Islamic and Arabian Developmental Studies
Durham, North Carolina, U.S.A.
May 30, 1985

Preface

I WAS cautioned by many upon undertaking the writing of this work concerning the scope of the topic I had committed myself to, and the need to narrow its focus as much as possible. If I had chosen to do so, I would have defeated my purpose. My cardinal objective is to introduce a comprehensive and up-to-date document covering the most important aspects of the political development of the Kingdom of Saudi Arabia. The lack of scholarly material on Saudi Arabia strengthened my determination to pursue my objective. Chapter I does emphasize the need for such a comprehensive study of Saudi Arabia, as a young Kingdom and a fairly new country does not have sufficient relevant research material. Existing material has been inadequate and relatively out of date.

This fact necessitated two field trips in Saudi Arabia to collect data. The first was for three months in 1974 and the second was from April to June, 1975. I had anticipated limiting my second field trip to a month and a half, but discovered that the time was insufficient: it required three full months. Most of those interviewed and contacted were cooperative and I would like to extend my appreciation for their constructive help. Space does not allow mention of each by name, but my personal and individual gratitude to all those who cooperated with me is no less keenly felt.

More than ninety per cent of the material I obtained from Saudi Arabia was written in Arabic, and its translation and sometimes transliteration became a major part of my task. Whenever my own translation appears, it is indicated by the designation "F.F. translation"; if this is not indicated, the translation was done by someone else or the source was originally written in English. The glossary at the end of this work was compiled by me and is intended to be a guide to Arabic words and expressions used throughout this work.

The translation of Arabic terms and transliteration of Arabic names generally follows the system used in *The Aramco Handbook, Oil and the Middle East* (Dhahran, Saudi Arabia, 1968). When the word could not be found in that source I used the *Area Handbook for Saudi Arabia* (Washington, D.C.: Superintendent of Documents, U.S. Government Printing Office, 2nd ed., 1971). In the few instances in which neither of these sources uses the word or expression, I have used my own translation.

Transliteration from script to Roman alphabet always poses problems. For a lengthy description of transliteration from Arabic script to English and for excellent analysis of the use of Arabic words, personal names, names, and suffixes thereto, see Marshall Hodgson, *The Venture of Islam* (Chicago: The University of Chicago Press, 1974), 1: 3–22.

At this point in the opening pages of this dissertation, I would like to extend my deepest appreciation, and to express my esteem and profound respect to my advisor, Professor Ralph Braibanti, and to Professors Calvin D. Davis, Kazimierz Gryzbowski, and Richard H. Leach for their valuable academic help and sincere advice through my years of study at Duke University.

Finally, I am grateful to Sheikh 'Abd Al'Rahman Aba Alkhail, former Minister of Labor and Social Affairs; Dr. Fayz Badr, then Deputy Minister of Planning; Sheikh Muhammed Al Harakan, former Minister of Justice; Sheikh Abdullah Kamel, former Director General of the Diwan of the Council of Ministers; Sheikh Hassan Kutbi, former Minister of Pilgrimage and Endowment; Sheikh Hashim Mattouk, Deputy Minister of Interior for Passports and Nationality; Dr. Ibrahim Obaied, Deputy Minister of Communications; and Dr. Soliman Al Solaim, Minister of Commerce, for their indispensable help and suggestions.

Fouad Al-Farsy
Riyadh, June 1978

Tables

Charts

Maps

Illustrations

Section following page 160

The publishers wish to thank Associated Press, Keystone Press, Aramco and the Ministry of Information, Riyadh for their pictures

Abbreviations

AH	Anno Hijria
ARAMCO	Arabian American Oil Company
ASPA CAG	American Society for Public Administration: Comparative Administration Group (Duke Series)
CPO	Central Planning Organization (now Ministry of Planning)
IPA	Institute of Public Administration
OAPEC	Organization of Arab Petroleum Exporting Countries
OPEC	Organization of Petroleum Exporting Countries
PETROMIN	General Petroleum and Mineral Organization
PLO	Palestine Liberation Organization
SAMA	Saudi Arabian Monetary Agency
SRG	Stanford Research Group
SR	Saudi Riyal
SSRC—CCP	Social Science Research Council—Committee on Comparative Politics (Princeton Series)
TAB	Technical Assistance Board

Introduction

FOR A variety of reasons, few would deny the vital importance of the Kingdom of Saudi Arabia. First, it is strategically located as a bridge between the Western World and Asia. With Africa on one side and Iran and South Asia on the other, it is in the middle of the strategically important Indian Ocean area which is a zone of contention between the Communist and non-Communist centers of power. Secondly, Saudi Arabia's unique form of government suggests its significance to comparative politics and to development studies generally. The only nation to use a sacred scripture, namely the *Quran*, as a Constitution, it is adjusting well to the conditions of the twentieth century while sustaining its distinctive Islamic identity. The fact that Islam appears not to be an obstacle or a hindrance towards progress and development suggests that a secular system is not necessarily a prerequisite for progress. King Faisal on a State visit to Malaysia stated that he felt

> sorry for those who think Islam . . . impedes progress or stands as an obstacle in the way of advanced development. Those who think so must have not understood [the] essential principles of Islam. The opposite is the truth. The most important requirements Islam calls for are: to maintain progress, to carry out justice, to create equality, and to breed in people good behavior and in nations moral conduct.[1]

A third reason for the importance of Saudi Arabia is the crucial importance of its vast petroleum deposits which add more political and economic weight to the Kingdom's position. This has been demonstrated successfully since 1974 and will be felt more strongly for decades to come. Saudi Arabia, at the end of 1974,

> ranked as the third largest oil producer in the world with a level of production reaching 3,095,088,427 barrels during 1974, averaging 8,479,694 barrels per day, [representing 15.2% of the total daily oil production of the world] an increase of 11.6% in comparison with that of 1973. . . . The government . . . revenue [throughout 1974 totaled] $22.6 billion, an amount equivalent to more than five times as much as that received during 1973. . . . [More important is the fact that] the Kingdom of Saudi Arabia is still in the leading position in the world

oil industry, [with a] proven crude oil reserve reaching 141 billion barrels at the end of 1974, representing the largest amount owned by any single oil producing country.[2]

These figures indicate the country's potential and strategic importance. This petroleum production creates a condition of development in the context of enormous wealth rather than abject poverty. Such developmental affluence is shared only by Kuwait, the United Arab Emirates, Bahrain and Qatar. But these are small states compared with Saudi Arabia which geographically and economically is a major state in the Middle East.

Fourthly, and most important, is the fact that Saudi Arabia is the religious site for more than 700 million Muslims all over the world. This cannot be overlooked, especially when it is realized that Islam to Muslims is a way of life closely intertwined with daily living. Religion plays a very important role in a Muslim's life. This significance of religion is starting to fade away in at least two major religions of the world: Christianity and Judaism. In brief, Saudi Arabia's political and religious impact is tremendous and should be accounted for when dealing with the status of the Kingdom domestically, regionally, and internationally.

Fifthly, Saudi Arabia is a unique model in nation building in which a country within two decades has been able to transform its polity from the conditions of the eighteenth century to those of the twentieth century. Modernization and development occurred and is still occurring at a slower but forceful pace and in a manner which will enable the Kingdom to maintain and preserve its culture, heritage, and distinctive identity. Most developing countries of the world risk the loss of their cultural identity while modern transformation takes place. Alien societal norms and values, not in harmony with these nations' heritages and cultures, seem to overwhelm indigenous values.

The author unequivocally agrees with Ralph Braibanti's profound appraisal of the significance of Saudi Arabia's unique political system among the developing nations.

Braibanti has stated that

It has long been a theoretical ideal that transnationally induced change should be carefully articulated to the cultural context of the recipient nation. . . . A prerequisite of this is that the recipient nation identify and evaluate its own values and control both the quality and the rate of introduction of outside ideas which will modify these values.

There are only three political systems in the world in which a conscious effort is made to control the admission of transnationally induced values in this way. . . . Saudi Arabia [is one of these three political systems].[3]

A final and no less important reason for treating Saudi Arabia as a unique case is the fact that the Kingdom has strongly maintained an equilibrium in the process of establishing its political system *vis-à-vis* the various sequences and stages of development.

Ideally a strong institutional base should be constructed before demands (inputs) escalate to a point at which they cannot easily be converted into effective governmental responses (output). This has not happened in most developing systems simply because the rapid expansion of mass participation and the idiosyncratic influences of foreign assistance which stimulate escalation of demands have made this impossible.[4]

Fortunately, Saudi Arabia's control over external influences on its own values and its ability to sponsor and finance its needed foreign assistance has made it possible to control—to a great extent—the process of its development. The freedom thus provided by enormous wealth is a condition not enjoyed by most developing countries.

The uniqueness of the Kingdom is manifested in its political developmental process which can be characterized by the relatively even development of institutions which have been selected as targets either by design or default. Braibanti characterizes it thus: "... [the] building of Saudi Arabian institutions start[ed] almost *de novo* [largely in the early 1950s]. The institutions which exist are of relatively equal organizational strength and viability."[5] In a sense there exist two separate spheres of legal validity in Saudi Arabia. The judicial system based on *Shari'ah* and the administrative, commercial, labor, and military institutions based on Western norms, each capable of coping with current needs, and each in its own sphere of influence.

The primary objective of this work is to deal as comprehensively as possible with the development of Saudi Arabia as a political system. The need for such a study is suggested, in part, by the findings in the Appendix, which demonstrate the critical inadequacy of materials dealing with Saudi Arabia.

Since the Kingdom of Saudi Arabia is a comparatively new country, access to documentary materials is particularly difficult. Very little research on government of the Kingdom has gone on in the past. Although organizations such as the Ministry of Planning and the Institute of Public Administration do exist, the opportunities for research are limited. A further drawback is the fact that virtually all materials are in Arabic and hence must be translated. Although there is now a trend to publish more materials in English, this was not the case at the time the research for this case study was done. A major contribution, therefore, of this case study is the translation of materials from Arabic to English. Most of the tables and charts in this case study appear here in English for the first time.

Translation took up a major portion of the total length of time spent on the research. The ordering and systematizing of materials and the description of institutions operating in Saudi Arabia's government are another contribution. When enough descriptive data have been compiled, further analysis can be made of the adequacy of the functioning of the system. But for the moment, the ordering of data, with whatever analysis is possible, seems to be the only feasible course of action.

F.A.F. (*Riyadh, 1980*)

[1] Kingdom of Saudi Arabia, Ministry of the Interior, General Directorate of Passports and Nationality, *Pilgrims' Statistics for 1391 A.H.–1971 A.D.*

[2] Sheikh Ahmad Zaki Yamani, *Petroleum Statistical Bulletin, 1975, No. 6,* Ministry of Petroleum and Mineral Resources, Economics Department, Kingdom of Saudi Arabia (Riyadh, Saudi Arabia: Al-Mutawa Press, 1975), p. 5.

[3] Ralph Braibanti, *Saudi Arabia: Contextual Considerations* (Report submitted to the Ford Foundation, Beirut, Lebanon, August, 1972), pp. 2–3 (typewritten).

[4] Ibid., p. 3.

[5] Braibanti, *Saudi Arabia: Contextual Considerations*, p. 4.

Introduction to the fourth edition (Riyadh, *1985*)

IN THE last ten years, the Kingdom of Saudi Arabia has undergone a remarkable transformation. A national development program has been conceived and implemented on a scale which is without parallel. A modern infrastructure has been built; social services and facilities have been developed; and the challenging process of diversifying the economy and sources of national income has been begun. Progress which in some other societies has taken a hundred years or more has been accomplished in Saudi Arabia in one decade.

This transformation is well-documented in facts and figures; and is amply demonstrated by the many new buildings in the cities and towns; by the roads that link them; by the schools and hospitals which serve them; by the new airports and seaports which facilitate the movement of people and goods.

It is one purpose of this book to give the reader some impression of the pace of this development and the scale of this achievement. At the same time, it would be foolish to pretend that a single volume can fully document what must be an unprecedented economic and social phenomenon. Furthermore, as changes and developments continue, even the more modest ambition of providing up-to-date statistics on the subjects which are treated is frustrated. Wherever possible, I have supplemented the data supplied in previous editions (and retained here for historical interest) with current information but, because of the rate of change, no work of this type can ever be entirely up-to-date.

Amidst all the statistical data, it should be remembered that the visible evidence of the Kingdom's development (the buildings and the roads, the ports and the industrial complexes) are effects, not causes. The causes are the skills and efforts of people and the vision of those who have planned what has now been achieved. At a crucial time in its history, when extraordinary demands were to be made upon its adaptability, its resilience and its good sense, the Kingdom of Saudi Arabia has been most fortunate in benefitting from the vision and wise government of King Fahd Ibn Abdul Aziz.

F.A.F. (Riyadh, 1985)

CHAPTER I

Historical and Cultural Background of Saudi Arabia

Only the Prophet Mohammed and his immediate successors in the seventh century had been able to unify the Arabian Peninsula, consolidate control and establish an enduring state. How had they managed to neutralize and subject to the requirements of stability and order the fierce conflicting loyalties of towns and tribes? Like the Prophet before him, like his eighteenth century forebears, Ibn Saud, King Abdul Aziz Al Saud in seeking an answer to his problem found an initial [yet utterly effective] ally in religion.[1]

Introduction

INDEED, IT was Islam that had led to the emergence of the Arabian Empire, and unified the Arabs not only in the Arabian Peninsula, but also from Asia to the Atlantic Ocean during the seventh and eighth centuries. Again in the early years of the twentieth century King Abdul Aziz Al Sa'ud, "by the name of God and the force of his right hand," consolidated his control over the major parts of the Arabian Peninsula. Saudi Arabia was officially proclaimed fully sovereign on September 22, 1932.

In unifying the Arab States into one cohesive nation it was Islam, which, like a spinning wheel, wove the various Arab peoples together in one strong fabric. It was the tie of faith rather than anything else which enabled King Abdul Aziz to found his kingdom; and if Arabs are ever destined to unite again in one nation or in a federation of nations it will be through their religion.

Something similar, though not identical, happened in the United States. In its early years, almost everybody had one thing in common: their religion. Moreover, in many colonies a religious perspective was a significant part of the culture. One could say that, in terms of their overall cultural philosophy and orientation, Americans were originally religious people, though not necessarily in terms of the practice of religion. Early leaders did not always practice religion or attend church regularly, but they thought of themselves as Christians. Briefly, a general belief in Christianity was and is the American consensus over religion. The American people's adherence to Judaeo-Christian ethics was influential in forming and solidifying the American nation of today.

This chapter deals first with geographical considerations relating to the Kingdom of Saudi Arabia. The second part of this chapter will discuss Islam, its rise and its foundations, together with Wahhabism, in order to develop a better understanding of the Wahhabi movement. The third part will survey Saudi Arabian foreign relations with the Western Powers from 1915 through 1953. The fourth and final part will treat the consolidation of the Saudi nation by King Abdul Aziz Al Sa'ud through a period of more than twenty years since the king's successful recapture of Riyadh in 1902.

Since the contemporary period of Saudi Arabia along with the history of its petroleum are of great importance, they will be dealt with in detail in the following chapter.

Geographical Considerations

The Kingdom of Saudi Arabia encompasses about four-fifths of the Arabian Peninsula. It had a population of just over seven million according to the census of 1974, a figure estimated to have risen by one million, including the immigrant workforce, by 1978. The Kingdom's area is just over a million square miles, one-third the size of the United States of America. Saudi Arabia has a population density of six persons per square mile, a figure roughly comparable to the population density of the United States in 1790. The Kingdom is bounded on the north by Jordan, Iraq and Kuwait; on the east by the Gulf, Bahrain, Qatar and the United Arab Emirates (consisting of Abu-Dhabi, Dubai, Sharjah, Ras Al-Khaimah, Fujairah, Umm Al-Qawain and Ajman); on the south by the Sultanate of Oman and the two Yemeni Republics (North and South), and on the west by the Red Sea. Aside from the country's religious and economic significance, "the potential importance of Saudi Arabia's geographical position is quickly apparent: it is strategically located between Africa and mainland Asia, lies close to the Suez Canal and has frontiers on both the Red Sea and the Arabian Gulf."[2]

Geographically, Saudi Arabia is divided into four (and if the Rub'al-Khali is included, five) major regions. The first is Najd, a high country in the heart of the Kingdom; secondly, Hijaz, the region along which lies the Red Sea coast. The region of Asir, in the southern Red Sea–Yemen border area, constitutes the third region. Finally, there is Al-Hasa, the sandy and stormy eastern part of Saudi Arabia, the richest of all the regions in petroleum (see map opposite).

The Asir region is the relatively fertile area of coastal mountains in the extreme southwest (near North Yemen). Mountain peaks rise to 10,000 feet, with ample rainfall for cultivation.

The Hijaz includes the balance of the west coast region, along with the

The potential importance of Saudi Arabia's geographical position is apparent: it is strategically located between Africa and mainland Asia, lies close to the Suez Canal and has frontiers on both the Red Sea and the Arabian Gulf.

mountain chain decreasing gradually in elevation as it moves northward, and the coastal plain bordering the Red Sea widening slightly. In this region is the busy seaport of Jiddah, known as Islamic Port of Jiddah, the major business center of the Kingdom. Most important is that the Hijaz region contains the holiest cities of Islam – Makkah and Medina – which are visited by well over a million Muslims annually.

The Najd region, considered the heart of the Arabian Peninsula, is a vast eroded plateau. At its center is the Royal capital of Riyadh. Most of the Najd region is arid, with some oases in the north around Buraydah and Unaizah.

The Al-Hasa region, also called the Eastern Province, is the country's wealthiest part, containing its massive petroleum resources. The head-quarters of the Arabian–American Oil Company (Aramco) is located in this region in Dhahran, a few miles from the administrative capital and port of Dammam. Ras Tanura, the world's largest petroleum port, is located to the north of Dhahran. Up the coast is the site of the Kingdom's new industrial complex at Jubail. The fertile oasis-cities of Qatif and Hofof are also located here.

Topographically, the Kingdom is a gently tilted plateau which slopes eastward from a coastal mountain range along its western edge bordering the Red Sea. In the south is the famous Rub'al-Khali (the Empty Quarter), a massive, trackless expanse of shifting sand dunes – the largest desert in the world (*see* Glossary).

The climate is basically hot and very dry. Along the Kingdom's coastal regions, such as at Jiddah and Dammam, there is a humid climate which prevails for almost six months of each year. There are also some temperate mountain locales as in Ta'if and Abha. During the long summer months, midday temperatures may soar to 120°F, though other seasons are generally mild and pleasant. The Kingdom does not include any lakes or permanent streams of water, and some areas may have to go without rainfall for long periods. Average precipitation ranges from three inches yearly up to twenty inches in the mountains of the country's southwest area.

For administrative purposes, Saudi Arabia is divided into five major provinces: the Western (Hijaz), the Central (Najd), Eastern (Al-Hasa), Southern (Asir) and the Northern Frontier provinces. The first of these is the Western Province (historically known as Hijaz and Asir) which is called in Arabic *Al-Mantika al-Gharbia*. This is a coastal plain confined within a narrow space by mountains dropping sharply toward the Red Sea. Four of Saudi Arabia's major cities are located in the Western Province. Makkah, which is the holiest city to all Muslims, is the first of these with a population over 350,000. This figure goes up to some two million during the pilgrimage season – the Hajj.[3] In the Hajj of 1974, the actual number of pilgrims was 1,122,545[4] and in 1977 1,627,589.

Makkah's climate is a dry one – very hot in the summer with mild weather during the night and never colder than fifty degrees in the winter. Jiddah, the second of the four cities, is a seaport on the Red Sea with a population of over 500,000. It is the Kingdom's leading commercial center. Jiddah has been the diplomatic capital of the Kingdom, though this role will be assumed by Riyadh with the removal of the diplomatic corps currently taking place. The forty-mile distance between Jiddah and Makkah is connected by a wide, modern highway. The climate in Jiddah, as a coastal city on the Red Sea, is hot and humid in the summer with a very mild winter. The third major city of the Western region, Medina, the second holiest to Muslims, has a population of 198,000 (1974). With very dry weather, Medina is extremely hot in the summer with mild weather at night, yet very cold in the winter. Another major city in the Western Province, Ta'if, with a population of 205,000 (1974), is the summer site of the Saudi government. It is approximately 6,000 feet above sea level with a pleasant climate in summer, cold and rainy in the winter. A new urban and industrial complex at Yanbu, north of Jiddah, is under construction, and will be connected by oil and gas pipe lines to Jubail on the east coast.

In the Central Province – *Al-Mantika al-Wosta* (Najd) – Riyadh, the Royal capital, is located. Riyadh's climate is a dry one, very much the same as that of Medina; that is, a desert climate.

The third is the Eastern Province, *Al-Mantika al-Sharkiya*, which is the richest of the Kingdom in petroleum. Most of the country's known petroleum reserves lie underneath its soil. The port city of Dammam on the Arabian Gulf is connected by a 600-kilometer railroad to Riyadh. Dammam and Dhahran, along with nearby Al-Khobar, are fast growing into a consolidated metropolitan area.

The fourth is the Southern Province, *Al-Mantika al-Janubiya* (Asir), which includes the major towns of Abha, Jizan and Najran. At the present time the emphasis in the Southern Province is focused on agriculture and on the modernization of the area to become one of the Kingdom's summer resort areas.

Finally, there is the Northern Province, *Al-Mantika al-Shamaliya*, which neighbors Jordan and Iraq at the most northern part of Saudi Arabia.

The Rise of Islam

Moslem Arabs, heirs of the Semitic tradition . . . held aloft the torch of enlightenment throughout a large portion of the civilized world. From their Syrian capital Damascus, they ruled an empire extending from the Atlantic to central Asia. From their subsequent capital Baghdad, they spread their translations and renditions of Greek, Persian and Indian philosophy, science and literature throughout the vast domain. From

Moslem Spain, Sicily and crusading Syria, some of these intellectual treasures passed on to Europe to become a vital force in its modern renaissance.[5]

The history of the Arabs since the Hijrah[6] (AD 622) reveals the salient fact that only under Islam did Muslims unite, consequently becoming more powerful. Once united, they ruled an empire for more than two hundred years. Before the rise of Islam in the seventh century, the Arabian Peninsula was under diverse and various external influences.

During the fifth and sixth centuries AD the northwest of Arabia was held by the Ghassanids,

> who claimed descent from one of the South Arabian tribes, and were under Byzantine influence; in the northeast the Lakhmids of the Kingdom of Hira were under the protection of the Sassanid Persians. In the south the remains of the Himyarite Kingdom was controlled first by the Christian Abyssinians and later by the Persians.[7]

It was only during the fourth century AD that towns began to take shape in South Arabia, due to the proximity of major trade routes, especially along the west and east coasts. Among these towns was Makkah, which was an aggregation of tribal groups, the most important of which was the Quraysh tribe. It was from the Quraysh that the Prophet Muhammad *Alayhi al-Salah wa Salam* (peace and prayer be upon him) was descended. Before the rise of Islam in Arabia

> the primitive religion of the desert was restricted to the worship of trees and streams and stones in which the deity was supposed to reside. . . . Nomads had naturally no temples or priesthoods, they usually carried their gods with them in a tent or tabernacle, and consulted them by casting lots with arrows, while their Kahins (high priests) or soothsayers delivered oracles in short rhymed sentences.[8]

Within Makkah itself tribes worshipped idols placed around and over the *Ka'bah*. In such a heterodox religious atmosphere, Muhammad was born in AD 570, in Makkah, of the Quraysh, the keepers and protectors of the *Ka'bah*.

Since the purpose of this part of the work is to familiarize the reader with the origins of Islam and is not a historical chronology of the religion, the following pages will deal with the five Pillars of the Islamic religion.

Al-Shahadah

The first of the five tenets of Islam is the testimony and the pronouncing of the words that "There is no God but Allah and Muhammad is His Prophet." This *Shahadah*, or testimony, when recited by a person of sincerity, sound capacity and without any mental reservations, consti-tutes the first major requirement for being a Muslim. Of parallel importance and in accordance with the *Shahadah* is the solemn belief in a general resurrection, in the final day of judgment, in all the prophets of God and in the Scriptures of God – that is, the *Quran* (widely referred to by Muslims as *Al-Quran Al-Karim*), the Pentateuch and the Christian Gospels.

Al-Salah (Prayer)

Prayers are of such great significance that some leading scholars of the religion describe them as the backbone of Islam. Each Muslim is required to pray five times daily, in a prescribed manner. The first prayer is at dawn, the next is at high noon. Then in the afternoon, after sunset and finally at night. The formalized prayer consists of a sequence of obeisances made first from a standing position and then from a kneeling one. Inseparable from prayers in Islam is the *Tahara*, that is, the complete cleanliness of clothes, body and place. Without the *Tahara*, a Muslim's prayers will be rendered null. It is the Muslim's obligation, therefore, to be clean at the time of each prayer before facing his Creator. Emphasizing the importance of bodily cleanliness, Allah is quoted in the *Quran*

> O ye who believe! When ye prepare for prayer, wash your faces, and your hands (and arms) to the elbows; rub your heads (with water); and (wash) your feet to the ankles. If ye are in a state of ceremonial impurity, bathe your whole body. But if ye are ill, or on a journey, or one of you cometh from offices of nature, or ye have been in contact with women, and ye find no water, then take for yourselves clean sand or earth, and rub there with your faces and hands. God doth not wish to place you in a difficulty, but to make you clean.[9]

Indeed, these verses of the *Quran* are but a small manifestation of the tremendous emphasis on cleanliness of Islam and its demand for purification. It should be noted here, and before moving to the third tenet of Islam, that the most important thing in prayer is total devotion and solemnity before God.

Al-Siyam (Fasting)

The imposition of fasting, which means complete abstention from food and drink from sunrise until sunset during the month of *Ramadan*, is the third basic tenet of the Islamic religion. *Ramadan* is the ninth month of the Arabian calendar, which consists of twelve lunar months. Therefore, the Arabian lunar month is either twenty-nine or thirty days but never thirty-one days.[10] Fasting in *Ramadan*, besides being a religious duty, is no doubt of great benefit as it trains one to be patient, wise, well disciplined and to share the feelings of others. In *Surat Al Baqara* of the *Quran* in speaking of fasting the Almighty Allah says

O ye who believe! Fasting is prescribed to you as it was prescribed to those before you, that ye may (learn) Self-restraint, . . . (Fasting) for a fixed number of days; but if any of you is ill, or on a journey, the prescribed number (should be made up) from days later. For those who can do it (with hardship), is a ransom, the feeding of one that is indigent. But he that will give more, of his own free will, . . . it is better for him. And it is better for you that ye fast, if ye only knew.[11]

Al-Zaka (Almsgiving)

In various parts of the *Quran* great stress is laid on the *Zaka*, that is, almsgiving to those who deserve it. Each able Muslim should give a certain percentage of his annual income, either in money or kind, to the poor and the indigent. In Saudi Arabia, the religious obligation of *Al-Zaka* has been officially recognized by the establishment of the Department of *Zaka* under the auspices of the Ministry of Finance. *Al-Zaka* on the individual's annual income from any legal source amounts to almost two and a half per cent. It is believed that one of the reasons for the imposition of *Al-Zaka* is the fact that Islam calls for the purity of both the soul and the body. Since it is required from the rich to satisfy the needs of the poor, the paying of *Al-Zaka*, no doubt, enhances amity and caring within society and strengthens the relationship between the wealthy and the indigent. It reflects fulfillment of an early concept of social justice, as it is taken from each person according to his capacity. The Book of God, the *Quran*, says "Take of their wealth a portion (as charity) to purify them by it", and who better qualified than God Almighty to stress the significance of *Al-Zaka* as a humanitarian source in Islam?

Al-Hajj (The Pilgrimage)

The fifth and last Pillar of Islam is the *Hajj*. It is explicitly stated in the Holy *Quran* that every physically and financially able Muslim should make the *Hajj* to Makkah once in his or her lifetime. The *Hajj* is considered the final culmination of each Muslim's religious duties and aspiration. Statistics obtained from the Saudi Ministry of *Al-Hajj* and *Awqaf* (Endowment) and the General Directorate of Passport and Nationality of the Saudi Ministry of Interior reveal the intensity of Islamic devotion within the ten countries under survey. Table 1.1 measures the flow of Muslims from various Islamic nations to Saudi Arabia during the *Hajj* season from 1964 to 1974. Table 1.2 shows the number (in millions) between 1970 and 1984. The countries surveyed are ranked according to the proportion of their population making the *Hajj*. The results reflect a single criterion of religious feeling, but this is nevertheless a helpful means by which to judge the degree of devotion among the Muslims of the different countries. Due to monetary and financial constraints adopted by some of the countries included in the

1.1 Number of Pilgrims Making the Hajj from Selected Muslim Countries

	Turkey	Iran	Nigeria	Egypt	Indonesia	Syria	Sudan	Libya	Jordan	Lebanon
1964	21602	19073	12299	18683	15234	20918	14050	12181	8771	4371
1965	25984	24937	7623	19495	15291	18458	6454	14788	10434	5409
1966	39309	35334	8535	10005	16130	19208	20168	18326	7380	4762
1967	41998	22903	10790	7134	17569	14521	18035	10444	4449	3563
1968	51055	13642	16177	12413	17062	12814	21649	16565	5179	3901
1969	56578	15132	24185	10875	10615	22383	20495	13547	6376	4570
1970	13269	48367	35187	11490	14633	42339	14865	11835	10909	6712
1971	23922	30299	14061	29171	22753	27045	29004	16861	15933	6404
1972	27235	45298	48981	39606	22659	31777	29506	23774	25819	6715
1973	36258	57230	38869	36452	40668	10448	33222	30705	12851	5355
1974	106045	57314	51764	89617	68872	31583	42084	30715	19391	9525
Total number of pilgrims (2,537,228)	443255	369529	298471	284941	261486	251494	239532	199741	127492	61287
Total population in millions	35563	28668	66174	33329	121198	6098	15312	1880	2317	2787
Country's % of Muslims	90	98	75	93	90	87	82	99	90	57

Note: Pilgrims figures of this table do not include the number of foreign pilgrims having residence permits in Saudi Arabia. The Hajj season starts officially on the first day of the Rajab month of each year.

Source: Figures were obtained by the author from the Office of the Saudi Minister of Pilgrimage and Endowment and from the Passports and Nationality Affairs of the Saudi Ministry of the Interior, Riyadh, Saudi Arabia, May–June 1975.

surveys, not everyone wishing to make the *Hajj* is able to go. In some of these countries, Muslims wishing to make the *Hajj* are required to submit an application to the local authorities. The authority in charge of the *Hajj* applications then selects at random up to a total for the year which the government concerned will authorize. The results shown in Table 1.1 reveal that the first three countries of the survey are Turkey, Iran and Nigeria – Muslim, but not Arab, countries. This finding is a manifestation of the strength of Islam in areas thousands of miles away from the Holy cities in Saudi Arabia. As for the next three ranking countries of the survey, Egypt, Indonesia and Syria, the figures in Table 1.1 show that Syria, despite being ranked as sixth, appears in a better position than both Egypt and Indonesia.

Lebanon, being in a unique situation because of its substantial Christian community, cannot be compared with the other countries.

When dealing with the *Hajj*, the fifth Pillar of Islam, one must pause and give special attention to its meaning and implications. The fulfillment of this corner of the Islamic religion is mandatory, providing that it is not financially or physically impossible. Perhaps more should be said about this principle. Muslims from all over the world seek to make the *Hajj* to Makkah, which occurs between the eighth and thirteenth days of the last month of the Islamic calendar – *Dhu al-Hijjah* – of each year. Muslims travel thousands of miles to reach Makkah for the *Hajj* and perform the rituals in the same manner as the Prophet Muhammad (*Alayhi al-Salah wa Salam*) almost fourteen centuries ago.

In Islam, the *Salah* (prayers) five times a day is considered the backbone of religion. It can be individually practised, although it is strongly urged that Muslims perform the *Salah* in groups whenever possible. Thus a delicate equilibrium between the importance of worshipping God in solitude and of individual worship in the company of others has been established.

Equally, *al-Shahadah*, the first tenet of the religion, may be considered an individual self-practice which is performed upon accepting the Islamic religion. The Faith does not require any rigid rules at certain times for its fulfillment. *Al-Zaka* (almsgiving), similarly, may be implemented by individuals and by the government; and in the former case, it is done at the person's own recognizance without any outside control. Therefore, this principle of Islam also is a self-practised duty.

Al-Siyam (fasting) must be observed during the *Ramadan* of each year. This pillar of the religion can be maintained in any part of the world with no difficulty at all. Consequently, *Al-Siyam* is also a self-practised religious duty which is fulfilled on an individual basis.

The performance of the *Hajj* is different from the other four Pillars of the faith. The *Hajj* must be performed between the eighth and the thirteenth day of *Dhu al-Hajjah* in Makkah and within an explicitly limited geographical area between *Mina-Muzdalfah* and *Arafat*. It is a true indication of a Muslim's dedication to his religion, involving personal, physical, and financial burdens.

The *Hajj* is a spiritual experience which a Muslim shares and practises jointly with the whole Islamic nation. Nonetheless,

> at no other place and on no other occasion in his [or her] lifetime does the believer feel so intensely and confidently that he is approaching a merciful, responsive and loving God. It is well-nigh impossible to convey the vividness of the experience and the sense of elation of the pilgrim during this [though conducted in a massive manner] essentially personal apprehension of Divine presence and grace. At Arafat, [where all the pilgrims gather en masse on the ninth day of Dhu al-Hijjah for the Wakfa (the standing) which is the culmination yet not the end of the Hajj] a Muslim's devotional life reaches its culmination. It is the feeling of many that this is [indeed] the closest man can come to an encounter with God on earth.[12]

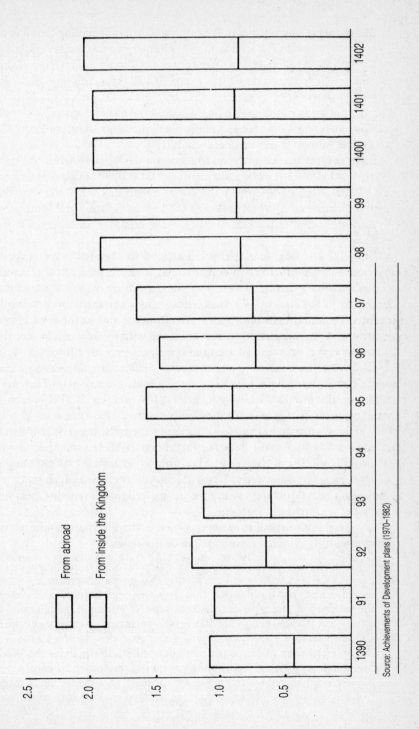

1.2 **Number of Pilgrims (in millions)**

From abroad

From inside the Kingdom

Source: Achievements of Development plans (1970–1982)

The *Hajj* truly reflects

that major, unparalleled contribution of Islam [which] is in the area of
racial harmony and the brotherhood of the faithful. The Hajj is Islam's
key instrument for creating and strengthening fraternal ties among
millions of its followers. Pilgrims representing every conceivable color,
country and tongue yearly converge upon Makkah. Here, they share
common objectives and beliefs, and perform the same devotions. . . .
The Hajj inspires in the believer an unrivalled sense of solidarity, a
feeling of identification in a world of alienation. The believer feels
himself a part of the whole system of the cosmos. Whether in Mina or
Michigan, Arafat or Zululand, no man, no woman, no nation is an island.
In this reunion convened annually by God from the time of Abraham,
ties of brotherhood and love are forged among people representing the
nations of the earth.[13]

Before proceeding to the third part of this chapter, it is perhaps
appropriate to make a brief reference to the Wahhabi movement of Saudi
Arabia. A brief examination of Wahhabism will be sufficient to inform
the reader of the essence, which has sometimes been misunderstood, of
the movement. Since Wahhabism is concomitant to the events which led
to the formation of Saudi Arabia by King Abdul Aziz Al Sa'ud, the
history of the Wahhabi movement will be dealt with concurrently, in the
fourth part of this chapter, with the consolidation of the Kingdom by
King Abdul Aziz at the opening of the current century. A survey of
various books, both in English and Arabic, that have dealt with Wahhabism demonstrates that no one could be better qualified than King Abdul
Aziz Al Sa'ud to explain the true significance and meaning of Wahhabism.
In a speech delivered by His Majesty King Abdul Aziz Al Sa'ud in
Makkah, at the Royal Palace on May 11, 1929, the King said that

They call us the "Wahhabis" and they call our creed a "Wahhabi" one as
if it were a special one . . . and this is an extremely erroneous allegation
that has arisen from the false propaganda launched by those who had ill
feelings as well as ill intentions towards the movement. We are not
proclaiming a new creed or a new dogma. Muhammad ibn Abdul
Wahhab did not come with anything new. Our creed is the creed of
those good people who preceded us and which came in the Book of God
(the *Quran*) as well as that of his Messenger (the prophet Muhammad,
prayer and peace be upon him).

And we respect the four Imams. We hold no preference between
Malike and al Shafie, Ahmad and Abu-Hanifa; in our view they are all
to be respected by us.

This is the creed which Sheikh al-Islam Muhammad ibn Abdul
Wahhab is calling for, and it is our creed. It is a creed built on the
oneness of the Almighty God, totally for His sake, and it is divorced from
any ills or false innovation. The Unitarian creed is the creed or dogma
which we are calling for, and it is the one which will save us from
calamity and catastrophe.[14]

Relations with Foreign Powers (1902–1953)

The significance of this period is that 1902 was the year in which King Abdul Aziz captured Riyadh, regaining for the Saudi dynasty control of their homeland which they had been forced to leave at the end of the nineteenth century, and that 1953 was the year in which King Abdul Aziz died. The Saudi dynasty had fled to Kuwait from Riyadh and had settled there for almost twelve years before King Abdul Aziz's brilliant maneuver.

For centuries, the Arabian Peninsula was so isolated that it had virtually no relations with any outside power except occasionally with Turkey and Egypt. The "almost-an-island" of Arabia, a synonym of the Arabian Peninsula, was divided between different tribes fighting each other; there was never a great need for foreign relations.

The first sign of contact with the Western powers came when Shakespeare, the British Consul, was sent to meet King Abdul Aziz in Riyadh in August, 1914. King Abdul Aziz had succeeded not only in consolidating his control in the Najd but also in Al-Hasa, the easternmost part of Arabia. Furthermore, by 1926 King Abdul Aziz gained control of the Hijaz and was proclaimed on the 8th of January of that year, with the widespread approval of the people of Al Hijaz, King of Hijaz and Sultan of Najd and its Dependencies. Thus after many centuries came the man who was destined to unite the greater part of the Arabian Peninsula into one state, the Kingdom of Saudi Arabia.

Saudi–British Relations

By 1915, the first major contact with a Western major power had occurred. "On December 26, 1915, Britain and Ibn Saud [King Abdul Aziz Al Sa'ud is widely known to the West as Ibn Saud] signed a treaty that secured the latter's benevolent neutrality."[15] In return, Britain recognized Ibn Saud's undisputed sovereignty over Najd and Al-Hasa. From 1915 through 1949, "Saudi Arabian-British relations [were] determined by the encircling presence of more than a dozen political entities, vestiges of former empires still under the suzerainty of Great Britain, which dot the rim of the Arabian Peninsula."[16]

Consequently, as events developed in the decade following 1915, King Abdul Aziz had become by 1926 the sole ruler of most of the Arabian Peninsula. In 1927, Saudi Arabia and Britain entered into full diplomatic relations at the ambassadorial level, when Britain recognized the sovereignty of Ibn Saud as the King of Hijaz and Sultan of Najd and its Dependencies. As a *quid pro quo*, Saudi Arabia acknowledged Britain's rights in Bahrain and other political entities in the area. Relations with Britain remained traditionally good up to the late 1940s during which period Britain gained no new political or military privileges in Saudi

Arabia – but British trade and business in Jiddah prospered. By 1949, relations had begun to deteriorate over the Buraimi Oasis issue, which was followed by unsuccessful boundary negotiations between the two countries. When the conflict was submitted to arbitration in Geneva in 1954–1955, the British representative withdrew from the tribunal panel, thus creating a deadlock in the talks. The Saudi government, in November 1956, severed its diplomatic relations with Britain because of the latter's invasion of Egypt. It was not until January 1963 that diplomatic relations were restored. In short, Saudi–British relations from 1915 through 1950 were mainly concerned with the fulfillment of boundary agreements concluded between them.

Saudi–United States Relations

Saudi–American relations began in 1933. During the thirties severe world-wide depression had a bad effect on Saudi Arabia. The *Hajj* season was Saudi Arabia's main source of revenue, and the depression of those years brought a drastic lessening of the pilgrimage traffic. Meanwhile, petroleum had been discovered in Bahrain in 1932. In the hope of increasing his country's revenues, King Abdul Aziz, in 1933, gave the Standard Oil Company of California a concession covering a large area in the eastern part of the country. Consequently, the California Arabian Standard Oil Company was founded. The Texas Oil Company joined in as well, in 1936. It became known as the Arabian American Oil Company (Aramco) in 1944. "Oil wells were drilled in Dhahran (Dammam) and Abu-Hadriya in the province of Hasa (currently the Eastern province), and both proven and estimated reserves surpassed the boldest expectations."[17] As a result of their success, a supplementary agreement between Aramco and Saudi Arabia's government was added to the original oil concession on May 31, 1939. When the Second World War broke out, the operations of the Arabian American Oil Company were seriously affected by wartime needs and priorities.

> It is noteworthy that in 1937 Ibn Saud had received a very advantageous offer from Japan, but believing it to be motivated by political considerations (and against the advice of his advisers) he rejected it. Germany also had designs on Saudi oil, and in the same year Dr. Fritz Grobba, German Minister to Iraq and Saudi Arabia . . . visited Jiddah. Nevertheless, Ibn Saud preferred to continue his association with the Americans.[18]

Saudi–American relations remained purely commercial up to 1940. This can be largely attributed to America's policy of isolation and non-involvement in world affairs at that time, which reflected a deep-rooted doctrine in the foreign policy of the United States. However, the war changed this situation and the United States began to take a more active role in the affairs of the world, especially in the post war era. During the first years of the war King Abdul Aziz remained neutral. By 1943, the United States decided to secure a strategic air base in the area of the Middle East to connect Cairo with Karachi, in order to strengthen the war effort against Japan. The United States joint chiefs of staff named Dhahran as their objective. After top secret negotiations, Ibn Saud granted an air-base lease to the United States; and in March 1945 he declared war on Germany. From that year on, "what followed could be described as a multiple increase of diplomatic, military, technical, and economic contacts between the United States and Saudi Arabia".[19] In February 1945 on board an American man-o'-war in the Great Bitter Lake of Egypt, King Abdul Aziz, in his first journey abroad, had met with President Roosevelt. It was reported that their meeting was mutually profitable. By 1948, diplomatic representation between the United States and the Kingdom of Saudi Arabia was upgraded to the status of an embassy (an American legation had been established on a permanent basis at Jiddah in 1943).

Cooperation between the two countries increased at all levels and in various fields through 1953. Britain and the United States were the only countries that had serious relations with King Abdul Aziz in the period from 1915 to 1953. As for the other great Powers, such as France, Germany, Russia and Italy, they had very little if anything to do with the Kingdom during those years.

Consolidation of the Nation

The consolidation of the Arabian Peninsula by King Abdul Aziz Al Sa'ud within a period of more than twenty years is an outstanding example of nation building. Before dealing with those events and circumstances, however, some reference should be made to the origins of the Saudi dynasty in the eighteenth century, to the alliance reached between Prince Muhammad Ibn Sa'ud and Sheikh Muhammad Ibn Abdul-Wahhab at Ad-Dir'iyah and to its later repercussions in the Peninsula. In 1703, Sheikh Muhammad Ibn Abdul Wahhab was born in the town of Ayaina in Najd of a highly respected and religious family. Showing a keen interest in religion and dismayed by contemporary deviations from Islamic teachings, the Sheikh started "preaching [the] . . . revival of Islam. . . . He ripped away the heresies and abuses which had grown up around Islam and he preached the Faith in its original simplicity."[20] For that he was prosecuted and was forced to leave his town. He took refuge at Ad-Dir'iyah, the home of Al Sa'ud, under the protection of Amir Muhammad Ibn Sa'ud, the ruler of Ad-Dir'iyah. Perceiving the value of Sheikh Muhammad Ibn Abdul Wahhab, Prince Muhammad concluded an agreement with him that together they would bring the Arabs of the peninsula back to the true faith of the Islamic religion. This alliance occurred in AD 1744 (1157 AH). They were successful. Within barely sixty years, Muhammad Ibn Sa'ud, and after him his son Abdul Aziz, extended the sovereignty of the House of Sa'ud over all Najd (presently the Central Province). The Turkish Empire, aware of these achievements by Al Sa'ud, felt threatened and ordered its Viceroy in Egypt, Muhammad Ali, to proceed to the Arabian Peninsula and put an end to the emerging nation. He launched a military campaign which lasted from 1812 through 1818, ending with the capture of Riyadh. Through 1824, the Ottoman Empire maintained a few garrisons in Najd as a gesture of their dominance.

In 1824, Turki Ibn Sa'ud, a cousin of Sa'ud Ibn Sa'ud, who ruled from 1803 through 1814, assumed the Amirship of Najd, with his capital in Riyadh. While continuing the Saudi drive for the consolidation of the area, he recognized the symbolic suzerainty of the Viceroy of Egypt, Muhammad Ali. Turki's son, Faisal Ibn Sa'ud, who refused to acknowledge the Viceroy of Egypt, was driven from power by an Egyptian force sent for that purpose in 1838. Later, when Muhammad Ali declared Egypt's independence from the Ottoman Empire, he was forced to recall his troops stationed at Najd in order to support his position in Egypt. Meanwhile, Faisal Ibn Sa'ud, who was held captive in Cairo, escaped and returned to Najd. So the House of Sa'ud reasserted its control over the area. After Faisal's death in 1865, a struggle for power between two of his sons led to the second weakening of the Saudi state. At the same time, a tribal leader of the Shammar, Muhammad Ibn Rashid, based in Hail, created a strong political body which rapidly covered the greater part of Najd, and by 1871, after concluding a pact with Turkey, captured Al-Hasa. In 1891 he completed his control over Najd by capturing Riyadh. Ibn Rashid's seizure of Riyadh, the citadel of the House of Sa'ud, forced the third son of Faisal Ibn Sa'ud, Abdul Rahman, to leave the city and settle for months with the Murra tribes at the Great Waste, in the outskirts of Rub' al-Khali, the Empty Quarter, accompanied by his son Abdul Aziz, the future King of Arabia. Eventually he left for Bahrain, to gather his family, and went to Kuwait to live there in exile.

Abdul Aziz was deeply concerned with thoughts of his home territory, Najd, the land of his ancestors. He anticipated that he would some day go back and regain control of that part of Arabia. When he reached the age of seventeen, Abdul Aziz realized that

> he had had enough of idling. For six years he had sat in Kuwait, eating out his heart, listening to the hopeless grumbles of the exiles. That was no life for a man. It might do for shopmen and clerks, but not for a Saud. He was a fighting man. . . . He wanted action . . . (and) with God's help he (knew that he) would win. He was sure of himself and of the people of

Najd. If he gave them the lead they would rise and join him and throw out the Rashid.[21]

When he was twenty-one, he decided to move on Riyadh with thirty of his devoted friends. Having departed from Kuwait in December 1901, Ibn Saud reached Riyadh in January. Using elements of surprise and stratagem, he overpowered the garrison of Al Rashid which consisted of eighty men. The Saudi dynasty became once more the rulers of Riyadh. "The population of Riad [sic] rose. They were tired of the Rashid and his injustices. They wiped out the other posts of Rashid soldiers in the town, and welcomed Ibn Saud with open arms. . . . Ibn Saud was master of Riad."[22] Naturally, this was not the end of the journey for Ibn Saud. It was merely the beginning. His father, Abdul Rahman, who was the legal and rightful ruler of Najd, was recalled from Kuwait, and in a council formed of the *Ulama* (religious leaders) and the notables, he abdicated his rights and declared Abdul Aziz his successor. From 1902 to 1904, through a sequence of military campaigns, Ibn Saud extended his authority all over the Najd. Ibn Saud, however, was now faced with a much greater task – unifying the various tribes in Arabia. Aside from marriage alliances, Abdul Aziz employed his unique personality in persuading the tribes to unite.

> The Saud talked much and eloquently, but when he appeared to be giving most he was in reality giving little. As he talked he concentrated on the man [to] whom he spoke as if he were his one interest in life. He had a smile, irresistible, all-absorbing, which swept his listeners up with him, blinding their judgment so that each one went away satisfied and only later found that he had come away empty handed, and even then did not resent the fact.[23]

Consequently, his drive for consolidation was quite successful to the extent that by the end of 1904 he had managed to break the stranglehold of the Rashid and pushed them to the area at Jabal Shammar in northern Najd. The Rashid, desperately, appealed to the Turks who sent them reinforcements. Nevertheless, Ibn Saud's desert fighters kept control of the situation in Najd. Through diplomatic negotiations at one time, and guerrilla warfare at another, Abdul Aziz forced the Ottoman Empire to recall its troops from Najd. Thus on the death of Al Rashid in 1906, Ibn Saud won complete control over Najd. Having accomplished this objective, he turned his attention to Al-Hasa and the area of the Arabian Gulf which was still under Turkish rule. Calculating on the Ottoman Empire's preoccupation with uprisings in Europe, and on his belief that Britain, considering the situation a domestic affair, would remain neutral, Ibn Saud launched a successful assault, and by 1913 his sovereignty was extended to both Najd and Al-Hasa. Having reached this goal, he once more confronted the perennial problem of the Bedouins and their practice of raiding and moving from place to place at will. This continual practice spelled insecurity and instability which Ibn Saud was determined to put an end to. Realizing "that any attempt to establish a stable, large-scale political organization in the conquered territories was impeded by the difficulty of creating loyalties beyond those of the local units, whether it was tribe or village",[24] he conceived a brilliant two-stage plan. First, he sent Wahhabi preachers to various tribes, teaching them the essence of Islam and encouraging them to engage in agricultural labor. Secondly, he settled the Bedouins in agricultural settlements established according to the Wahhabi teachings, in Najd. The first of these projects was a success, and was followed by many others (sixty) so that by 1916 the tribes constituted a formidable political–military force which enabled Ibn Saud to further solidify his rule over Najd and Al-Hasa. These settlers, known as the *Ikhwan* (meaning "brethren" in Arabic), became such a powerful force that Ibn Saud assumed personal command of them. In 1916, he concluded another treaty with Britain, recognizing him as the sole ruler of Najd and Al-Hasa. This agreement gave Abdul Aziz the tacit right to destroy the remaining members of the Rashid family. He did so, and by 1918 his authority was extended to reach the outskirts of Ha'il, the capital of the Rashid. During the next year clashes occurred between the forces of Sherif Hussein of Makkah and a force of the *Ikhwan*. Nevertheless, Abdul Aziz withheld his troops from attacking the Hijaz. In 1920, he moved further south and annexed Asir. The following year, he completed his campaign against the Rashid in Ha'il which fell under his control. Restraining himself time and time again from proceeding to Hijaz because of his word to Britain, Abdul Aziz "Ibn Saud" adopted a policy of sitting and waiting. During the following three years, relations between the Sherif of Makkah and Britain began to deteriorate. The Sherif's maladministration of the holy cities further isolated him from other Arab countries. When, in March 1924, the Sherif proclaimed himself King of Arabia and Caliph of Islam, Ibn Saud's patience ceased. And in September of that year an army of the *Ikhwan* captured the city of Ta'if. With little delay and only minor resistance, Makkah, Medina and the whole area of Hijaz came under the sovereignty of Ibn Saud. This final consolidation of the Arabian Kingdom was accomplished by the end of 1925. In the following year, Ibn Saud, responding to a popular demand from the people of Makkah, became the King of Hijaz and the Sultan of Najd and its Dependencies. Thus,

> with the exception of the Yemen and the territory far to the south beyond the Great Waste on the coast of the Indian Ocean, Ibn Saud . . . ruled all Arabia from the Red Sea to the (Arabian) Gulf and from the Great Waste to the edges of Syria. He was Guardian of the Sacred Cities of Islam and Imam of the Wahhabis. He was Lord of Arabia.[25]

[1] Richard H. Nolte, "From Nomad Society to New Nation: Saudi Arabia," in K. H. Silvert, ed., *Expectant Peoples* (New York: Random House, 1963), p. 82.

[2] George Lipsky, *Saudi Arabia, Its People Its Society Its Culture* (New Haven: HRAF Press, 1959), p. 19.

[3] For further details consult the special issue on the Hajj, *Aramco World Magazine*, 25, no. 6 (1974).

[4] Kingdom of Saudi Arabia, Ministry of Interior, Passports and Nationality-Affairs, *Pilgrims Statistics for 1393 AH (1974 AD)*. (Riyadh: Da'ar al-Asfahani & Co. Al'as'fahani Printing Co., 1974), p. 37.

[5] Philip K. Hitti, *A Short History of the Near East* (Princeton: D. Van Nostrand Co., 1966), p. 3.

[6] The year in which the Prophet was forced to flee from Makkah to Medina marks the beginning of the Islamic calendar.

[7] *Area Handbook for Saudi Arabia* (Washington, DC: US Government Printing Office, 1971), p. 26.

[8] J. J. Saunders, *A History of Medieval Islam* (New York: Barnes and Noble, 1965), pp. 9–16.

[9] *Al Quran Al Karim, Surat Al Ma'ida*, verse 7, pp. 242–243. The *Quran* used in this dissertation is a copy authenticated by the Muslim World League, Secretariat-General at Makkah, Saudi Arabia. It was presented as a gift upon completion of this dissertation to Perkins Library at Duke University.

[10] The Prophet's immigration in AD 622 from Makkah to Medina became the starting year of the Muslim calendar and it is called Hijra. The twelve lunar months are Muharram, Safar, Rabi al-Awwal, Rabi al-Thani, Jumada al-Ula, Jumada al-Thaneiya, Rajab, Sha'ban, Ramadan, Shawwal, Dhu al Qa'adah and Dhu al-Hijjah.

[11] *Al Quran Al Karim, Surat al Baqara*, p. 72.

[12] Ibrahim Ismail Nawwab, "The Hajj: An Appreciation," *Aramco World Magazine*, 25 (1974): p. 13.

[13] *Ibid.*

[14] Mohyeldin al Qaissy, *Al Mu'Shaf w'a Alsa'yf, The Quran and the Sword* (Riyadh: The National Press, n.d.), p. 85. (F.F. translation.) The founders of the four schools of jurisprudence in Islam. The schools named after them are known as the Hanifite, Malekite, Shafiite and Hanbalite. Further analysis of these schools can be found in Marshall Hodgson, *The Venture of Islam*, 3 vols. (Chicago: The University of Chicago Press, 1974).

[15] George Lenczowski, *The Middle East in World Affairs*, 2nd ed. (Ithaca, N.Y.: Cornell University Press, 1956), p. 431.

[16] *Area Handbook for Saudi Arabia*, p. 170.

[17] Lenczowski, *The Middle East in World Affairs*, p. 439.

[18] *Ibid.*, p. 439.

[19] *Ibid.*, p. 444.

[20] H. C. Armstrong, *Lord of Arabia: Ibn Saud, an Intimate Study of a King* (London: Arthur Barker, Ltd., 1934), pp. 13–14.

[21] Armstrong, *Lord of Arabia*, pp. 48–49.

[22] *Ibid.*, p. 60.

[23] *Ibid.*, pp. 200–201.

[24] *Area Handbook for Saudi Arabia*, p. 35.

[25] Armstrong, *Lord of Arabia*, p. 262.

CHAPTER II

Saudi Arabia and Petroleum

1 *The rights of peoples and nations to permanent sovereignty over their natural wealth and resources must be exercised in the interest of their national development and of the well-being of the people of the state concerned.*

2 *The exploration, development and disposition of such resources, as well as the import of the foreign capital required for these purposes, should be in conformity with the rules and conditions which the peoples and nations freely consider to be necessary or desirable with regard to the authorization, restriction or prohibition of such activities.*

United Nations General Assembly, Resolution 1803 (XVII of 14 December 1962) *Permanent Sovereignty over Natural Resources.*[1]

Introduction

A COMPLETE chapter devoted to the role of petroleum in Saudi Arabia is justified simply because petroleum is imperative to the development of the Kingdom. The focus will be on Saudi–Aramco relations and the establishment of Petromin. Since Saudi Arabia is a founding member of both the Organization of Petroleum Exporting Countries (OPEC) and the Organization of Arab Petroleum Exporting Countries (OAPEC), the history and composition of both organizations will be treated in this chapter. Finally, an analysis will be made of one of the leading universities concerned with petroleum, not only in Saudi Arabia but also in the world – the University of Petroleum and Minerals in Dhahran.

The history of petroleum in the Middle East and the Arab world goes back many centuries during which seepage oils and tar were used for a multitude of purposes. A mission of German experts, in 1871, visited Iraq and reported plentiful supplies of petroleum. In 1907 another mission said Iraq was a veritable "lake of petroleum". In Iran, petroleum was found in quantity in 1908. The major Iraqi field was discovered at Kirkuk in 1927 and began producing petroleum in commercial quantities; petroleum flowed abroad in 1934. In 1932, petroleum was discovered in Bahrain. In 1938, the Dammam field was discovered in Saudi Arabia. The Biergon field, in Kuwait, the largest oil field in the world at that time, was discovered in the same year. Petroleum was discovered in Qatar in 1940; in Algeria in 1948; in Kuwait Neutral Zone in

1953; in Syria in 1956; in Abu Dhabi in 1958; in Libya in 1959, and in Tunisia and Oman in 1965.[2] Quite apart from the religious significance of the Middle East as the cradle of Islam, Christianity and Judaism, this area is one of the most strategically important regions of the world, geographically and economically:

> The Middle East is a land bridge connecting Europe, Asia, and Africa.
> Its soil has borne the travelers, merchants, and conquering armies of the
> centuries. Three of the world's religions were founded there – Judaism,
> Christianity, and Islam – and under its surface lies the world's largest
> known oil reserves, the "black gold" of our machine age. The Middle
> East is, with good reason, often called the crossroads of the world.[3]

The region of the Middle East, more specifically the area of the Gulf, is witnessing a great shift of power which, if wisely utilized, will have an extremely important effect, not only on regional, but also on world affairs.

Saudi–Aramco Relations

The Saudi–American agreement over petroleum is in a class by itself in terms of its economic magnitude. It was, however, preceded by other petroleum agreements between the government of Saudi Arabia and various petroleum companies representing different nationalities.

The first petroleum concession ever given in Saudi Arabia was extended to a British company by King Abdul Aziz in 1923 for the exploration of petroleum in the Eastern province, which is now known to contain the world's largest petroleum reserves. Four years later, having failed to strike oil, the British did not renew their option and the agreement lapsed. When petroleum was discovered in neighboring Bahrain, Ibn Saud granted a second petroleum concession for exploration in Saudi Arabia, this time to an American company. His concession to the American firm at that time represented a major break with what was virtually a British monopoly of petroleum concessions in that part of the world. This agreement, signed on May 29, 1933, granted the Standard Oil Company of California a sixty-year concession.[4] Articles 1 and 2 of the agreement define the nature and geographical limits of this concession. Article 2 states:

> The area cover[s] . . . all of eastern Saudi Arabia, from its eastern
> boundary (including islands and territorial waters) westward to the
> westerly edge of Dahana and from the northern boundary to the southern
> boundary of Saudi Arabia, provided that from the northern end of the
> western edge of the Dahana the westerly boundary of the area in question
> shall continue in a straight line north thirty degrees west to the northern
> boundary of Saudi Arabia, and from the southern end of the westerly
> edge of the Dahana such boundary shall continue in a straight line south
> thirty degrees east to the southern boundary of Saudi Arabia.
> For convenience this area may be referred to as "the exclusive area".[5]

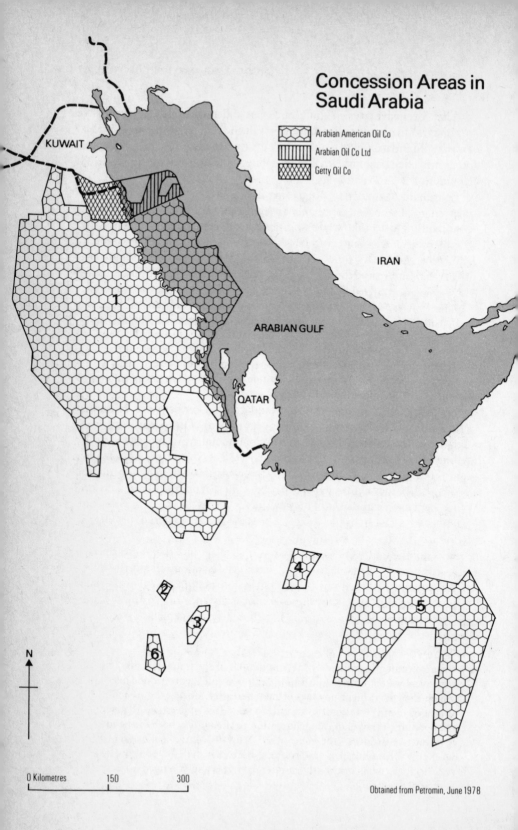

Concession Areas in
Saudi Arabia

Arabian American Oil Co
Arabian Oil Co Ltd
Getty Oil Co

KUWAIT

IRAN

ARABIAN GULF

QATAR

1

4

2

3

6

5

N

0 Kilometres   150   300

Obtained from Petromin, June 1978

The "exclusive area" rights, however, did not include the exclusive privilege to market petroleum products in the Kingdom of Saudi Arabia. In 1936, Standard Oil of California, putting Article 32 of the 1933 agreement into effect, sold one-half of its concession's interest to the Texas Oil Company.

Petroleum having been discovered in commercial quantities at Dammam in 1938, another supplementary agreement was signed on May 31, 1939, adding 6 to the 60 years. This second instrument, known as the Supplemental Agreement, enlarged the company's concession area by almost 80,000 square miles. It also included rights in the Saudi government's half interest in the two neutral zones shared with Iraq and Kuwait.

> It is noteworthy that in 1937 Ibn Saud had received a very advantageous offer from Japan, but believing it to be motivated by political considerations he rejected it. Germany also had designs on Saudi oil, and in the same year Dr. Fritz Grobba, German minister to Iraq and Saudi Arabia, who was stationed in Baghdad, visited Jidda [sic]. Nevertheless, Ibn Saud preferred to continue his association with the Americans; it had the advantage of assuring the economic development of the country without incurring political liabilities.[6]

In 1944, the California-Arabian Standard Oil Company was re-named the Arabian American Oil Company (Aramco). Once more, in 1948, Aramco enforced an Article of the Supplemental Agreement of 1939 by selling a thirty per cent interest to Standard Oil of New Jersey and a ten per cent interest to Socony Vacuum, redistributing the ownership of Aramco as follows: Texas Oil Company, thirty per cent; Standard Oil of California, thirty per cent; Standard Oil of New Jersey, thirty per cent; and Socony Vacuum the last ten per cent (currently named Texaco, California Standard, Exxon, and Mobil Oil).

In 1949, the Getty Oil Company was able to acquire a sixty year petroleum concession in the neutral zone where the Saudi government shared rights equally with Kuwait. This concession included exploration and production rights in territorial waters for a distance of six miles. Later, the government of Saudi Arabia concluded an agreement by which it granted the Japan Petroleum Trading Company, Ltd, a forty-four year concession covering

> the government's undivided share in all that offshore area outside the territorial waters limit of the Saudi Arab–Kuwait Neutral Zone over which the government now has or may hereafter, during the period of this agreement, have right, title and interest. It is understood that such offshore area extends to the delimitation in the middle both of the mean low water coastlines of the Saudi Arab–Kuwait Neutral Zone and of Iran on the Arabian Gulf, and that such offshore area shall include shoals, reefs, waters, wholly or partly submerged lands and submarine areas, seabed and sub-soil.[7]

Drilling started in 1959: petroleum was discovered in January 1960.

In January 1965, the Saudi government concluded another concession agreement with the French-owned Société Auxiliaire de la Régie Autonome des Petroles (Auxirap) to explore for petroleum in the Red Sea. It was agreed that the French company would bear all exploration costs until petroleum was discovered. Then a joint operating company would be founded in which Petromin (the Saudi National Oil Company) would acquire forty per cent equity, but would enjoy fifty per cent of the voting power. Furthermore

> under this agreement [with Auxirap] the government will receive a 15% royalty which will be increased to 20% if production exceeds 80,000 barrels a day. Other payments are bonuses amounting to $5.5 million, $4 million of which is payable only when production reaches the level of 70 barrels of crude oil a day for 90 consecutive days, and rental charges ranging from $5 per square kilometer for the first 5 years to $500 during the last 5 years of a 30-year period. In addition, the company will pay a 40% income tax.[8]

It is important to trace the financial and economic aspects of Saudi–Aramco relations as a necessary preface to discussing the creation of OPEC, later in this chapter. Both the first "Saudi Arab Concession" of 1933 and the Supplemental Agreement of 1939 had separate articles dealing with the financial aspects of Saudi-Aramco relations. Article 14 of the Saudi Arab concession of 1933 stated that

> The company shall pay the government a royalty on all net crude oil produced and saved and run from field storage, after first deducting:
>
> 1 water and foreign substances; and
> 2 oil required for the customary operations of the company's installations within Saudi Arabia and
> 3 the oil required for manufacturing the amounts of gasoline and kerosene to be provided free each year to the government in accordance with Article 19 hereof. The royalty portion of such net crude oil shall be either:
>   a four shillings gold; or its equivalent; or
>   b at the election of the company at the time of making each royalty payment, one dollar, United States currency, plus the amount, if any, by which the average rate of exchange of four shillings gold, during the last half of the semester for which the royalty payment is due, may exceed one dollar and ten cents, United States currency. Thus, for example, if such average rate should be one dollar and fourteen cents, United States currency (that is to say, five dollars and seventy cents per gold pound), the royalty rate would be one dollar and four cents, United States currency, per ton of such net crude oil. [After the payment of the United States tax which, *a priori*, means less revenues for the Saudi government.][9]

Article 4 of the Supplemental Agreement of 1939, concerned the new financial situation that had developed due to the enlargement of the area of concession in Saudi Arabia along with the new rights in the Saudi-Iraqi-Kuwaiti Neutral Zones. Yet no conflict occurred between articles dealing with the financial arrangements in the Saudi Arab concession and the Supplemental Agreement of 1939. It was not until

> December 30, 1950, [that] Aramco and Saudi Arabia [had] made a major change in the concession by concluding a fifty-fifty profit-sharing agreement. This agreement was of great importance inasmuch as it set a precedent for similar formulas in other oil-producing countries of the Middle East. A further [significant] step was the agreement of both parties on October 2, 1951, to apply the new formula before the payment of United States taxes rather than after, as had been done until then.[10]

Equally relevant was the fact that it was only in November 1950 that the first income tax law was issued by a Royal Decree. The imposition of taxes affected both personal income and corporate profits with minimum exemptions in both categories. Thus, by 1951, Aramco in addition to paying royalties at the rate of about 22 cents a barrel, was paying a fifty per cent income tax on its net profits. Moreover,

> it was agreed upon by 1952 that the Saudi government should be represented in the company's policy deliberations and that the company's headquarters should be located in Saudi Arabia . . . [consequently], Aramco's headquarters were moved to Dhahran, and in1959 two Saudi government representatives were elected to Aramco's 15-man board of directors.[11]

It is crucial to the following part of this chapter, which deals with OPEC, to make mention of the Saudi–Iraqi agreement of 1953, which provided for the exchange of petroleum data as well as for the holding of periodic consultations regarding petroleum policy. This agreement may very well be considered as an early catalyst towards the subsequent establishment of OPEC. From the late 1940s through the late 1950s, relations between the Saudi government and Aramco went smoothly. It was not until the 1959–1960 unilateral reductions in petroleum prices by the major petroleum companies in the area of the Gulf, that relations began to change. A more complete analysis of these cuts will be made in the OPEC section of this chapter since they became the most influential factor leading to the creation of the Organization of Petroleum Exporting Countries in 1960.

At this point in the discussion of Saudi-Aramco relations it is important to note the creation of the General Petroleum and Mineral Organization (Petromin) in 1962, the nation's first national petroleum company, which is empowered to formulate and execute projects for the development of the petroleum, petrochemical and mineral industries of the nation, and to deal

> with the progressive relinquishment of acreage by Aramco and the entry of new oil companies in the country. Petromin is acquiring growing importance. Its stature was further enhanced and its responsibilities widely extended with the implementation of the principle of participation in the equity of Aramco.[12]

Petromin

To develop the entire natural resource sector and harness it to the service of overall development, the Government established the organization of Petromin.

Petromin's role is to maximize the usefulness of the Kingdom's oil, gas and minerals. It is thus engaged in the production of natural resources (including, for example, the engagement of foreign partners), in the exploitation of natural resources (such as the evolution of a wide range of hydro-carbon products, like petroleum, LPG, and asphalt), and in the marketing, both domestically and internationally, of these products. Its range of activity is therefore vast. Refining, pipelines, storage, power generation – all fall within Petromin's province.

For the period 1975–80 Petromin's activities were governed by its own five year plan. This in turn was circumscribed by a number of basic governmental policies. These included that of avoiding adverse influence on local life through excessive concentrations of population; hence, decentralization has prevailed in development. At the same time, industrial development would take place with as much vertical and horizontal integration as possible. Good husbandry was stimulated by the emphasis on profitability. Long-term planning – beyond the span of any five year period – was a further requirement. There was the caution that Petromin, with all its potential, should not encroach into fields already within the authority of other Government bodies or Ministries, but should integrate its planning with theirs. Lastly, Petromin would give priority to projects which might provide opportunities for private Saudi investment, and wherever possible look to the expansion of job opportunities for Saudis.

Under its plan, Petromin listed five principal areas of activity: the exploitation of gas; the diversification of industries within the field of fossil fuels and minerals; developing the refining of oil, including the production of benzene, toluene and xylene for the Kingdom's burgeoning petro-chemical plants; the marketing and transportation, at home and abroad, of LPG; and the speeding up of the production of mineral industries and of the prospection and development of precious metal resources.

No doubt it will play an even greater role once Aramco becomes one hundred per cent Saudi in ownership. In 1979 there were ongoing negotiations between the Saudi government and Aramco in order eventually to finalize full Saudi ownership.

There appear to have been no significant legal changes in the May 31, 1939 Supplemental Agreement until 1972. In that year, Sheikh Ahmad Zaki Yamani, the Saudi petroleum minister, concluded an agreement with the western petroleum companies operating in Saudi Arabia regarding the participation formula.

On December 20, 1972, the governments of Abu Dhabi and Saudi Arabia, in accordance with resolutions passed by the conference of OPEC for the participation of member states in existing crude petroleum concessions within member states signed a "General Agreement" with major petroleum companies operating in their countries providing for such participation. Annex 1 of that agreement appears below. Article 3, Section (a) of this General Agreement on Participation states:

> Each Gulf State shall have an initial percentage level of participation equal to twenty-five per cent (25%) in each concession as provided in paragraph (b) of this Article; thereafter, it shall have the right to acquire percentage increments and resulting percentage levels of participation in accordance with Annex 2. . . .[13]

Annex I Table of General Agreement

Countries	Concession holders or parties to Government Agreements	Shareholders, direct or indirect, or Concession Holders or of parties to Government Agreements
1 Abu Dhabi	1 Abu Dhabi Marine Limited	1 The British Petroleum Ltd, Compagnie Française des Pétrôles
	2 Abu Dhabi Petroleum Company Limited	2 The British Petroleum Ltd, Compagnie Française des Pétrôles, Exxon Corporation, Mobil Oil Corporation, The Shell Oil Petroleum Co Ltd, and Shell Petroleum NV, Participations Explorations Corporation
2 Saudi Arabia	3 Arabian American Oil Company	3 Mobil Oil Corporation, Standard Oil Company of California, Exxon Corporation, Texaco Inc

Source: Kingdom of Saudi Arabia, Ministry of Petroleum and Mineral Resources, Legal Department, **General Agreement, 1972.** A copy of the agreement was obtained by the author from the Legal Department of the said Ministry in May of 1975.

Annex 2 of the agreement required the first twenty-five per cent initial level of participation [effective January 1, 1973] to be enforced through January 1, 1978. By January 1, 1978, the first five percentage increment was due, making the level of participation thirty per cent. The second five percentage increment was due on January 1, 1979; the third five percentage increment on January 1, 1980; the fourth five percentage increment on January 1, 1981. By January 1, 1982, the final or last five percentage increment of this General Agreement was made.

It is important to specify that the effective date of participation under this General Agreement was January 1, 1973. [See Annex 2 below.]

Talks between the government of Saudi Arabia and Aramco were under way in 1978 with the Saudi objective of a one hundred per cent ownership of Aramco. It is significant that the government of Saudi Arabia in 1974 decided to sign another sixty–forty per cent participation agreement, pending the conclusion of complete ownership in order to keep pace with other Gulf States and similar participation deals concluded

Annex 2 Table of General Agreement

Increments and Percentage Levels of Participation

Increment	Percentage increments	Percentage levels of participation	Earliest dates for acquisition of percentage increments
First	5	30	1 January 1978
Second	5	35	1 January 1979
Third	5	40	1 January 1980
Fourth	5	45	1 January 1981
Fifth	6	51	1 January 1982

In respect of each percentage increment each Gulf State will give notice to the Company or Companies concerned of its intention to exercise its right to acquire such increments, such notice to be given on or before the date on which notice of the phase-in quantities is given pursuant to Paragraph E (2) (b) of Annex 3 for the year when such increment is to become effective. Only one percentage increment may be acquired in any one year and the Effective Date for each increment shall be 1 January. If a Gulf State has not given notice as above provided, or has not satisfied all payment obligations due under paragraphs (c) (i) and (ii) and (d) of Annex 4 and paragraph (a) of Article Seven prior to 31 December of the year preceding the year when such increment would have become effective, the earliest date for acquisition of such increment and for each succeeding percentage increment shall be postponed one year.

Source : Kingdom of Saudi Arabia, Ministry of Petroleum and Mineral Resources, Legal Department, **General Agreement, 1972.** A copy of the agreement was obtained by the author from the Legal Department of the said Ministry in May 1975.

previously. It is likely that such an agreement will occur sometime in the near future.

A brief examination of the production potential of petroleum seems appropriate at this point.[14] An examination of the history of petroleum of the Kingdom of Saudi Arabia shows that petroleum production rates reached a new peak, though not at full capacity, in October 1973, at 8.5 million barrels per day, and maintained that rate through 1974, thus making Saudi Arabia the third largest petroleum producer in the world. In 1975, Saudi Arabia's petroleum production rate began a decline induced by the law of supply and demand in the international market. The Saudi daily petroleum production during 1975 fluctuated between five and six million barrels per day. This decline in petroleum production enabled Saudi Arabia and other state members of OPEC to maintain their prices at a high level.

To accentuate Saudi Arabia's impressive achievements in the realm of petroleum, it should be noted that in 1938 the Kingdom's daily production was a mere 11,000 barrels per day. In 1950, production reached 547,000 barrels, and in 1960 grew to 1,315,000 barrels per day. In 1970 it increased to 3,799,000 barrels. From October of 1973 through 1974, petroleum production[15] reached its highest level in the history of the country. Later, in 1975, due to world wide economic and financial considerations, petroleum production was deliberately curtailed. The 1978–79 daily production average ranged between 9 and 9.5 million barrels, and in subsequent years production has been cut back still further to less than 6 million barrels.

Organization of Petroleum Exporting Countries (OPEC)
Historical Background
Since its creation in 1945 in Cairo, the League of Arab States had considered establishing a petroleum organization to develop a common policy towards major petroleum companies operating within their boundaries. After some study it became evident that such an organization would have to include non-Arab exporters of petroleum, such as Iran and Venezuela. Serious diplomatic negotiations with these countries started in Washington, DC, in 1947, aimed at achieving a coordinated petroleum policy among large exporters. Another major step occurred in 1949 on the initiative of the Venezuelan government, which, in an effort to ally itself with the petroleum states of the Gulf, dispatched a special three-man delegation to visit Iran, Iraq, Kuwait and Saudi Arabia. This Venezuelan delegation exchanged views on petroleum policies and explored the possibilities of developing a permanent channel of communication between both sides. The Venezuelan government also extended an invitation to both Iranian and Saudi Arabian petroleum experts to visit Venezuela in 1951.

The fruitful result of such contacts first became evident in Iraq, Kuwait and Saudi Arabia, when these countries demanded fifty per cent of the companies' net profits instead of a fixed royalty on each barrel of petroleum produced.

Another step towards the establishment of an OPEC-like body was the Saudi–Iraqi Agreement of 1953. But perhaps the most important preliminary event was the convening of the first Arab Petroleum Congress in Cairo in 1959, under the auspices of the League of Arab States. Both Iran and Venezuela were invited to attend as observers. This Congress is considered by many leading petroleum experts to have been the immediate predecessor of OPEC.

Establishment of OPEC

During 1959, the existence of a large global petroleum surplus led to the weakening of the international market. In addition, the United States, in the same year, imposed import controls in an effort to lessen its dependency on foreign petroleum. For the major companies operating in the Gulf area, this decision meant the closure of the profitable United States market. Faced with such a situation, the petroleum companies

> had either to risk angering their host countries and at the same time increase their own profits by lowering posted prices, or to maintain good relations with the producing nations by freezing prices at their current levels, even if it meant angering the consumers and foregoing some profits. The companies chose the first alternative. In February 1959, they decided, without prior consultation with the governments concerned, to cut the prices of Middle Eastern oil by about 18 cents per barrel. [Furthermore, the oil companies, ignoring the serious situation developed by the cut and the calling of the Arab states on them for prior consultation in such events], [they] decided to cut prices again in August, 1960, by an average of about 9 cents per barrel.[16]

These two cuts meant that, using 1960 as a base, Kuwait, Iran, Iraq and Saudi Arabia were losing $231,241,000 annually in the value of their exports.[17]

These two successive unilateral and arbitrary cuts in 1959 and 1960 by the petroleum companies operating in the Middle East were important determinants towards establishing OPEC. They "generated a feeling of economic insecurity in oil exporting countries and emphasized the need for a collective defense to arrest the downward drift of prices and government per barrel revenues".[18]

Structural Organization of OPEC

The governments of Saudi Arabia and Venezuela, in accordance with the objectives of the Arab Petroleum Congress of 1959, issued a declaration on May 13, 1960, recommending that petroleum exporting countries pursue a common policy in order to protect their rightful interests. The declaration also advanced the idea of establishing an organization to achieve this end. Nonetheless, the countries concerned did not take

IIa Structure of the Organization of Petroleum Exporting Countries (OPEC)

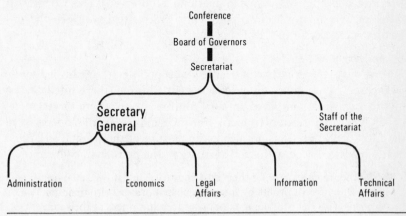

Source: Synthesized by author from Abdul Amir Kubbah, **'OPEC: Past and Present'**, pp. 25–32.

Note: For explanation of terms of reference and composition of Conference and Board of Governors see footnote 19

immediate action. It was the sudden and arbitrary decrease in petroleum prices for the second time in 1960 that made them feel the danger which encouraged them to unite in a common front.[20] Consequently, the major petroleum producing countries declared, after the Baghdad Conference of August 10–14, 1960 (at which the Kingdom of Saudi Arabia, Republic of Iraq, Iran, Venezuela and Kuwait were represented), their intention to establish the organization which became known as the Organization of Petroleum Exporting Countries (OPEC). One of the major decisions of that meeting declared a cardinal objective of the organization to be the standardization of petroleum prices among its members and agreement on the best methods of protecting its individual and collective interests.[21] As a result, OPEC was founded in September 1960

as a permanent intergovernmental organization with an international status. In accordance with Article 102 of the United Nations Charter, the agreement creating OPEC was duly registered with the Secretariat of the United Nations on November 6, 1962, under No. 6363. [Moreover, it is quite important to refer to the fact that] OPEC is not a business entity; it does not engage in any commercial transactions. [It concerns itself with the formulation of a common policy toward the industrialized countries of the world and the fixing of petroleum prices in a unified manner.] The legally authorized representative of the organization is its Secretary General. The staff of the Secretariat are international civil servants.[22]

2.1 Member States of the Organization of Petroleum Exporting Countries

State membership	Date of membership	Remarks or status
Iran	September 1960	Founder Member
Iraq	September 1960	Founder Member
Kuwait	September 1960	Founder Member
Saudi Arabia	September 1960	Founder Member
Venezuela	September 1960	Founder Member
Qatar	December 1960	Full Member
Libya	December 1962	Full Member
Indonesia	December 1962	Full Member
United Arab Emirates	November 1967	Full Member
Algeria	July 1969	Full Member
Nigeria	July 1971	Full Member
Ecuador	November 1973	Full Member
Gabon	December 1973	Associate Member

Source : Author's design. Drawn from Abdul Amir Kubbah, **OPEC: Past and Present**, pp. 17–18.

OPEC's headquarters were in Geneva, Switzerland, from January 21, 1961, through August 1965, but, in the latter year, moved to Vienna. Both sites were chosen because of the host country's political neutrality.

As can be seen from Table 2.1, only seven of OPEC's thirteen members are Arab states.

The criteria governing the admission of new member states are set forth in Article 7, para. C., of OPEC's statute of November, 1971:

Any other country with a substantial net export of crude petroleum, which has fundamentally similar interests to those of Member Countries, may become a Full Member of the Organization, if accepted by a majority of three-fourths of Full Members, including the concurrent vote of all Founder Members.[23]

For a state to qualify, it must first possess a "substantial net export of crude petroleum". Secondly and more significantly, the state applying for membership must "[have] fundamentally similar interests to those of Member Countries".

Any member state has the right to withdraw from OPEC. According to Article 8, section A,

No member of the Organization may withdraw from membership without giving notice of its intention to do so to the conference. Such notice shall take effect at the beginning of the next calendar year after the date of its receipt by the conference, subject to the Member having at that time fulfilled all financial obligations arising from its membership.[24]

Article 2, section A/B/C of OPEC's statute, delineates the aims and objectives of the Organization:

A The principal aim of the Organization shall be the coordination and unification of petroleum policies of the Member Countries and the determination of the best means for safeguarding their interests individually and collectively.
B The Organization shall devise ways and means of ensuring the stabilization of prices in international oil markets with a view to eliminating harmful and unnecessary fluctuations.
C Due regard shall be given at all times to the interests of the producing nations and to the necessity of securing a steady income to the producing countries; an efficient, economical and regular supply of petroleum to consuming nations; and a fair return on their capital to those investing in the petroleum industry.[25]

The global impact of the Organization of Petroleum Exporting Countries was clearly felt during and in the aftermath of the Ramadan War of 1973, when the Arab petroleum-producing countries imposed a gradual embargo with an initial five per cent cut of their total production. This was to be followed by another five per cent cut each month, until a peaceful and just solution for the Middle East conflict was found. But President Nixon's decision to provide Israel with military aid of over $2 billion caused the Arab petroleum-producing nations to impose a total embargo against the United States while maintaining the previous policy of successive five per cent cuts towards the rest of the Western world. The effect of the embargo is best illustrated by the fact that the Arab petroleum-producing countries' normal production of 20 million barrels per day was cut back to between 13 and 14 million barrels per day, as a result. Of that reduction of 6 to 6.5 million barrels, United States cuts amounted to 2 million barrels per day. The rest was split between Europe and Japan. The total production of the members of OPEC normally runs at 30 million barrels per day, so the 6–6.5 million the Arabs cut represented a twenty per cent reduction in what was available for the world market. Although the reduction was minimal, the effect was widespread.[26] The embargo was lifted in March 1974. Previously OPEC had existed and functioned without much attention from the rest of the world. But 1973 revealed the actual and potential influence of OPEC on the world economy.

Controversial theories emerged regarding OPEC's prospects. The first of these theories, held by the United States Secretary of the Treasury, William Simon, argued that OPEC was soon destined to decline. Simon repeatedly declared that the laws of supply and demand, along with the conditions of the international petroleum market, would bring about a lower price for petroleum. Consequently, the power of OPEC in world affairs would gradually diminish.

Three years after Secretary Simon's prediction relating to the future of OPEC none of his prophecies had been fulfilled. It is true that most of the OPEC members had been forced to reduce their petroleum production because of a relative decline in world demand. Nevertheless, such a decline provided most of the member states of OPEC with a success in reverse; that is, the reduction of their petroleum production enabled them to maintain their posted price for petroleum.

Five eminent analysts from Iran, Japan and the United States similarly speculated that

the United States seems to expect consuming countries to shrink their consumption of oil quite naturally as they proceed further in adapting to the increase of the oil price. It is apparently expect[ed] that the producing countries will be unable to agree on shares of a shrinking market [due to a relative decrease in petroleum] consumption and will consequently begin competing among themselves at declining oil prices [and] that the "cartel" will break apart.[27]

An alternative theory was that OPEC would maintain a relatively strong posture for some length of time. Therefore, a common and firm policy by the western industrialized nations had to be developed in order to cope forcefully with OPEC. Such a policy, it was argued, could only be developed by the western powers alone and without any previous consultation with the world's major petroleum producers; that is, the OPEC member states. In other words, "the United States propose[d] to organize the developed countries first, as a prerequisite to other contacts and negotiations involving either the developing countries or the oil-producing countries".[28] This approach was supported by United States Secretary of State Henry Kissinger. By 1978 OPEC still wielded considerable power in the world economy and was expected to maintain such a lead for a considerable time to come. It must be admitted, at this point, that Secretary Kissinger's statement regarding the future of OPEC was not specific; it made no precise predictions like those of Secretary Simon in regard to the future.

A third approach was for the western industrialized world to pursue a policy of accommodation and cooperation with the OPEC member states rather than a policy of confrontation. This approach assumed that the post-1973 events proved that confrontation with OPEC had failed. The collapse of the Energy Conference, which the United States convened in Washington, DC during the first quarter of 1975 attested to this fact. That conference included all the western European industrialized countries, Japan and the United States of America. The ulterior motive was to develop a confrontation policy against the OPEC nations. Instead, another conference was held in Paris in April of 1975 between the leading industrial nations and the OPEC representatives to establish an on-going dialogue that would serve the objectives and interests of all parties.

> The inability of [that] preparatory meeting called by President Giscard d'Estaing in April [1975] to agree on a concept for future discussions between producers and consumers [should under no circumstances dissuade the parties from constructive future talks]. [This is illustrated by the] bilateral contacts to organize a new meeting [which] are already under way, and the search for that concept will go on, for there can be no equilibrium in the world economy or in the world until a more balanced relation of power between oil producers and industrial countries is reached, defined, institutionalized.[29]

The Organization of Arab Petroleum Exporting Countries (OAPEC)

In the summer of 1967, the Kingdom of Saudi Arabia submitted a proposal to both Kuwait and Libya for establishing an Arab organization of petroleum exporting countries. As a result, and after further studies, the three Arab countries met in Beirut and signed an agreement on January 9, 1968, initiating the first institutionalized Arab cooperation in the field of petroleum – the Organization of Arab Petroleum Exporting Countries (OAPEC). It was agreed that Kuwait would be the organization's headquarters. Article 7 of OAPEC's statute sets forth the criteria for admission. The principal criterion is that petroleum must constitute the main source of the applicant state's national income. Later it was realized that such a condition was highly selective and would restrict the membership of the organization to some, rather than most, of the Arab countries. This was not in harmony with the basic objective of the organization; that is, greater cooperation between all Arab states. Consequently the Saudi government, represented by Sheikh Ahmad Zaki Yamani, suggested an amendment to Article 7 whereby any Arab petroleum exporting country in which petroleum represents an important (rather than the main) source of income may join. Abu Dhabi, now the capital of the United Arab Emirates (UAE), Algeria, Bahrain and Qatar were admitted to the organization during an extraordinary ministerial board meeting on May 24, 1970, as a direct result of this amendment to

Article 7. Another group of new member states, Egypt, Iraq and Syria, joined the organization during 1972. Both Iraq and Syria became full members during 1972, but, because of the late deposition of Egypt's ratification documents at the Kuwaiti Foreign Ministry, Egypt did not officially become a member of OAPEC until 1973. So the members of the Organization of Arab Petroleum Exporting Countries are: Algeria, Bahrain, Egypt, Iraq, Kuwait, Libya, Qatar, Saudi Arabia, Syria and the United Arab Emirates.

The organization's objectives can be summed up in these three main aims:

A To carry out common projects that would achieve a diversified economic investment for the members. This, in turn, would lessen their dependency on petroleum as a sole source of income. And consequently, this would slow down the consumption of their petroleum and prolong the period of its investment for future generations.
B To consider the legitimate rights of the consumer by making sure that petroleum reaches the market under just and reasonable conditions.
C To develop and promote the international petroleum industry by means of providing suitable circumstances for capital and experience to be invested in the member countries. The text, in this general sense, is applied to both national and foreign capital and experience as long as it is invested in the petroleum industry of member states.[30]

Since its creation, the Organization of Arab Petroleum Exporting Countries has made great efforts toward achieving its goals and serving the economies of all Arab, as well as member, countries. Among the most important projects which the Organization has carried out are the following:

1 The establishment of Maritime Oil Transportation. This Company began its activities in 1974 with a capital of US $500 million.
2 Ship Building and Repairs. The Company was officially launched in 1974 with a capital of US $120 million.
3 The Petroleum Investment Company. The Company was officially inaugurated in September of 1974 with capital of almost $1 billion.
4 The Petroleum Services Project. This Company is still under intensive study and may become a reality in the near future.

Article 8 of the Organization's statutes sets out its organizational structure. OAPEC consists of:

Ministerial Board [referred to as the Council]
Executive Bureau (or office) [referred to as the Office]
Secretary General [referred to as the Secretary]
Judicial Organization [referred to as the Organization][31]

The economic strength of the member countries of OAPEC is obvious. Its total proven petroleum reserve – as of the beginning of 1975 – was about 382 billion barrels, which then equalled 56.9 per cent of the world's proven reserves (estimated at 672 billion barrels of petroleum in the same year). The Organization of Petroleum Exporting Countries' daily production of petroleum according to the 1975 statistics, reached a capacity of 30,917.6 (thousands of barrels per day)[32] compared to 18,090.2 (thousands of barrels per day) from the Organization of Arab Petroleum Exporting Countries. The latter's annual production for the same year amounted to thirty-two per cent of the world's total production of petroleum.[33]

University of Petroleum and Minerals, Dhahran[34]

Since the University of Petroleum and Minerals was established to train the manpower to staff the country's oil industry, it may be appropriate to deal briefly with this institution of learning in this chapter as well as in Chapter IV which explores the many educational facets of Saudi Arabia.

The University of Petroleum and Minerals was established in 1963.[35] During the following year, 1964, the University decided to admit other Arab and Muslim students along with Saudi students. The University was officially inaugurated in 1965 by King Faisal, who, on that occasion, declared that "it is great pleasure for us to take part in inaugurating this great institution, of which the least that can be said is that it represents one of the pillars of our scientific, economic and industrial development".

The University of Petroleum and Minerals is composed of the following schools (or colleges):

1 The College of Sciences
   Offers Bachelor of Science degrees in chemistry, geology, mathematics and physics.
2 The College of Engineering Sciences
   Offers six programs leading to Bachelor of Science degrees in chemical, civil, electrical, mechanical, systems, architectural and petroleum engineering.
3 The College of Applied Engineering
   Offers Bachelor of Applied Engineering degrees in chemical, civil, electrical and mechanical engineering.
4 College of Industrial Management
   Started its studies in the second semester of 1974. Offers a Bachelor of Science and a Master of Science degree in the following majors: science management; accounting; marketing and economics; supply and methodology.
5 Graduate School
   Started its program of studies in the academic year 1973–1974.

Currently, Masters' degrees are offered in chemical, electrical, civil, mechanical and petroleum engineering, mathematics, and industrial management.

6 Center of Applied Geology

The Center, located in the city of Jiddah, was under the administration of the University of Petroleum and Minerals, but came under King Abdul Aziz University's administration in 1975. It was established in 1970 with the cooperation of the United Nations Economic, Social and Cultural Organization (UNESCO). The objective of this center is to offer graduate studies in the field of applied geology leading to the Master of Science degree in that field. It encourages scientific and research work in the same field.

7 Data Processing Center

The University of Petroleum and Minerals was the first scientific institution in the Kingdom to establish a center for data processing which is indispensable for any modern university. The Center includes an IBM 370/158 complex, along with other subsidiary units necessary for educational and research purposes.

When the University (then a college) first started in 1963, student enrollment was sixty-seven and there was a faculty strength of fourteen. In 1978, student enrollment was 2,350 of whom eight per cent were non-Saudi students from twenty-five Arabian–Islamic countries. The faculty strength reached 388 from twenty-five different countries, including thirty-seven Saudi professors with PhD degrees. Over one hundred Saudi "faculty" members were in training in the United States, working for their PhDs. By 1983 3,814 students had enrolled.

Saudi students enrolled at the University receive generous financial aid from the government (free tuition, monthly allowance, subsidized meals at the University's cafeteria, essential medical care, furnished and air conditioned accommodation, free textbooks and round-trip air transportation to the student's place of residence once each academic year). The University offers similar scholarships to non-Saudi students from the Arab and Islamic world. It has students from Bahrain, Egypt, Ethiopia, Indonesia, Iraq, Jordan, Lebanon, Morocco, Pakistan, Qatar, Sudan, Syria, Tunisia and Yemen.

The University is governed by a Board consisting of prominent Saudi and non-Saudi scholars and government officials. The Saudi Minister of Petroleum and Mineral Resources was its chairman until 1976, when the Minister of Higher Education became Chairman of the Board.

UPM's academic program to train the manpower for the petroleum and related industries was complemented by the decision to set up a major applied Research Institute to help solve technical problems in this field. The Institute's program includes six areas of focus – petroleum and gas; alternative sources of energy (such as solar power); minerals; water and the environment; standards metrology; and economic and industrial research.

A SR 900 million ($260 million) expansion of campus facilities began in 1977, including a 24,000-square-meter building for the Research Institute; a building for the Graduate School, College of Industrial Management and the Data Processing Center; a Conference Center within the Department of Architecture; a 10,000-seat stadium; and a doubling of family and student housing.

By 1978, UPM had graduated one thousand engineers and industrial managers. By 1982 it planned to be graduating over five hundred engineers annually.

Status of Oil: Present and Future

Following the 1974 price increases, the Kingdom of Saudi Arabia has consistently exerted a moderating influence on oil pricing. By accepting the dollar as the currency for oil payments, Saudi Arabia has shared the consequences of dollar inflation and the devaluation of the money paid for oil. The government has shown itself to be peculiarly sensitive to world economic problems, aiming for a degree of oil price stability against the natural volatility of the market. Such volatility, while benefitting producer or consumer from time to time, does little, from a global economic viewpoint, to encourage international cooperation and sustained development.

The readiness of Saudi Arabia to reduce its own production of oil in order to stabilize prices is a striking feature of the history of oil pricing over the last decade. From 10,000,000 barrels a day in 1980/81, Saudi Arabia had reduced production to less than half that level in 1984. The consequences for Saudi Arabia's revenue are obvious and the more modest development program envisaged in the fourth Five Year Plan (covering the years 1985–1990) indicates that the Kingdom is prepared to accept the consequences of attempting to stabilize oil prices by limiting oil production in future.

Nevertheless, despite Saudi Arabia's moderating influence, the oil price has not been stable. The Iranian crisis at the end of 1978 led to Western fears of serious shortages of crude oil supplies. As governments increased their own oil stocks, the official price of crude oil rose from US$ 12.70 bbl in 1978 to US$ 30.00 bbl in 1980. In 1981, a high of US$ 42.00 was reached on the spot market. Since then crude oil prices have dropped reaching lows on the spot market of US$ 26.00 bbl in 1983 and 1984. At the same time, actual demand for oil in the non-communist world has

2.2 World Oil Production 1974–1983

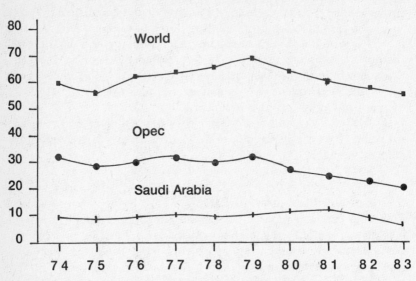

Source: BP Statistical Review of World Energy, June, 1984

fallen, from more than 50 million barrels a day in 1979 to about 45 million barrels a day in 1983.

What will happen next? What are the likely future developments in the oil market? Even with the moderating influence of Saudi Arabia, will the current oil price remain relatively stable? Or will it, as some predict, drop substantially to its "true" market value? Will uncertainties in the world political scene cause such price volatility that any form of prediction is impossible?

There is, of course, no single, simple answer to such questions. There are, however, underlying factors which are relevant and can be identified. First, there is, at present, no shortage of oil. This factor is clearly most important in attempting to assess the "true" market price of oil. To some extent, it is a buyers market. Secondly, new or increased reserves of oil are being discovered, in Saudi Arabia and elsewhere, as existing reserves diminish. Thirdly, the industrialized nations have made a major effort to diversify their sources of energy, including major investment in nuclear energy programs, in order to reduce their reliance on oil and vulnerability to price increases.

These three factors would suggest that, unless there is a major political upheaval, the price of oil will decrease in real terms over the next few years. On the other hand, oil remains an essential source of energy in all parts of the world and, if OPEC continues to function as a cohesive body, adjusting production levels as the need arises, any reductions in the oil price can be modest and well-ordered.

In the long term, the price of oil is likely to increase. Oil is a finite resource. In the end, the resource will become depleted. Unless, by then, alternative sources of energy have been developed which can satisfactorily fulfil all the energy roles of oil, the price of oil will rise.

No-one can be sure how the complex equation of supply and demand, economics and politics, technological developments and environmental considerations will be resolved. It is perhaps worth quoting World Oil (November, 1984) for an informed, oil industry-orientated view of likely future trends:

> Throughout this decade and the next, OPEC and the Middle East will continue to be of strategic importance to the industrialized nations. By 1990, world oil demand is expected to be 63 million barrels a day, approaching the peak demand level of 1979. The Middle East will continue to capture world attention because of its vast oil reserves and the production ability it represents.

> With increased demand for petroleum, OPEC will be able to produce 23 to 26 million barrels a day in 1990 . . . The countries of Saudi Arabia, Iran and Iraq are capable of meeting a 9 million barrel a day increase in world demand simply by opening up existing oil wells, oil system clean-up work and further oil developments which could be accomplished in about a two to three year time frame.

If this view is correct, clearly the oil policy of Saudi Arabia will continue to be of considerable importance to the industrialized nations of the West. Saudi Arabia's powerful voice, supported by deeds in terms of adjusting production to preserve a stable price structure, will be heard, loud and clear, for many years to come.

2.3 Oil: Official crude prices 1973–83* US dollars a barrel

	Saudi Arabia (Light)	Saudi Arabia (Heavy)	Iran (Light)	Nigeria† (Light)	Indonesia (Minas)	Venezuela (Tia Juana Med)	Mexico (Isthmus)	UK (Forties)
1973								
January 1st	—	—	—	—	—	—	—	—
April 1st	—	—	—	—	—	—	—	—
July 1st	2.75	2.48	—	—	3.73	—	—	—
October 1st	2.80	2.53	—	—	4.75	—	—	—
1974								
January 1st	10.84	10.64	11.16	—	10.80	—	—	—
April 1st	10.84	10.64	11.16	—	11.70	—	—	—
July 1st	10.84	10.64	11.26	—	12.60	—	—	—
October 1st	10.84	10.64	11.04	—	12.60	—	—	—
1975								
January 1st	10.46	10.27	10.67	11.72	12.60	—	11.30	—
April 1st	10.46	10.27	10.67	11.67	12.60	—	11.15	—
July 1st	10.46	10.27	10.67	11.45	12.60	—	11.10	—
October 1st	11.51	11.14	11.62	12.72	12.80	—	12.15	—
1976								
January 1st	11.51	11.14	11.62	12.86	12.80	11.12	12.15	12.60
April 1st	11.51	11.14	11.62	12.91	12.80	11.22	12.15	12.60
July 1st	11.51	11.04	11.62	13.12	12.80	11.32	12.15	12.80
October 1st	11.51	11.04	11.62	13.27	12.80	11.65	12.30	12.85
1977								
January 1st	12.09	11.37	12.81	14.33	13.55	12.72	13.35	14.00
April 1st	12.09	11.37	12.81	14.63	13.55	12.72	13.35	14.25
July 1st	12.70	12.02	12.81	14.63	13.55	12.72	13.40	14.18
October 1st	12.70	12.02	12.81	14.63	13.55	12.82	13.40	13.90
1978								
January 1st	12.70	12.02	12.81	14.33	13.55	12.82	13.40	13.70
April 1st	12.70	12.02	12.81	14.12	13.55	12.72	13.40	13.60
July 1st	12.70	12.02	12.81	14.12	13.55	12.72	13.10	13.70
October 1st	12.70	12.02	12.81	14.12	13.55	12.72	13.10	14.00
1979								
January 1st	13.34	12.51	13.45	14.82	13.90	13.36	14.10	15.45
April 1st	14.55	13.64	16.57	18.52	15.65	15.76	17.10	18.25
July 1st	18.00	17.17	22.00	23.49	18.25	19.31	22.60	23.20
October 1st	18.00	17.17	23.71	23.49	21.12	19.48	24.60	23.20
1980								
January 1st	26.00	25.00	30.37	29.99	27.50	25.20	32.00	29.75
April 1st	28.00	27.00	35.37	34.71	29.50	26.78	32.00	34.25
July 1st	28.00	27.00	35.37	37.02	31.50	29.88	34.50	36.25
October 1st	30.00	29.00	35.37	37.02	31.50	29.88	34.50	36.25
1981								
January 1st	32.00	31.00	37.00	40.02	35.00	32.88	38.50	39.25
April 1st	32.00	31.00	37.00	40.02	35.00	32.88	38.50	39.25
July 1st	32.00	31.00	37.00	40.02	35.00	32.88	36.50	35.00
October 1st	34.00	31.50	37.00	34.52	35.00	32.88	34.00	35.00
1982								
January 1st	34.00	31.00	34.20	36.52	35.00	32.88	35.00	36.50
April 1st	34.00	31.00	30.20	35.52	35.00	32.88	32.50	31.00
July 1st	34.00	31.00	31.20	35.52	35.00	32.88	32.50	33.50
October 1st	34.00	31.00	31.20	35.52	35.00	32.88	32.50	33.50
1983								
January 1st	34.00	31.00	31.20	35.52	34.53	32.88	32.50	33.50
April 1st	29.00	26.00	28.00	30.02	29.53	27.88	29.00	29.75
July 1st	29.00	26.00	28.00	30.02	29.53	27.88	29.00	29.75
October 1st	29.00	26.00	28.00	30.02	29.53	27.88	29.00	29.90

* Official Government Selling Prices ruling on the first day of each quarter (except for UK where BPBNOC prices are given). Prices are reported only from the port where Official Government Selling Prices were first established for the crudes in question.

† Including 2 cents/barrel port dues.

Source: BP Statistical Review of World Energy, June 1984.

The table below shows the relative importance of the different sources of energy broken down by country (1982–83).

2.4 Primary energy: Consumption (1982–83) by fuel (million tonnes oil equivalent)

	Oil 1982	Natural gas 1982	Coal 1982	Hydro-electric 1982	Nuclear energy 1982	Total 1982	Oil 1983	Natural gas 1983	Coal 1983	Hydro electric 1983	Nuclear energy 1983	Total 1983
North America												
USA	705.5	459.2	394.6	90.1	77.7	1 727.1	700.3	432.3	400.3	95.4	80.0	1 708.3
Canada	72.9	48.9	27.3	56.7	9.1	214.9	66.5	46.7	28.3	55.7	11.5	208.7
Total North America	778.4	508.1	421.9	146.8	86.8	1 942.0	766.8	479.0	428.6	151.1	91.5	1 917.0
Latin America	223.5	60.0	17.1	52.0	0.5	353.1	217.9	60.7	17.2	52.6	0.6	349.0
Western Europe												
Austria	10.5	3.8	3.0	7.1	—	24.4	10.0	3.9	2.8	7.1	—	23.8
Belgium & Luxembourg	23.3	7.8	11.1	0.1	3.7	46.0	21.2	8.2	9.1	0.1	5.3	43.9
Denmark	11.0	—	5.7	—	⁺ —	16.7	10.4	.	5.4	—	—	15.8
Finland	11.3	0.6	1.9	3.5	4.1	21.4	10.4	0.6	2.2	3.3	4.2	20.7
France	91.5	24.0	28.6	15.2	22.5	181.8	89.3	24.8	24.3	15.2	27.4	181.0
Greece	11.9	—	4.0	0.9	—	16.8	11.5	—	4.8	1.1	—	17.4
Iceland	0.5	—	—	1.0	—	1.5	0.5	—	—	1.0	—	1.5
Republic of Ireland	4.6	1.4	2.1	0.2	—	8.3	4.2	1.9	2.2	0.2	—	8.5
Italy	90.7	22.0	14.4	11.0	2.4	140.5	88.7	22.6	13.0	11.1	2.1	137.5
Netherlands	31.0	30.4	5.4	—	0.9	67.7	29.1	32.3	5.4	—	0.9	67.7
Norway	7.7	—	0.5	23.7	—	31.9	7.6	—	0.6	25.3	—	33.5
Portugal	9.5	—	0.4	2.5	—	12.4	9.4	—	0.4	2.3	—	12.1
Spain	47.8	2.3	18.0	5.6	2.0	75.7	47.6	2.3	18.9	6.8	2.4	78.0
Sweden	21.8	—	1.6	9.5	6.8	39.7	20.0	—	1.6	10.9	7.0	39.5
Switzerland	11.2	0.8	0.4	9.6	3.7	25.7	12.3	0.9	0.3	9.3	3.8	26.6
Turkey	16.5	—	8.0	3.2	—	27.7	16.7	—	8.6	3.4	—	28.7
United Kingdom	75.6	42.2	65.3	1.4	9.4	193.9	72.4	43.3	65.6	1.4	10.7	193.4
West Germany	112.2	38.0	79.4	5.6	14.4	249.6	109.8	38.8	80.5	6.2	14.8	250.1
Yugoslavia	14.1	3.8	15.9	6.2	0.6	40.6	13.0	3.9	16.7	6.0	0.9	40.5
Cyprus/Gibraltar/ Malta	1.6	—	⁺	—	—	1.6	1.6	—	⁺	—	—	1.6
Total Western Europe	604.3	177.1	265.7	106.3	70.5	1 223.9	585.7	183.5	262.4	110.7	79.5	1 221.8
Middle East	87.9	37.8	⁺	1.3	—	127.0	90.4	38.5	⁺	1.6	—	130.5
Africa	79.5	18.0	70.1	15.9	—	183.5	80.3	17.6	74.4	17.2	—	189.5
Japan	207.8	24.7	62.0	19.5	27.0	341.0	205.8	25.2	63.0	19.5	27.5	341.0
South East Asia	113.5	7.6	21.7	3.8	4.4	151.0	114.5	7.8	24.1	4.1	7.2	157.7
South Asia	45.6	11.8	91.5	14.0	0.6	163.5	46.4	13.0	97.0	16.0	0.7	173.1
Australasia	34.4	12.2	33.2	8.9	—	88.7	33.2	13.4	32.3	9.2	—	88.1
Total NCW	2 174.9	857.3	983.2	368.5	189.8	4 573.7	2 141.0	838.7	999.0	382.0	207.0	4 567.7
Centrally-Planned Economies (CPEs)												
China	82.4	9.5	412.2	19.0	—	523.1	84.7	10.7	463.0	21.9	—	553.3
USSR	448.5	380.0	345.0	49.5	20.5	1 243.5	450.5	405.0	358.0	51.0	22.0	1 286.5
Others	119.1	70.1	306.8	14.1	7.2	517.3	117.8	74.5	304.1	14.3	7.3	518.0
Total CPEs	650.0	459.6	1 064.0	82.6	27.7	2 283.9	653.0	490.2	1 098.1	87.2	29.3	2 357.8
Total World	2 824.9	1 316.9	2 047.2	451.1	217.5	6 857.6	2 794.0	1 328.9	2 097.1	469.2	236.3	6 925.5

⁺ Less than 0.05

Source: BP Statistical Review of World Energy, June 1984

[1] Ashraf Lutfi, *OPEC Oil* (Beirut: The Middle East Research and Publishing Center, 1968), p. 116.

[2] Kamal Sayegh, *Oil and Arab Regional Development* (New York: Frederick A. Praeger, 1968), pp. 25–26.

[3] Dwight D. Eisenhower, *Waging Peace 1956–1961* (New York: Doubleday, 1965), p. 20.

[4] Hereafter referred to as the "Saudi Arab [*sic*] Concession".

[5] *Agreement between the Saudi Arab Government and the Arabian American Oil Company*, 2nd ed. (Makkah: Government Press, 1383 AH/1964 AD), p. 5.

[6] George Lenczowski, *The Middle East in World Affairs*, 3rd ed. (Ithaca, N.Y.: Cornell University Press, 1962), p. 549.

[7] *Agreement between the Saudi Arab Government and the Japan Petroleum Trading Company, Ltd*, 2nd ed. (Makkah: Government Press, 1384 AH/1964 AD), p. 4.

[8] *Area Handbook for Saudi Arabia*, 2nd ed. (Washington, DC: US Government Printing Office, 1971), p. 317.

[9] *Agreement between the Saudi Arab Government and the Arabian American Oil Company*, p. 9.

[10] George Lenczowski, *Oil and State in the Middle East* (Ithaca, NY: Cornell University Press, 1960), p. 19.

[11] *Area Handbook for Saudi Arabia*, p. 246.

[12] Abdul Amir Kubbah, *OPEC: Past and Present* (Vienna: Petro-Economic Research Center, 1974), p. 156.

[13] A copy of this General Agreement was obtained by the Author through the courtesy of the Legal Department of the Ministry of Petroleum and Mineral Resources of Saudi Arabia in May 1975 at Riyadh.

[14] Statistics obtained by Author from the Saudi Ministry of Petroleum and Mineral Resources, Economics Department, Riyadh, June, 1975.

[15] Kingdom of Saudi Arabia, Ministry of Petroleum and Mineral Resources, Economics Department, *Petroleum Statistical Bulletin* 2 (1971): 12.

[16] Kubbah, *OPEC: Past and Present*, p. 12.

[17] *Ibid*, p. 13.

[18] *Ibid*, p. 9.

[19] THE CONFERENCE Basic Rules:
  1. It holds two ordinary meetings annually – June, November, or December.
  2. Each member country has one vote.
  3. All decisions of the conference must be unanimous.
  4. A quorum of three-quarters of member countries is necessary for holding a conference (currently ten members constitute a quorum).
  5. Resolutions become effective after 30 days from the conclusion of the meeting.
  THE BOARD OF GOVERNORS General Rules:
  1. A simple majority is sufficient for making decisions.
  2. Meets twice annually.
  3. Term of each Governor for two years.
  4. The Chairman and alternate Chairman are appointed from the Governors of the Conference for one year term.
  Synthesized by author from Abdul Amir Kubbah, *OPEC: Past and Present*, pp. 25–32.

[20] Mohammed T. Algohonami, *Al A'Hkam Ala' Ama F' Ka'Nun Al U'mam* ("General Rules in the Law of Nations") (Alexandria, Egypt: Al Ma'arif Publishing House, n.d.), pp. 1218–1219. (F.F. translation.)

[21] *Ibid*, p. 1219.

[22] Kubbah, *OPEC: Past and Present*, p. 17.

[23] *The Statute of the Organization of the Petroleum Exporting Countries* (Vienna, 1971), p. 7.

[24] *Ibid.*

[25] *Ibid.*

[26] "The Gazelles and the Lions", *The Economist* 249 (November 17, 1973): 14.

[27] Khodadad Farmanfarmaian, Armin Gutowski, Saburo Okita, Robert V. Roosa, and Carroll L. Wilson, "How Can the World Afford OPEC Oil?" *Foreign Affairs*, 53 (January 1975): 206.

[28] *Ibid.*

[29] Thomas O. Enders, "OPEC and the Industrial Countries," *Foreign Affairs* 53 (July 1975): 637.

[30] Algohonami, *Al A'Hkam Ala' Ama*, pp. 1241–1245. (F.F. translation.)

[31] *It' Fakiyat Mu'nazimat Al' Aktar Al' Arabia Al Musadera Lil Petrol* ("Agreement: Organization of Arab Petroleum Exporting Countries") (Kuwait: OAPEC, n.d.), p. 7. (F.F. translation.)

[32] Kubbah, *OPEC: Past and Present*, p. 162.

[33] *Mu'nazimat Al' Aktar Al' Arabia Al Musadera Lil Petrol* ("Organization of Arab Petroleum Exporting Countries: A Brief Report on its Activities, 1968–1973") (Kuwait: Fahd al Marzok Printing Press, 1974), p. 14. (F.F. translation.)

[34] All the information and data on the University of Petroleum and Minerals of Dhahran, Saudi Arabia, in this Section, was received through mail in a letter dated 15–8 1395 AH (1975 AD), from the Director of Public Relations of the University, Mr. Abdul Rhaman Algandan. All the material is the Author's translation.

[35] By Royal Decree No. 397 of September 23, 1963 (1383 AH).

CHAPTER III

The Polity and Organization of the Kingdom

O ye who believe!
Obey God, and obey the Apostle
And those charged
With authority among you
If ye differ in anything
Among yourselves, refer it
To God and His Apostle
If ye do believe in God
And the last day:
That is best, and most suitable
For final determination.

Holy Quran, *Sura Nisaa* [The Women], verse 59.[1]

Introduction

THIS CHAPTER deals with the various aspects of the Saudi government's polity and organization. The first part will deal with the Royal Family as the head of the government. The *Ulama*, religious leaders, will be treated briefly in the second part of the chapter. The military institutions of Saudi Arabia will be discussed in the third part. The fourth will be devoted to a very important mechanism in the government of Saudi Arabia – the Ministry of Planning (formerly the Central Planning Organization – CPO), which is entrusted with the formulation and implementation of the country's development plans. The final part of this chapter will examine the concept of polycommunality and how it can be related to the polity of Saudi Arabia.

Saudi Arabia's Royal Family

The history of the House of Sa'ud, the Royal Family of the Kingdom of Saudi Arabia, goes back over two centuries. As part of this chapter we have designed three charts dealing with the Royal family's structure and political leadership. The first chart covers the period starting with the first ruler of the Saudi Dynasty from 1744 through 1818. The second chart deals with the continued succession of the Saudi House from 1824 through 1891. The final chart traces the third ascendancy of the Royal Family, the period starting in 1902 and continuing through the current era.

Actually, "the name of Al-Sa'ud, which means 'Family of Sa'ud' or 'House of Sa'ud', comes from Sa'ud Ibn Muhammad Ibn Mugrin, who lived in the early 18th century."[2]

IIIa

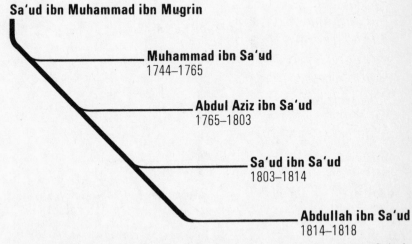

Sa'ud ibn Muhammad ibn Mugrin

Muhammad ibn Sa'ud
1744–1765

Abdul Aziz ibn Sa'ud
1765–1803

Sa'ud ibn Sa'ud
1803–1814

Abdullah ibn Sa'ud
1814–1818

The first ruler of the First House of Sa'ud was Muhammad Ibn Sa'ud, who joined forces with Imam Muhammad Ibn Abdul Wahhab, the eminent religious leader, in what could be called the first alliance, which laid down the early foundations of the Kingdom of Saudi Arabia. Most important is the fact that Muhammad Ibn Sa'ud started first as the ruler of the town of Ad-Dir'iyah, in the heart of Najd; his reign lasted through 1765.

His son, Abdul Aziz Ibn Muhammad Ibn Sa'ud, ruled from 1765 through 1803, retaining the association with Imam Muhammad Ibn Abdul Wahhab in the same capacity as his father and continuing to reform Islam in that part of the world. Abdul Aziz successfully captured the city of Riyadh in 1773. As a result, the Saudi state began to spread rapidly and within fifteen years had extended its authority all over Najd.

After the death of Abdul Aziz, his son, Sa'ud, ruled from 1802 through 1814.

In 1814 Sa'ud's son, Abdullah, ruled until 1818, when the Viceroy of Egypt, Muhammed Ali, sent troops to Ad-Dir'iyah and captured Abdullah Ibn Sa'ud. Thus, the first temporary decline in the House of Sa'ud occurred.

The second chart traces the reemergence and rise of the House of Sa'ud after a brief decline of a few years, and shows its continuation with Turki Ibn Sa'ud from 1824, through 1834. The succession of his son Faisal to the leadership of the House lasted through 1865. From 1865 until 1889, disagreements between the four sons of Faisal Ibn Sa'ud led to another decline in the House of Sa'ud. Fortunately, Abdul-Rahman Ibn Faisal,

III b

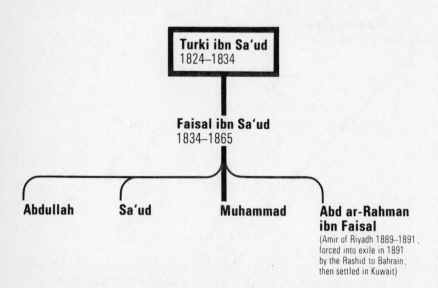

the third son of Faisal Ibn Sa'ud, managed to confirm and enhance the rule of the Saudi Dynasty by assuming the leadership of the family in 1889. By that time, the authority of the Saudi family extended to Riyadh, which became the center of their domain. In 1891, another decline occurred in the House of Sa'ud when the Rashid family and tribes of northern Arabia forced Abdul-Rahman Ibn Faisal to leave Riyadh and live in exile in Kuwait.

The following chart traces the third rise of the House of Sa'ud, from 1902 onward, and the eventual establishment of the Kingdom of Saudi Arabia.

This third period began in 1902 when King Abdul Aziz Al Sa'ud recaptured the city of Riyadh and established his rule over that area. From 1902 through 1926, King Abdul Aziz vigorously and brilliantly extended his authority over most of the Arabian Peninsula. In September 1932, the Kingdom of Saudi Arabia officially acquired its present name.

From Chart IIIc one can deduce a basic political phenomenon in the structure of the Royal Family; that is, in the dynamics of succession to the leadership of the Kingdom. Since the first Saudi rule in 1744 by Muhammad Ibn Sa'ud, through 1902, the succession process was from father to son. But from 1953, after the death of King Abdul Aziz, the father–son succession ended. In 1964 King Faisal Ibn Abdul Aziz became the third of the modern kings of Saudi Arabia. In 1975 King Khalid succeeded his brother, King Faisal; thus a new process of succession to

III c

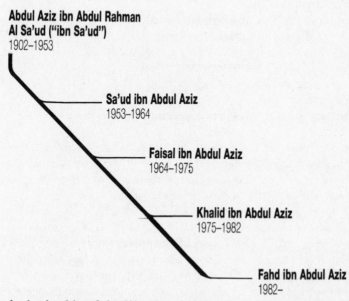

Abdul Aziz ibn Abdul Rahman Al Sa'ud ("ibn Sa'ud")
1902–1953

Sa'ud ibn Abdul Aziz
1953–1964

Faisal ibn Abdul Aziz
1964–1975

Khalid ibn Abdul Aziz
1975–1982

Fahd ibn Abdul Aziz
1982–

the leadership of the Kingdom is being established – succession among the sons of King Abdul Aziz Al Sa'ud in order of their ages. There are over thirty-five sons of Ibn Saud. Another new political factor, equally important, is the majestic size of the Kingdom founded by Ibn Saud. Currently, members of the Royal Family hold positions in the government at all levels.

The Ulama (Religious Leaders)

The role of the *Ulama* in Saudi Arabia has a long history and great significance. A brief summary will have to suffice.

The first alliance between Muhammad Ibn Sa'ud and Imam Muhammad Ibn Abdul Wahhab, and its continued success through the years reflect the important role played by the *Ulama* in Saudi Arabia. That first alliance was both political and religious in nature and clearly emphasized the true notion of the state in Islam; that is, state and religion are inseparable. The Kingdom of Saudi Arabia is an example of an Islamic state governed by the Holy *Quran*. This fact reflects the important role of the *Ulama*. They play an influential part in the following fields of government:

1 The judicial system of Saudi Arabia.
2 The implementation of the rules of the Islamic *Shari'ah*.
3 Religious Guidance Group with affiliated offices all over the Kingdom.
4 Religious education, that is, Islamic legal education and theology at all levels in Saudi Arabia.
5 Religious jurisprudence.
6 Preaching and guidance throughout the nation.
7 Supervision of girls' education.
8 Religious supervision of all Mosques in the Kingdom.
9 Preaching for Islam abroad.
10 Continuous scientific and Islamic research.
11 Notaries public.
12 The handling of legal cases in courts according to Islamic law.

The administration and application of the judicial system of Saudi Arabia illustrates the importance of the *Ulama*. When King Abdul Aziz extended his rule over the western part of the Kingdom, the Hijaz, he was faced with the existence of three separate judicial systems. The first was that of the Hijaz, with an Ottoman orientation. The second was that of the small towns of Najd. Under this system, an Amir (similar to a regional governor), with the assistance of one judge, represented the law. The Amir would try to solve the disputes submitted to him or refer them to the judge for a final ruling. The implementation of the judge's decisions was the Amir's duty.

The third, more primitive and indigenous, was the tribal law. Here, the conflicting parties would refer their disputes to the individual tribe's law, and its own lawyers would give a final decision according to precedent.

While recommending temporary measures to cope with the current situation, King Abdul Aziz did not allow the persistence of such perplexing and impeding judicial systems. A Royal Decree was issued in 1927 with the aim of unifying the judicial system of the nation. Its institutions were classified into three hierarchical categories: "expeditious courts, *Shari'ah* courts, and the Commission on Judicial Supervision".[3] The first courts

> handled the more simple criminal and civil cases and were divided into first expeditious courts and second expeditious courts. The latter dealt with cases involving nomads. All other cases were within the jurisdiction of the *Shari'ah* courts. In addition to inspecting and supervising the courts, the commission had the function of judicial review.[4]

This classification of courts in the Kingdom of Saudi Arabia is basically the same today, and the latest important legislation on the subject, the Attributions of *Shari'ah* Jurisprudence Responsibilities of 1952, though more detailed, and covering such subjects as the Notaries Public, the

Property Departments and Summoning Officers, has not signified any radical departure.

The organizational framework remained as below:[5]

III d

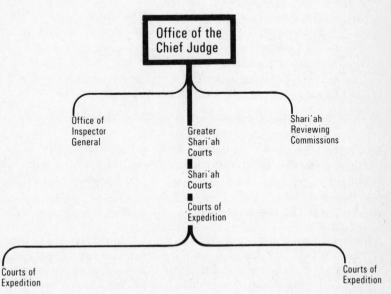

Underlying the judicial structure are the four schools of thought in Islamic law. They are: the *Hanbali* school; the *Shafii* school; the *Hanafi* school; and, finally, the *Ma'liki* school. Before the unification of the Saudi judicial system, the courts, as well as individual judges, used to derive their legal judgments from these various schools. That is to say, in Hijaz there were two dominant schools of thought – the *Hanafi*, and the *Shafii*, whereas in Najd, the *Hanbali* school had been the only major source of legal guidance. After 1927, all the courts of Saudi Arabia were instructed to use six *Hanbali* books for their legal decisions in an effort to establish one sound judicial system. Judges have recourse to the other three schools of legal thought, as well as to their personal discretion, in cases for which no provision is available in the six *Hanbali* books. This has added more flexibility to the judicial system. The general rule that "the diversity of the four Imams for whom these four schools of thought were named is a god-send for the Islamic nation"[6] indeed reflects the elastic nature of Islamic law in general.

As the Kingdom of Saudi Arabia began to keep pace with twentieth century developments, it became evident that the judicial system needed more workable subsidiary organs to cope with the increase of litigation.

As a result, various judicial organs were created. The following are the most important:

The Grievance Board
The Committee on Cases of Forgery
The Commission on Cases of Bribery
The Commission on the Impeachment of Ministers
The Commission on the Settlement of Commercial Disputes
The Central Committee on Cases of Adulteration
The Supreme Commission on Labor Disputes
The Disciplinary Councils for Civil Servants
The Disciplinary Councils for Military Personnel

While some of these organs, such as the Grievance Board, function on a continuous basis, others, such as the various disciplinary Councils, are of an *ad hoc* character.[7]

Undoubtedly the Saudi Arabian *Ulama* enjoyed a unique status while developing, reforming and unifying the judicial system of the country. The *Ulama* were never handicapped by a situation which confronted various Muslim countries; they

were not faced with an imposed foreign law as the country was never under any colonial rule which would confront them with the dilemma of either calling for its repeal and thus creating a vacuum, or producing an instant Islamic alternative, something beyond their human reach.[8]

The *Ulama* of Saudi Arabia were not imitators "picking isolated fragments of opinions from the early centuries of Islamic law, arranging them into a kind of arbitrary mosaic, and concealing behind this screen an essentially different structure of ideas borrowed from the West".[9] Rather, they were faithful, broad-minded followers of the teachings of the Holy *Quran* and the *Sunnah* (tradition), and implemented Islamic laws according to one of the accepted trends of law in Islam, the *Hanbali* school of thought.

Military Institutions in Saudi Arabia[10]
The government of Saudi Arabia consists of several major elements. The first is the Royal Family; the second the *Ulama*; the third, its military institutions.

A brief reference should be made to the National Guard, which is an independent force presided over by Crown Prince Abdullah Ibn Abdul Aziz, the Deputy Prime Minister. The Saudi National Guard's duties parallel those of the National Guard of the United States. In case of emergency, it can join with the armed forces for the defense of the Kingdom.

The current Minister of Defense and Aviation is the Second Deputy Prime Minister, Prince Sultan ibn Abdul Aziz. The Minister and the Vice

IIIe **Ministry of Defense and Aviation**

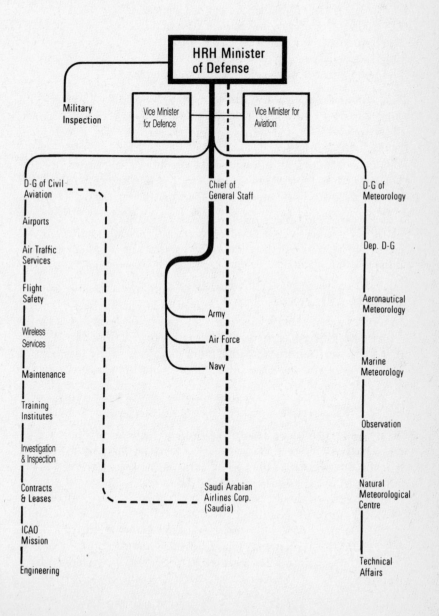

Ministers perform similar functions and exercise similar authority, despite the fact that, in the foregoing chart, the Vice Ministers come second on the administrative scale of the Ministry of Defense. His Royal Highness, the Minister, delegates his authority to the Vice Ministers at all times, whether the Minister is in the country or abroad.

A similar delegation of authority applies to the General Chief of Staff and the Assistant Chief of Staff.

Saudi Arabia's armed forces, according to seniority, are composed of

1 The Army
2 The Air Force
3 The Navy

There is no compulsory draft; recruiting is conducted purely on a voluntary basis. Once a person is recruited, he joins a training center; then, as a private, he is referred to one of the army's special units according to the needs of the army.

A candidate seeking to join one of the Saudi military academies after high school, enrols for a period of three years, graduating at the end of the third year as a second lieutenant without specific specialty. He would then be sent to one of the army's schools for specialization, after which he would become a member of one of the army's corps. Currently, in Saudi Arabia, there are four military academies. These are:

1 King Abdul Aziz Military College (Riyadh)
   It confers a Bachelor of Military Science degree.
2 King Faisal Air Force College (Riyadh)
   It offers a Bachelor's degree.
3 Command and Staff College (Riyadh)
   Offers a degree which equals a Master of Science degree in Military Science.
4 Internal Security College
   Offers a Bachelor's degree in Internal Security Science. This college is under the supervision of the Ministry of Interior.[11]

This part of the chapter will be restricted to the Army of Saudi Arabia. There will be no elaboration on either the Navy or the Air Force as they were not included in the interviews conducted by the author.[12]

The Saudi Arabian Army consists of the following units:

Combat Units
A Infantry
B Artillery
C Armored
D Air Defense

Support Units
E Signal
F Maintenance
G Transportation
H Engineering

Supply Units
I Ordnance
J Supply

Naturally there are various schools in the army which train men for the ten major units of the army. These schools are as follows:

1 Maintenance
2 Infantry
3 Artillery
4 Armored
5 Air Defense
6 Engineering Corps
7 Signal Corps
8 Airborne Corps
9 Administrative Affairs

Moreover, the Saudi Arabian Army, believing strongly in good quality education at all levels and in various fields, incorporates within its structure, the following institutes and schools:

a Foreign Languages Institute
b Technical Institute of the Air Force
c Musical Institute of the Armed Forces

As for the other general schools of the army, they are:

1 School of Medical Services
2 School for Clerical Training
3 School of Physical Education
4 Military Police School

The period of training at these four general schools varies from two to two and a half years. They graduate Non-Commissioned Officers (NCOs).

Moreover, the Ministry of Defense carries the burden of further educating its military personnel as well as spreading and making available adult education throughout the various units of the armed forces.

It also sends men for further training in different countries – to Belgium, Britain, France, West Germany and the United States, and in Asia to Pakistan and Nationalist China (Taiwan). Within the countries of the Middle East, some Ministry of Defense Personnel are sent to the

Arab Republic of Egypt and to Jordan. By 1980, in accordance with the Second Five Year Plan, the Ministry of Defense and its armed forces achieved a level of efficiency which has enabled the Kingdom to pursue with greater ease its perceived role in the Gulf area.

1. Ministry of Planning[13]

The Ministry of Planning plays a key role in the development of the country. The CPO had already executed with moderate success the First Five Year Plan (1390–1395 AH 1970–1975 AD). The Ministry of Planning then engaged in the implementation of the Second Five Year Plan which started with the budget of 1975–1976. The Second Five Year Plan's allocations are about US $141 billion.

A supreme planning board was established in 1960.[14] This was replaced by the Central Planning Organization in 1964 in accordance with the Council of Ministers' Resolution No. 430.

This Resolution sets out the CPO's basic functions and objectives. Article 4 of the Resolution reads:

4 The said Organization [CPO] shall be charged with the following functions:

a To prepare a periodic economic report on the Kingdom, containing an economic analysis and showing the scope of progress achieved and prospective developments.

b To prepare economic development plans, provided that the first plan be a five year plan and be approved by the Council of Ministers before being put into effect.

c To estimate the total funds required for the implementation of the development plans approved by the Council of Ministers.

d To conduct economic studies required for relevant projects and to submit its recommendations thereon.

e To assist Ministers and independent agencies in their planning affairs. To submit technical advice on matters raised by His Majesty the King.[15]

Members of the Organization's staff, as at May 1975, numbered 194 persons.[16] Work in the CPO was divided into two categories, administrative and technical. Out of the total number of CPO employees, ninety-three held administrative jobs; their educational level was beneath that of Bachelor's degree. Another 101 occupied technical or specialized positions in the CPO. All of these were university graduates and a moderate percentage had a Master's degree in various fields (eg, Engineering, Economics, Public Administration, Business Administration). The Central Planning Organization also cooperated with foreign advisory groups in the field of planning and development.

IIIf **Ministry of Planning**

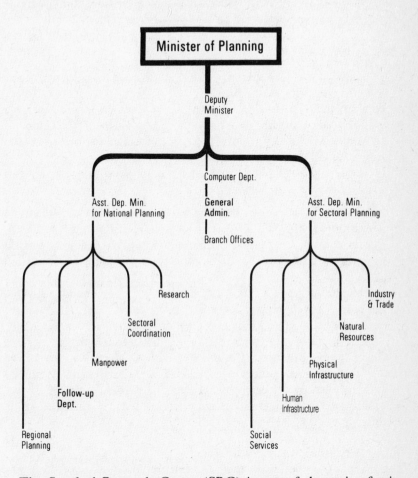

The Stanford Research Group (SRG) is one of the major foreign advisory groups which has worked within the CPO/Ministry of Planning since 1967. According to Dr. Fayz Badr, then Vice President of the Central Planning Organization, the status of the Stanford Research Group is unique. It did not function as an independent body within the CPO; rather, the Stanford Research Group was part of the CPO staff. Dr. Badr explained that the Central Planning Organization would submit assignments to the Stanford Research Group for study. In other words, the CPO initiated development programs, because it knew best the needs of the country. This approach is a mechanism for implementing appropriate technology.[17]

Previously, the Saudi approach to foreign advice had been contrary to the current policy; foreign advisory groups enjoyed independent status and initiated programs in the country. These often proved to be incompatible with Saudi perceptions of developmental needs.

The role of the Stanford Research Group within the Ministry may be described as follows:[18]

1 To assist in the formulation of the country's developmental plans under the direction of the Ministry.
2 To assist the Ministry in recruiting the proper personnel needed for its staff in a direct manner; direct contracting on behalf of the Ministry.
3 To assist the Ministry in its follow-up and evaluation of the various projects and plans.
4 To render advice and conduct research on specific subjects when asked to do so by the Ministry.

Another foreign advisory group working within the Central Planning Organization was the SCET International, a French group engaged in making a study of economic impediments in the Kingdom.[19] Such a study was crucially needed in a country undergoing an industrial revolution.

The Kingdom's astronomical 1978 budget of US $30 billion reflected the ambitious developments occurring in the country. Sheikh Mohammad Aba Al Kail, the Minister of Finance and National Economy, stated that the 1975–1976 budget (1395–1396 AH) constituted an increase of over fifty per cent from the previous year's. Moreover, sixty-seven per cent of the total budget was allocated for developmental projects while only nineteen per cent was devoted to defense allocations. *In toto*, the Saudi Arabian budget multiplied one hundred and ten times within the decade to 1975.[20]

Polycommunality and Manpower

The fifth, and by no means the least, integrated sequence of the polity and organization of Saudi Arabia is the ethnicity phenomenon. In many developing countries, any study of their ethnic composition would immediately involve the concept of polycommunality. By this we mean that in countries like India, Lebanon, Nigeria and Pakistan, where problems of cultural and religious heritage, language and ethnic origin exist, the concept of polycommunality

allows for the varying mixtures and interlacings of ethnic, caste, tribal, religious, and different systems. It . . . has the qualities of range and precision. The prefix "poly-" directs attention to the inter- rather than the intra- group nature of the problem.[21]

Since we are examining Saudi Arabia which is among the

few polities [of the world] whose political culture ... approximates homogeneity [a condition which can largely be attributed to the cohesiveness of Islam],[22]

the term polycommunality is not as pertinent as it is elsewhere.[23] The population of Saudi Arabia falls conveniently into three categories. The first and second are indigenous, the third are the aliens.

The first category contains the major tribes of the country. The second contains the bulk of the population: native residents of cities, towns and villages. The final category includes all the foreigners living and working in the country.

In this section we have relied on an authoritative work dealing with Arabian tribes.[24] The author, Fouad Hamza, was for some time a Deputy Minister of Foreign Affairs in the reign of King Abdul Aziz Al Sa'ud. All his work on the tribes of Saudi Arabia had received the approbation of the late Prince Abdullah Ibn Abdul Rahman, King Khalid's uncle, who was himself considered to be a leading authority on tribal affairs. As Hamza rightly said,

it is very difficult for a researcher to comprehend and account for the origin of all the Arabian tribes that exist at the present time, due to the loss of a rather large section of the genealogical records which their predecessors wrote, and [to] the loss of several links in the lineage chain during the middle ages, a period of decline for Arabian states [as well as of] disagreement among its princes and tribes.[25]

For obvious reasons, no effort was made to trace the branches of these various tribes back to their ancient roots.

Tribes, according to Fouad Hamza, may be divided into five classes:

1 Tribe   *Kabila*
2 Group   *Batin*
3 Division   *Fakhed*
4 Clan   *Fasila*
5 Family   *Raht*

As an example, the family (*Raht*) of Sahlan belongs to the Al Mir'ad clan (*Fasila*), of the group of Al Rola, of the division (*Fakhed*) of Dani Muslim of the tribe (*Kabila*) Anza.

The following names of the tribes of the entire country were arranged alphabetically according to the Arabic alphabet, disregarding the alternative categories of pride, wealth, ability and lineage.[26]

The two tables designate respectively the major tribes of the Arabian Peninsula and the main ones of Saudi Arabia.

3.1 Names of Major Arab Tribes in the Arabian Peninsula (arranged in alphabetical order)

Ahmar	Rabiy'ah al Tihham	Awof
Asmar	Rabiy'ah Warfidah	Awazim
	Rabiy'ah at Yaman	Ayr
Barik	Rashaydah	
Bahr bin Sukayna	al Rayesh	Gamed
Baqum	Rigal al Ma'a	
Bili		Fodole
	Zubeid	Fahme
Tamim	Zahran	
	Zeid	Qahtan
Thaqif		Karne or Garne
Thamalah	Subel'a	Quraysh[1]
Thawab	Sa'd	
	Sufyan	Malek
Gahadlah	Su'kaynah	Malek Asir
Ga'afrah	Sahl	Muhammad
Go'dah		Marwan
Gohaynah	Shoubail	Masarehah
	Shararat	Motair
Harith	Shareef	Ma'a
Ho'rath	Shou'abah	Me'gyed
Harb	Shamran	Manaseer
Hasan	Shammar	Mongehah
Hala	Shehre	Mahdy
Howaytat	Shahran	Mosa
	Shalawah	Morrah
Khaled		
Kath'am	Salboh	Hager
Kotha'ah		Hotaym
Kidayr	Zufayer	Hothayl
Kamiseen		Helal
	Abse	
Doriab	Utaybah	Nogo'a
Da'Kaiyah	Ogman	Nashar
Dawasir	Aryan	Nomoor
	Asir	Nagran
Zabyan or Thabyan	Atayah	
	al Kam al Howl	Ya'la
Rabiy'ah	Amre	Yam
Rabiy'al Mokatirah	Anzah	

[1] Descendants of the Prophet Muhammad

Source Hamza, **Qalb, Al-Jazira Al-Arabia**, pp. 136–137. Author's transliteration.

3.2 Names of Major Tribes in Saudi Arabia

Belahmer	Kath'am	Kabilat al Ogman
Belasmer	Kotha'ah	Kabilat Harb
Ahle Bareg[q]	Kamiseen	Kabilat al Howaytat
Bahr bin Sukayna	Bano Kidayr	Ahle Hala
Baqum	Al-Aldorayeb	Thoo Hasan
Bili	D'akyah	Khaled
Bano Tamim	Dawasir	Shamran
Bano Thawa'h	Rabiy'ah	Bano Shehre
Thamalah	Rigal al Ma'a	Shahran
Thaqif	Al Rashaydah	Al Sha'lawah
Al Gahadlah	Al Raysh	Shammar
Al Ga'afrah	Zubeid	Al Selbeh
Go'dah	Zahran	Kabilat Twowayreg[q]
Gohaynah	Bano Zeid	Al Zufayer
Belhareth	Saby'a	Kabilat Anzah
Kabilat al Howaytat	Bano Sa'ad	Kabilat Utaybah
Asir	Sufyan	Kabilat Bani Atayah
Al Kam al Howle	Al Sahol	Al Awazim
Al Ashraf	Al Shararat	Bano Abse
Quraysh	Kabilat Fahme	Bano Shobayl
Bano Malek	Belgarn	Qahtan
Al Masarehah	Bano Malek Asir	Al Mahdy
Kabilat al Morrah	Bano Muhammad	Bano Marwan
Al Mongehah	Me'gyed	Kabilat Motayer
Al Nogo'a	Al Mosa	Al Manasir
Amre	Bano Nashar	Nagran
Kabilat Bani Hager	Bal'eyre	Al Nomoor
Hothayl	Kabilat Bani Hager	Gamid
	Helal	Hotaym
	Bano Ya'ly	Yam

Source: Hamza, **Qalb Al-Jazira Al-Arabia**, pp. 138–212. Author's transliteration.

In general

there has never been a steady trend toward settlement on the part of
nomads, who pass through semi-nomadic stages. There may be no more
than 200,000 to 300,000 wholly nomadic bedouin in the Kingdom of
Saudi Arabia out of a total population of approximately six to seven
million. . . .[27]

Perhaps five per cent of the Saudi population are wholly nomadic today.
    As to native residents of cities, towns and villages, little can be said
except that the population of Saudi Arabia is ethnically homogeneous.
The most conspicuous difference is that of dialect, by which one can

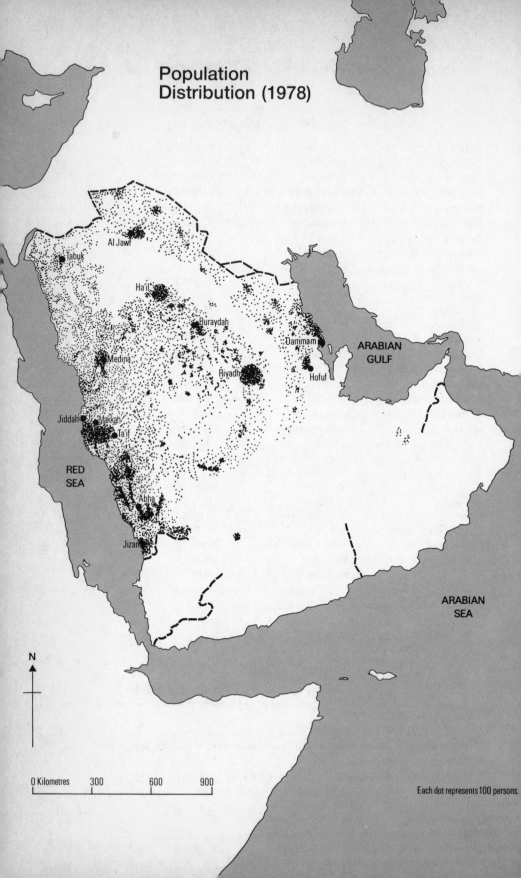

Population
Distribution (1978)

Tabuk

Al Jawf

Ha'il

Buraydah

Dammam

ARABIAN
GULF

Medina

Riyadh

Hofuf

Jiddah Makkah

Ta'if

RED
SEA

Abha

ARABIAN
SEA

Jizan

N

0 Kilometres   300   600   900

Each dot represents 100 persons.

distinguish whether a person is from the Western Province (Medina, Makkah, or Jiddah) or from the Central or Eastern Provinces (Riyadh, Dammam, or Al-Hasa).

In recent times the trend has been towards further urbanization and away from nomadism, a trend encouraged by the Government. Saudi Arabia's estimated population is between seven and nine million out of which more than half are under twenty years of age. Although no official population growth rates are available, it is believed that the 1978 rate was around two per cent.

Population is concentrated not only in the major cities of the Kingdom but in approximately parallel north–south bands down the middle of the Peninsula. The foregoing map indicates this distribution. The first band includes the cities of Hijaz and the settled agricultural areas of Asir and Hijaz oases. The second comprises the belt of oases in the Tuwaiq escarpment area. The third includes the Al-Hasa (Hofof and environs) oases, which had a total population in the late 1970s of about 160,000, and the oases and towns in the Arabian Gulf coastal plain, of which the agricultural center of Qatif, the administrative capital of Dammam and the Aramco headquarters of Dhahran are the most important.[28]

The third stratum of population raises an issue of considerable significance to the future of the country: foreign manpower, the minority ethnic groups. These groups can be divided into Arabic and non-Arabic speaking people. Any review of the numbers of these expatriates during the past decade reveals a significant increase. In 1962–1963 the Saudi Ministry of Finance and National Economy sponsored a census, limited to the five largest cities of the country, which revealed that the foreign population of those cities comprised from fifteen to thirty-five per cent of the total number of residents and about thirty per cent of the owners and employers of businesses and service establishments.[29] The tremendous wealth of the nation at the beginning of the 1970s, along with the critical and crucial need for foreign manpower, has contributed to a significant increase in the number of aliens working in Saudi Arabia. The Second Five Year Plan (1975–1980) projected a further increase in imported foreign manpower. The Plan's objectives were to:

1 Maintain the religious and moral values of Islam.
2 Assure the internal security of the Kingdom.
3 Maintain a high rate of economic growth by developing resources, maximizing earnings from oil over the long-term and conserving depletable resources.
4 Reduce economic dependence on the export of crude oil.
5 Develop human resources by education, training and raising standards of health.
6 Increase the well-being of all groups within the society and foster social stability under circumstances of rapid social change.

7 Develop the physical infrastructure to support the achievement of the above goals.

8 This endeavor will be done with an economic system based on the principles of a free economy.[30]

The implementation of this Plan was basically contingent upon the increase of both Saudi and non-Saudi manpower through the following five years. The Plan's goal was to increase "the Saudi work force from 1,236,000 to 1,518,000, while the non-Saudi work force would more than double – from 314,000 to 812,000."[31] The increase of Saudi manpower would require more time for reaching its optimum capacity. Training and educating Saudis in the various fields of industrial technology according to the plan would need about ten years. The focus was therefore on foreign manpower to satisfy the immediate and foreseeable industrial needs of the Kingdom.

Besides importing this urgently needed foreign manpower from the Arab and Muslim world, Saudi Arabia sought a labor force from the Western countries as well as from Asia and, more recently, from North Africa. The manpower of the countries of North Africa was doubly useful. These were Western-trained workers who speak Arabic, so there was no communication barrier at the lower level of the industrial base. *Al-Hawadith* of Beirut, Lebanon, stated that "the Kingdom of Saudi Arabia has declared its need of a quarter of a million workers in addition to various kinds of experts". The British *Daily Telegraph* indicated that the shortage of manpower in the Arabian states forced those who were in charge of planning in Saudi Arabia to turn towards the North African workers, among whom unemployment was increasing.[32]

The then Saudi Central Planning Organization which sought the aid of the International Bank to help it in studying its labor force needs, estimated that between 180,000 and 250,000 skilled and semi-skilled workers were needed for the Second Five Year Plan.[33] Dr. Fayz Badr, the then Vice President of CPO, hoped that Saudi Arabia might acquire those "guest workers" from Morocco and Algeria, where a large number of expert laborers with experience of European industry existed. And a plan was made to draw up contracts with those workers through an international advisory consultative company specializing in labor affairs.

Table 3.3 indicates the volume of foreign manpower in Saudi Arabia in 1973/74 as well as the nationality of the groups constituting this foreign labor force. Table 3.4. shows the number of dependents of foreign manpower in Saudi Arabia during the same period.

Examination of Table 3.3 reveals that foreign manpower in Saudi Arabia in 1973/74 increased significantly. Of one hundred different foreign and ethnic minorities, only thirty-six showed a decrease; most of the other sixty-four showed significant increases.

3.3 Foreign Manpower in Saudi Arabia, 1973–1974

(Workers only; not dependants)

Country of nationality	1973AD 1393AH	1974 1394	Increase/ Decrease 74/73	1978 1398	Increase/ Decrease 78/74
Afghanistan	88	51	−37	1,037	+986
Algeria	62	140	+78	297	+157
Argentina	0	1	+1	64	+63
Austria	0	0	0	225	+225
Australia	0	0	0	236	+236
Bahrain	1	1	0	0	−1
Bangladesh	0	0	0	2,319	+2,319
Belgium	37	57	+20	733	+676
Barbados	0	0	0	2	+2
Bolivia	0	0	0	1	+1
Burundi	2	3	+1	0	−3
Brazil	6	4	−2	166	+162
Britain	4,493	5,002	+509	12,139	+7,137
Burma	12	151	+139	6	−145
Cambodia	1	1	0	0	−1
Cameroon	13	7	−6	11	+4
Canada	163	179	+16	1,451	+1,272
Ceylon	24	21	−3	2,777	+2,756
Chad	19	77	+58	219	+142
Chile	1	10	+9	5	−5
China (Taiwan)	73	193	+122	4,629	+4,436
Colombia	0	0	0	24	+24
Costa Rica	0	0	0	4	+4
Cyprus	46	72	+26	1,062	+990
Dahomey	10	4	−6		−4
Denmark	27	44	+17	359	+315
Dominican R.	0			2	+2
Ecuador	0	1	+1	6	+5
El Salvador	0	0	0	136	+136
Egypt	17,491	23,086	+5,595	92,956	+69,870
Eritrea	3		−3	3,753	+3,753
Ethiopia	619	1,318	+699	1,295	−23
Fiji	1	0	−1	0	0
Finland	17	8	−9	330	+322
France	454	532	+78	2,980	2,448
Gambia	4	1	−3	0	−1
Germany (F.R.)	558	723	+165	4,333	+3,610
Ghana	16	10	−6	38	+28
Greece	240	359	+119	3,228	+2,869
Guinea	2	2	0	15	+13
Guyana	3	4	+1	0	−4
Holland	271	183	−88	1,959	+1,776
Hong Kong		2	+2	10	+8
Hungary	7		−7	0	0
India	1,130	1,912	+782	32,842	+30,930

Country of nationality	1973AD 1393AH	1974 1394	Increase/ Decrease 74/73	1978 1398	Increase/ Decrease 78/74
Indonesia	251	383	+132	3,326	+2,943
Iran	110	120	+10	414	+294
Iraq	782	919	+137	898	−21
Ireland	60	76	+16	204	+128
Italy	531	733	+202	7,206	+6,473
Ivory Coast	0	0	0	4	+4
Jamaica	0	1	+1	3	+2
Japan	612	405	−207	1,833	+1,428
Jordan	12,199	15,211	+3,012	14,036	−1,175
Kenya	16	35	+19	263	+228
Lebanon	2,784	3,683	+899	18,396	+14,713
Liberia	0	2	+2	1	−1
Libya	0	2	+2	4	+2
Malagasy R.	1	0	−1	1	+1
Mali	37	78	+41	43	−35
Maldive Islands	2	4	+2	0	−4
Malta	7	20	+13	57	+37
Malaysia	0	0	0	622	+622
Mauritania	50	42	−8	64	+22
Mauritius	0	3	+3	1	0
Mexico	0	1	+1	3	+2
Morocco	62	48	−14	1,188	+1,140
Nepal	0	1	+1	0	−1
New Zealand	23	22	−1	62	+40
Niger	12	19	+7	289	+270
Nigeria	40	47	+7	341	+294
N. Korea	0	29	+29	0	−29
Norway	0	0	0	104	+104
Oman	32	39	+7	5	−34
Pakistan	5,401	8,884	+3,483	59,400	+50,516
Palestine	5,723	8,541	+2,818	3,570	−4,971
Panama	0	0	0	1	+1
Peru	1	1	0	1	0
Philippines	363	206	−157	16,672	+16,466
Poland	0	1	+1	3	+2
Portugal	5	1	−4	1,965	+1,964
Qatar	1	2	+1	0	−2
Rwanda	1	3	+2	0	−3
Senegal	15	13	−2	84	+71
Sierra Leone	5	4	−1	38	+34
Singapore	3	6	+3	497	+491
Somalia	228	743	+515	2,542	+1,799
S. Africa	30	22	−8	53	+31
S. W. Africa	0	0	0	10	+10
S. Korea	8	277	+269	41,035	+40,758
Spain	25	15	−10	327	+312
Sudan	n/a	n/a	n/a	12,933	
Sweden	54	145	+91	641	+496
Syria	3,991	5,599	+1,608	20,878	+15,279
Switzerland	n/a	n/a	n/a	1,098	
Tanzania	12	11	−1	35	+24
Thailand	59	52	−7	13,159	+13,107
Togoland	3	4	+1	0	+4

Country of nationality	1973AD 1393AH	1974 1394	Increase/ Decrease 74/73	1978 1398	Increase/ Decrease 78/74
Trinidad	1	1	0	7	+6
Tunisia	85	170	+85	354	+184
Turkey	231	235	+4	7,404	+7,169
Uganda	7	14	+7	10	−4
U.A.E.	5		−5	1	+1
Upper Volta	16	11	−5	7	−4
Uruguay	0	0	0	38	+38
U.S.A.	2,552	4,319	+1,767	14,701	+10,382
Vietnam	53	2	−51	0	−2
Venezuela	0	0	0	3	+3
W. Somalia	0	0	0	95	+95
N. Yemen	62,091	90,006	+27,915	66,998	−23,008
S. Yemen	6,573	7,077	+504	3,092	−3,985
Yugoslavia	0	0	0	7	+7
Zaire	0	0	0	9	+9
Unknown or Non-Nationality	3	20	+17		
Totals	131,050	182,449	+51,339	488,685	+306,236

Source : Figures for 1978 derived from completed data sheets supplied to the author through the courtesy of the Deputy Minister of Interior (Passport and Immigration Affairs) Government of Saudi Arabia, June 1979.
(F. F. translation)

3.4 Dependants of Foreign Manpower in Saudi Arabia, 1973–1974

	1973	1974	Increase or decrease 1974 over 1973
Workers	131,148	182,505	+51,357
Dependants	66,124	97,872	+31,748
Total	197,272	280,377	+83,105

Source : Figures for 1973 and 1974 derived from handwritten data supplied to the author through the courtesy of the Deputy Minister of Interior (passport and immigration affairs) Government of Saudi Arabia, in an interview in Riyadh, June 1975.
(F. F. translation)

Among most developing countries

data on the labor force are limited and of poor quality. . . . Furthermore, it would be inappropriate to criticize strongly the data base for the region [of the Gulf area] because, for any country, developing a reliable systematic data collection system is expensive and requires years of effort. Moreover [it is quite true to assert that] the rationale for such a system has until recent times been lacking.[34]

Since there were no official figures available from the Ministry of Labor and Social Affairs, it seemed that the best way of calculating the foreign labor force was to obtain the figures of aliens residing in Saudi Arabia during 1973 and 1974. The figures in these tables are for aliens granted annually renewable residence permits. Arab Muslims and non-Arab Muslims, along with Christian Arab workers, were those most needed to carry out the Kingdom's development needs. Manpower from the Western world was needed for its technical know-how and efficiency. The figures in both categories show an increase in 1974 over 1973. The inflow of Western manpower has increased steadily over the years following the country's Second Five Year Plan.

The categories of professional foreign manpower also showed an increase in the Arab Muslim and non-Arab Muslim labor force. The increase in Egyptian manpower in 1974 was almost forty per cent over that of 1973. This reflected an impressive undertaking in the educational system of the Kingdom, since most of these Egyptians worked as teachers at all levels of the system.

The high increase of Lebanese, Syrian and Palestinian manpower indicated the growth in trade and business. The third, and most important, element was the increase in the inflow of American, British, French, Italian, Swedish and Nationalist Chinese manpower in 1974 over that of 1973. These groups, to which have to be added a very substantial Korean element, represented a potential factor in the development of Saudi Arabia at the highest industrial, technical and commercial level. Indeed, the increase or decrease of this foreign labor force was seen as a good index of the economic development of the Kingdom.

In spite of the critical need for more foreign manpower in order to achieve the objectives and projects of the Second Five Year Plan, the ratio of foreign manpower to the total population of the country had to be kept at a certain level which, for all practical purposes, should not have exceeded one-fifth of the total population of the nation – that is, 1.25 million. While it is true that Saudi Arabia was not confronted with the problem Kuwait was experiencing, of its citizens possibly becoming a minority within their own country, a carefully thought out manpower policy was certainly required.[35]

The most crucial problem arising from this massive need for foreign manpower was the social impact which such an alien labor force might have on the country. Too many foreigners with their own alien customs and way of life could have disturbed the existing unique Islamic social pattern of the Kingdom. Despite the fact that most foreign workers were and are drawn from the Islamic countries, there was no precedent in history for the idea that a commonly shared creed – Islam – would suffice to prevent or delay rapid social change. Ralph Braibanti's assertion that "[occasionally] advisers and other agents of change from similar cultures are less respectful of the indigenous context in which they work than are foreigners from a totally different society"[36] underlined the need for concern.

The problem of the effect of alien social customs and habits on the country's social mores, posed a critical challenge for the future. Over the previous two decades there had always been a foreign labor force residing in Saudi Arabia, but the issue was never raised. The situation then did not involve a small foreign community, as it had done in the past; it arose from the need for a huge foreign labor force over the next decade. At the most conservative estimate, the figure would reach a million; but if dependants were included, it would be much higher. Saudi Arabia was, indeed, confronted with a critical dilemma: whether to strive for this crucially needed foreign manpower in order to carry out developmental projects essential to future prosperity, or whether to curtail the inflow of foreign laborers in order to safeguard a social system based on "orthodox" Islam.

Undoubtedly, this was the most grave choice which the country had to face. Concern over the adverse social impact which the massive foreign labor force could have had on Saudi Islamic society might justify a recommendation to slow down the country's urgently needed developmental projects. On the other hand, future prosperity was largely dependent upon rapid implementation of the Second Five Year Plan. The enormous wealth of Saudi Arabia derived totally from a depletable natural resource – petroleum. All the existing signs, such as the trend towards conserving energy, and the industrialized world's vigorous efforts to develop other sources of petroleum or alternative sources of energy, suggested that Saudi Arabia had only until the turn of the century to develop a new industrial and economic base, not entirely dependent upon petroleum. It was an awesome task, to be completed within a relatively short period of time.

The second alternative therefore seemed preferable; namely, the rapid and sound industrialization of the country, even if an excessive influx of foreign manpower was required.

This decision should, by no means, be construed as acceptance of the unwanted, anticipated social change which might have occured as a result. On the contrary, the problem was treated with great urgency by the Saudi planners.

It was not possible to prescribe an exact formula for solving this critical problem. But an important factor which helped to minimize the impact of alien social customs and norms was that once the purpose of each individual or group had been accomplished their services would be terminated. In other words, there would be a pre-designed policy for their dispersal rather than allowing them to settle permanently in the country.

Another recommendation was the maintenance of a fixed and balanced ratio between the inflow of foreign manpower and the total population. This would serve to control leverage against the spread of alien social norms, and thus, help the Kingdom to preserve its existing way of life.

Perhaps the final answer lies in the resilience and strength of the Saudi ethos. Saudis must accept, absorb and perceive the necessary measures for the development of their country without losing their enormous pride in a truly distinctive Islamic social order.

Only time will tell how this crucial problem will present itself in the future. Now that the Third Five Year Plan has ended, the awesome task of building the Kingdom's infrastructure is more or less complete and the requirement for foreign manpower is diminishing. It is forecast that during the Fourth Five Year Plan the figure for foreign manpower will drop substantially while development of the indigenous workforce will be sustained and enhanced. The industrial advance now occurring in the Kingdom must be used to maintain the existing Islamic society rather than weakening its base.

[1] *The Holy Quran*, Text, translation and commentary A. Yusaf Ali (Beirut: *Dar Al'Arabia*, 1968), p. 198. (Copy approved by the Muslim World League, Secretariat General, Makkah)

[2] "Saudi Arabia: Kingdom's Foreign Policy Remains Unchanged," *The Link*, 8 (Summer, 1975): 4.

[3] Kingdom of Saudi Arabia, *Majmo'at al-Nuzum* ("Collections of Regulations") (Makkah: Umm al-Qura Press, 1958), p. 8. Cited in Soliman A. Solaim, "Saudi Arabia's Judicial System," *Middle East Journal* 25 (Washington, DC, Summer 1971), no. 18: 404.

[4] Solaim, "Saudi Arabia's Judicial System," p. 404.

[5] *Ibid.*

[6] The author has studied *Shari'ah* courses at the law schools of Beirut Arab University. Thus, he is in a position to cite such a rule of law based on his own knowledge as a lawyer.

[7] Solaim, "Saudi Arabia's Judicial System," p. 406.

[8] *Ibid.*

[9] Joseph Schacht, "Problems of Modern Islamic Legislation," in Richard H. Nolte, ed., *The Modern Middle East* (New York: Atherton Press, 1963), p. 191.

[10] All the material and information on the military institutions of the Kingdom of Saudi Arabia were obtained by the author through two interviews conducted in June 1975 at the Ministry of Defense, Riyadh. The first interview was with the Director of the Department of Public Affairs; the second with the Director of the Department of Planning and Budgeting. Both departments were courteous and fully cooperative. All material appears in the Author's translation.

[11] The Saudi Ministry of Interior also supervises the following units:
1 Public Security, which, in turn, contains the following:
  a Traffic department
  b Police force, which also includes Special forces
  c Emergency Mobile Force
2 Civil Defense
3 Coast Guard
4 General Investigation Department
5 Department of Prisons.

[12] After completing this stage of its development the Saudi Air Force is presently pursuing its final stage (late 1970s). It is currently operating a large advanced technical and administrative system and apparatus (see p. 12 of source below).

The Navy was inaugurated in 1960 (1380 AH), starting with a single naval vessel. At the present time, it is expanding rapidly and planning is focused on making the Saudi Royal

Navy first class in the near future (see p. 16 of source below). (F.F. translation.)

Saudi Ministry of Defence, *Al Ta'liem Fe' Al Ko'wat Al Arabia Al Saudia* (*Education in the Saudi Arabian Armed Forces*), 1st ed. (Riyadh: The Army Press, 1974 [1394 AH]), pp. 12–16.

[13] This governmental body was known before 1975 as the Central Planning Organization (CPO).

[14] Royal Decree No. 50 dated 17 September 1960 (17/7/1380 AH).

[15] Presidency Office of the Council of Ministers, *Resolution No. 430 dated 11/12–9/1384 AH* (*1964 AD*), Riyadh, pp. 1–2.

[16] Information received in an interview with Mr. Muhammad Mufti, Director of the General Administration of the CPO at Riyadh, May 1975.

[17] For an analysis of the concept of appropriate technology, see Ralph Braibanti, "Conceptual Prerequisites for the Reconstruction of Asian Bureaucratic Systems," in Inayatullah, ed., *Management Training for Development: The Asian Experience* (Kuala Lumpur, 1975), pp. 185–231, especially pp. 211–215.

[18] Data obtained by the author in an interview with Dr. Fayz Badr, then Vice President of the Central Planning Organization at the CPO Building in Riyadh, Saudi Arabia, May 1975. (F.F. translation)

[19] Data as in footnote 18.

[20] Interview with the Saudi Minister of State for Financial Affairs and National Economy, *Al Ahram* (Cairo, July 26, 1975), p. 5.

[21] Ralph Braibanti, "External Inducement of Political-Administrative Development: An Institutional Strategy," in Ralph Braibanti, ed., *Political and Administrative Development* (Durham, N. C.: Duke University Press, 1969), p. 4.

[22] Gabriel Almond and James Coleman, eds., *The Politics of the Developing Areas* (Princeton, N.J.: Princeton University Press, 1960), p. 544.

[23] See footnote 2, above, for more details of this phenomenon.

[24] Fouad Hamza, *Qalb Al-Jazira Al Arabia* (*The Heart of the Arab's Peninsula*), 2nd ed. (Riyadh: Alnasr Publishing House, 1968), in Arabic. (F.F. translation and transliteration.)

[25] *Ibid.* p. 131.

[26] *Ibid.* p. 134.

While visiting the Ministry of the Interior in Riyadh, the Author learned that a new Department for Bedouin Affairs had been established. This department is collecting important data on the tribes of Saudi Arabia for official use.

[27] *Area Handbook for Saudi Arabia*, p. 49.

[28] *Ibid.* pp. 19–20.

[29] *Ibid.* p. 51.

[30] *The Wall Street Journal*, October 6, 1975, 10.

[31] *Ibid.*

[32] *Al-Hawadith* (Beirut), March 17, 1975, p. 24. (F.F. translation.)

[33] *Ibid.*

[34] Lee L. Bean, *Demographic Changes in Iran, Pakistan and the Gulf Area with Particular Emphasis on the Developing Labor Force Need* (paper submitted to the International Conference on Islam, Pakistan, Iran and the Gulf States, Bellagio Conference and Study Center, Bellagio, Italy, August 13–18, 1975), typewritten, p. 7.

[35] *Ibid.*, p. 30.

[36] Ralph Braibanti, *Recovery of Islamic Identity in Global Perspective* (paper presented to International Conference on Islam, Pakistan, Iran and the Gulf States, Bellagio Conference and Study Center, Bellagio, Italy, August 13–18, 1975), typewritten, p. 12.

CHAPTER IV

Institutional Base of the Political System

... Prudence, indeed, will dictate that governments long established, should not be changed for light and transient causes; and, accordingly, all experience hath shown, that mankind are more disposed to suffer, while evils are sufferable, than to right themselves by abolishing the forms to which they are accustomed.

Declaration of Independence of the United States of America

Introduction

THIS CHAPTER has four objectives. The first will analyze how the Holy *Quran*, as the Constitution[1] of Saudi Arabia, provides an effective flexible ground for a governmental system, despite allegations from both East and West that after almost fourteen centuries, the Holy *Quran* may not be adaptable to modern conditions and that, consequently, it would be best to resort to an organic secular constitution. Secondly, the two constitutions, functions, duties and divisions of the Saudi Council of Ministers will be examined as the paramount central administrative body of the Kingdom. The various ministries in Saudi Arabia that constitute the Council of Ministers is the concern of the third part of this chapter.

The Institute of Public Administration (IPA), an advanced and sophisticated governmental entity dealing with fundamental administrative reforms and training, will be treated in the fourth and final part of this chapter.

The Constitution: The Holy Quran

It is the fundamental assumption of the polity of Saudi Arabia that the Holy *Quran*, correctly implemented, is more suitable for Saudi Muslims than any secular constitution. This assumption must be viewed in the context that the nation is completely Islamic. Hence, no churches, synagogues, temples or shrines of other religions exist. No proselytizing by other faiths is allowed. The entire Saudi population is Muslim; the only non-Muslims in the country are foreigners engaged in diplomacy, technical assistance or international commerce. If they are non-Muslims, they may practice the rituals of their religion only in the privacy of their homes. So there is no problem of ethnic, religious or linguistic pluralism or (to use Braibanti's term) polycommunality, such as is found in virtually all other developing countries. It may, however, be worth considering the commonly advanced argument that, since the Holy *Quran* is almost fourteen centuries old, it does not meet current circumstances, is out of date and should be replaced by an organic constitution which presumably would suit these needs and conditions. The Author considers that the Holy *Quran*, which Muslims believe is the divine word of God, does suffice to cope with the events and matters of all times if it is rightly followed. Let us look, nevertheless, at the argument that the Holy *Quran* should be replaced by an organic constitution to fit modern times. To begin with, Islam is a distinctive religion in that according to Islamic doctrine

> the very text and wording of the Holy Book, the *Quran*, has remained unchanged, being neither reworded nor interpolated, for God has undertaken to safeguard it. Other [sacred scriptures], on the other hand, have undergone many influences that have led to discrepancies between their texts as well as divisions among their followers. In spite of the changed wording which these [scriptures] have undergone, they often fit with similar doctrines adopted by the various nations of the world. These are ascribed to reformers belonging to these people. For the basis of these doctrines is that they fit with the fundamental human nature with which Allah has created mankind.[2]

It must also be noted that the Holy *Quran* was written originally in Arabic and that this same Arabic is a living language among over 700 million Muslims. The *Quran* has been translated, but only the Arabic version is used in religious ceremonies and education throughout the world. This is in marked contrast to the scriptural languages of other religions – Pali for Buddhism, Sanskrit for Hinduism, Aramaic and ancient Greek for Christianity – which are no longer spoken by the multitudes. Even Hebrew, the language of Judaism, is regarded as a scriptural language and orthodox Jews view its everyday colloquial (as opposed to liturgical) use as a sacrilege.

Islam, governed by the Holy *Quran*, is not just another religious doctrine; rather, it is unique among other religions as it

> penetrates into the whole spirit of its adherents through the Holy *Quran* whether individually or collectively, for it has put together authority in the form of the political state. It has been protected against division between religious affairs and state affairs. Religion has been given the authority for legislation and jurisprudence.[3]

In response to a request to the Saudi Embassy in Paris, the Saudi Ministry of Justice sponsored a seminar dealing with the Islamic *Shari'ah* (law) and human rights in Islam in March 1972 (Safar 7, 1392 AH). Among the major interests of the group of Western jurists who participated was a desire to study further the Kingdom's total reliance on the Holy *Quran* for all matters of state.[4] Examining this crucial issue, a member of the Saudi group replied that, in order to answer this question, we must first realize the basic difference between the two groups – Muslims and Christians – in their understanding of the essence of religion. He noted that the article on religion in the French *Grande Encyclopédie des Sciences, des Lettres et des Arts* included a hundred definitions of religion, and said that, in a similar conference at Paris, sponsored by the French government in 1951, ninety-eight definitions out of the existing hundred had been excluded by the participants as being incoherent. They had agreed to discuss only the following two definitions of religion:

First: Religion is the way by which mankind achieves its relations with the supernatural forces.
Second: Religion is that which includes everything known and a power not coincident with science.

As for the first definition, the same member stated that the Muslim delegation to the 1951 conference disagreed with their Western counterparts since Islam simultaneously deals with everything known regarding men's relations with one another as well as with God. Muslims would also disagree with the second definition, because Islam, based on the Holy *Quran*, is compatible with science and intellect. So it does not seem strange that Muslims believe all their affairs should be derived from the Holy *Quran*. One of the prominent *Ulama* of the Islamic *Shari'ah* said, "whenever there is common interest, there exists the *Shari'ah* of God" – even when there are no divine revelations or the Prophet's tradition (*Sunna*). According to this view, Islamic laws are compatible with science, and, therefore, should be able to cope with civil, criminal and personal affairs in the light of existing conditions.

When dealing with the Islamic *Shari'ah*, a distinction should be made between those general rules which are unamendable and unchangeable and those which are interpretive applications of the general rules. The latter may be modified according to changing times and circumstances. As for the general rules, embodied in the Holy *Quran*, they are the Constitution and major system of the Islamic *Shari'ah*, from which are derived the explanatory and detailed rules.[5] There exist a few man-made constitutions, such as that of the United States of America, which are expected to continue indefinitely as the supreme law of the land; *a fortiori*, the divine Constitution of Islam, the Holy *Quran*, is held in

Saudi Arabia to be capable of governing the affairs of Muslims all over the world suitably, relevantly and for all time.

The Saudi Council of Ministers (Majlis al-Wuzara)
"Of all the agencies and organized bodies of the government of Saudi Arabia, the Council of Ministers is the most potent. It derives the power directly from the King. It can examine almost any matters in the Kingdom."[6] Despite its relatively recent origin, the Saudi Council of Ministers emerged in 1953 as the natural political outcome of Ibn Saud's final consolidation of power and unity over the young Kingdom.

Since the establishment of Saudi Arabia, King Abdul Aziz divided the administration. He took personal and direct charge of the affairs of both the Central and Eastern Provinces while appointing his second son, Faisal, later to be King, as Viceroy of the Western Province. It was in that Western Province that the grassroots of the present Council of Ministers originated. King Abdul Aziz established two major bodies to govern the affairs of the Hijaz, the Western Province. The first body, which still exists, was the Consultative Council (*Majlis Al-Shura*). A second body, created later, was the Council of Deputies (*Majlis Al-Wukala*) which, in 1953, evolved into the Council of Ministers.

The more important of these two governing bodies was the Council of Deputies (*Majlis Al-Wukala*), established by a Royal Decree in December of 1931. This decree authorized the establishment of a four member council consisting of a president, the Viceroy of Hijaz (then Prince Faisal), a deputy for foreign affairs, a deputy for finance, and the vice-president of the consultative council. In retrospect, the Council of Deputies was a stronger governing body than the Council of Ministers. According to the decree establishing it, the Council of Deputies derived its authority directly from the King and was able to issue direct instructions originated in the Council to various government departments and agencies.

The Council, upon reaching a decision which concerned a government department, would transmit its policy directly to that body rather than to the King for approval, as the Council of Ministers under its 1954 constitution had to do. It is believed that the need for a decisive and centralized governmental body to deal directly with the affairs of the Hijaz, which was then being gradually but firmly incorporated to the Kingdom, was the reason behind such a move. In fact, the basic difference between the Council of Deputies and its predecessor was that while the former confined its authority to the Hijaz, the latter became the central administration for the whole Kingdom.

In the early 1940s, having achieved its immediate objective, namely the elimination of the dual administration, the Council of Deputies began to decline, while the central Government began to exercise more comprehensive authority over the whole country, as well as provide more services at the national and local levels. With expansion of the area centrally administered and of services provided by the central Government, new ministries and departments had to be established. Ministries of Foreign Affairs and Finance had already existed since 1930 and 1932 respectively. In 1944, the Ministry of Defense was established, replacing the previous defense agency. In 1951, the jurisdiction of the Ministry of the Interior was extended to the whole of the nation; previously it had been limited to Hijaz Province, functioning as an agency of the interior rather than as a ministry. In 1953, the Ministries of Communications, Education and Agriculture were established, and the Ministry of Commerce was inaugurated in 1954. In the same year, the Ministry of Health was detached from the Ministry of Interior and given separate status.

The successful integration of the Hijaz within the Kingdom enhanced the efforts of King Abdul Aziz to establish the country's first central administrative body, the Saudi Council of Ministers. It was the last stage in the national consolidation of the Kingdom. And since "functions were being assembled under new ministries, it remained for the ministries to be assembled into a coordinating body."[7] A Royal Decree issued by King Abdul Aziz established the first Saudi Council of Ministers.[8] The Royal Decree dealt with five issues: (1) organization of the Council; (2) jurisdiction of the Council; (3) the Council's procedures; (4) jurisdiction of the President of the Council; (5) divisions of the Council of Ministers, council cabinet (staff facilities).

Articles 1 and 2 of Part I, Article 7 of Part II and Article 8 of Part III of the constitution of the Council of Ministers delineated the Council's main provisions.

Article 1
A council of ministers shall be created under our presidency and, in our absence, under the presidency of our viceroy and Crown Prince.

Article 2
The Council of Ministers shall consist of:
A His Majesty's active Ministers who are appointed by a Royal Order.
B His Majesty's Advisers who are appointed by a Royal Order as active members in the Council of Ministers as Ministers of His Majesty.
C Those whose attendance at the Council of Ministers is desired by His Majesty, the King.

Article 7
State policy within the country and abroad shall be under the surveillance of the Council of Ministers.

Article 8
However, the decisions of the Council of Ministers shall not come into effect until they have been sanctioned by His Majesty the King.[9]

Article 8 reflected a very important aspect of the overall authority of the Council of Ministers. Although the Council of Deputies' competence had been limited to the Hijaz, it exercised more authority than the Council of Ministers, as its decisions were not subject to a Royal sanction. This can be attributed to the events and circumstances that surrounded the creation of the Council of Deputies.[10] First its authority was geographically limited; secondly, it existed at a time when the need was great for a direct and prompt decision making process. Also, the fact that King Abdul Aziz used to spend most of his time governing the Central and Eastern provinces while his son, Prince Faisal, was his viceroy in Hijaz, justified the extra measure of authority granted to the Council of Deputies. On the other hand, the establishment of the Council of Ministers came at a time when the central Government had completed the administrative consolidation of the Kingdom. *Mutatis mutandis*, the King's final approval of the Council of Ministers' resolutions paralleled that of the President of the United States' final signature on bills to become law. But this analogy is valid only when restricted to the final signature as the last phase of the decision making process. Article 18 of Part IV of the constitution of the Council of 1954, in describing the mechanism of the Council of Ministers, enumerated the President of the Council's (the King's) functions:

Article 18
The President of the Council of Ministers shall:

First: Supervise the Council of Ministers, the Ministers, and the Public Departments;

Second: Supervise the execution of Royal Orders and Decrees, and the laws and decisions issued by the Council of Ministers;

Third: Supervise the carrying out of the budget, through the Office of the Comptroller of State Accounts;

Fourth: Issue the regulating decisions, instructions, and rules required to execute Royal Orders and Decrees and laws and decisions approved by the Council of Ministers and sanctioned by His Majesty the King.[11]

In essence, the King, as the President of the Council of Ministers, can veto the Council's resolutions. In addition, both the First Deputy and the Second Deputy are responsible to the President of the Council (1958 constitution of the Council of Ministers). As for the member ministers, they are responsible to the Council of Ministers and its President as well. Both the resignation and dismissal of ministers are subject to the approval of the President of the Council through a Royal Order.

Article 7 of Part III of the Council's constitution enumerated its spheres of authority. These duties and functions are:

1 The annual budget, the approval of the year-end balance sheet of the State . . ., and the making of new appropriations;
2 international treaties and agreements, and authorizing the Minister of Foreign Affairs to sign them;
3 concession and monopoly contracts granted to individual companies;
4 any contract, measure . . . or obligation for which there is an appropriation in the provisions of the public budget and which involves thirty thousand Saudi Riyals or more if the Ministry concerned deems it necessary, in executing it, to go beyond the established laws of the State. Any appropriation provided for in the authorized budget, however, shall be executed by the Ministry concerned in accordance with the established regulations of the State without reference to the Council of Ministers.
5 The formation of stock companies and the authorization of foreign companies to operate in the Kingdom.
6 Conciliation in disputes to which the State is a party, when such conciliation involves a charge to the State Treasury or a waiver of amounts payable to the State in excess of fifty thousand Saudi Riyals regardless of the origin of the obligation.
7 The appointment and dismissal of directors of Departments and of officials of grade four and above.
8 The creation of new positions, jobs, or grades not included in the budget.
9 All contracts for the employment of foreigners. The employment of foreigners, however, shall be permissible only in case of necessity and when no Saudi national can be found to fill the position or perform the work stipulated in the contract.
10 Agreement to conditional donations. Ministries or departments may not dispose of State funds, whether by way of donation, sale, exchange, or otherwise, or grant a lease for a period exceeding one year, under the terms of the contract or by way of renewal, unless permission has been requested from the Council of Ministers and its consent to the said contracts has been obtained before they are signed.

    The Council of Ministers shall consider those matters which the president of the Council or the Council itself decides to ask (to have referred to it) by the source concerned for discussion and settlement, and it shall also consider the regulations enacted by the Consultative Council or the Department concerned, in order to approve, amend, or reject them.[12]

These wide and comprehensive functions enabled the Council to achieve a great deal in the administration of the Kingdom.

To a considerable extent, the Saudi Council of Ministers is analogous to the presidential cabinet of the United States as it

IVa **The Saudi Council of Ministers**

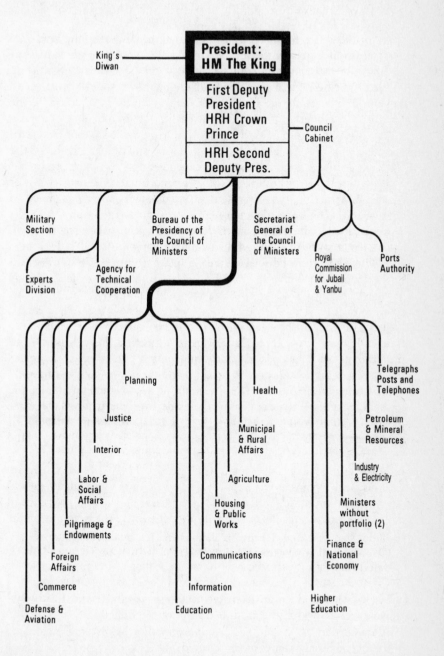

President: HM The King

First Deputy President HRH Crown Prince

HRH Second Deputy Pres.

King's Diwan

Council Cabinet

Military Section

Experts Division

Agency for Technical Cooperation

Bureau of the Presidency of the Council of Ministers

Secretariat General of the Council of Ministers

Royal Commission for Jubail & Yanbu

Ports Authority

Planning

Justice

Interior

Labor & Social Affairs

Pilgrimage & Endowments

Foreign Affairs

Commerce

Defense & Aviation

Health

Municipal & Rural Affairs

Agriculture

Housing & Public Works

Communications

Information

Education

Telegraphs Posts and Telephones

Petroleum & Mineral Resources

Industry & Electricity

Ministers without portfolio (2)

Finance & National Economy

Higher Education

does not have independent authority any more than the presidential cabinet has. The Council derives its powers from the King. He has delegated to the Council authority to examine, decide and recommend on almost any phase of Saudi government administration.[13]

As to procedures followed by the Council of Ministers, the tendency has been towards greater flexibility. Fixed rules regulating procedures at meetings are thus not found in Part III of the Council's constitution. Article 8 specified[14] that two-thirds of the members should constitute a quorum for a meeting and that its decisions were to be voted on by the majority of members present. An affirmative vote of a majority of those present is essential to ratify a decision. These decisions are not final until sanctioned by His Majesty, the Council's president. Article 10 of the 1954 constitution stated that the Council's meetings were to be conducted monthly, but the King could call for an extraordinary meeting whenever he deemed it necessary. At present, it is customary for the Council to meet weekly. The Council's deliberations are not made public as a rule. However, its decisions are usually announced except when the Council, in accordance with Article 11 of the Council's constitution, decides otherwise. Articles 12 and 13 discussed the Council's agenda and it was decided by the Council that the agenda should be submitted to the Council's members for study a week prior to a meeting. However, in practice, this requirement of a week's advance notice was not always met. The agenda, due to its urgency or the intensive nature of the Council's work, was sometimes only distributed three days prior to a meeting. Very important or urgent items could be handed out to the Council's members at the opening of the meeting. According to practice and the new 1958 constitution[15] of the Council of Ministers, the President of the Council and (since the era of King Faisal) his deputy may preside over the Council, regulate debate, conduct voting, announce the Council's decisions and adjourn its meetings. In the 1970s, it became customary for the First Deputy of the President's Council to preside over the Council in its weekly meetings by authority of the King. The King himself presided only over extraordinary sessions, such as those for the approval of the country's annual budget and the inauguration of the Kingdom's development plans. The President of the Council may preside over all its meetings at the discretion of the King.

The final part of the constitution deals with the Council of Ministers' four divisions: the Secretariat General, the Office of the Comptroller of the State Accounts, Technical Experts and the Board of Grievance.[16]

The differences between the 1954 and 1958 constitutions of the Council of Ministers are as follows:

1 While the constitution of the Council of Ministers of 1958 abrogated that of 1954, it maintained the four divisions of the Council.

2 In the new constitution, the post of Vice President (now First Deputy President) was made permanent. The Crown Prince, according to previous and present practice, is usually the First Deputy of the Council of Ministers.

3 The 1958 constitution does not specify the number of sessions of the Council. In the case of the constitution of 1954, Article 10, Part III, explicitly required monthly sessions.

4 A significant new rule on voting was introduced in the 1958 constitution: the President of the Council casts the decisive vote in the event of a tie.[17]

5 A new rule for making Council's decisions final was also introduced in the 1958 constitution. The Kingdom's statutes, treaties, international agreements, concessions and contracts for government loans are subject to Royal approval and the approval of the President of the Council. Such approval is announced by Royal Decrees. Aside from these affairs, the Council's approval of other resolutions suffices to render its decisions final.

6 The Council's authority was enlarged by Article 48 of the 1958 constitution. This article authorized the Council to promulgate regulations for internal rules for the Council of Ministers, as well as internal rules for each of the ministries, for the State's municipalities, regulations for impeachment of ministers, regulations for selling and leasing state property and, finally, regulations for provincial administration.

7 The new constitution is composed of fifty articles while that of 1954 consisted of twenty-one articles.

The Cabinet

The phenomenal expansion in the government activities, along with the Government's continued effort to enhance the development of the Kingdom and the wide-ranging program for providing better and expanded services to its citizens, has resulted in the establishment of more ministries, departments and governmental agencies.

Until recently, the Saudi Cabinet consisted of fourteen ministries represented in the Council of Ministers. But the new cabinet[18] formed on October 13, 1975 (Sh'awal 8, 1395 AH) increased the ministries from fourteen to twenty.[19]

This was the largest cabinet in the Kingdom's history. A more significant and encouraging precedent established in the cabinet of 1975 was the fact that out of the twenty-three ministers appointed, eight of them held a Doctor of Philosophy degree from the United States or England.

Three others had a Master's degree from abroad. This decision to include new well trained young ministers in the Council further enhances its performance and quality, and yields dividends for the country. The Royal Decree appointed three more ministers of state without portfolio as members of the Council of Ministers. It has long been a practice of the King to appoint by Royal Decree ministers of state who are not members of the Council of Ministers. In appointing a minister of state, the Royal Decree must explicitly indicate that the appointed minister is a member of the Council of Ministers; otherwise he is automatically excluded.

The fourteen ministries which existed before the recent new expansion of the cabinet were as follows:

1 Defense
2 Foreign Affairs
3 Labor and Social Affairs
4 Interior
5 Education
6 Communications
7 Agriculture
8 Finance and National Economy
9 Petroleum and Mineral Resources
10 Health
11 Commerce and Industry
12 Pilgrimage and Endowments
13 Justice
14 Information

The cabinet of October 1975 established six new ministries for the first time. These ministries are:

1 Public Works and Housing
2 Municipal and Rural Affairs
3 Higher Education
4 Industry and Electricity
5 Telegraphs, Posts and Telephones
6 Planning

With the Minister of Planning and the three Ministers of State without portfolio, the number of ministers in the Council of Ministers became twenty-three.[20]

The following pages provide the organizational charts of all ministries except Defense and Planning, which have already been dealt with in Chapter Three, along with the major government independent agencies. These four independent agencies are usually presided over by an official with the rank of Minister of State. They are not members of the Council of Ministers. These agencies are:

1 Civil Service Bureau
2 General Audit Bureau
3 Investigation and Control Board
4 Organization for Public Services and Discipline

IVb **Ministry of Foreign Affairs**

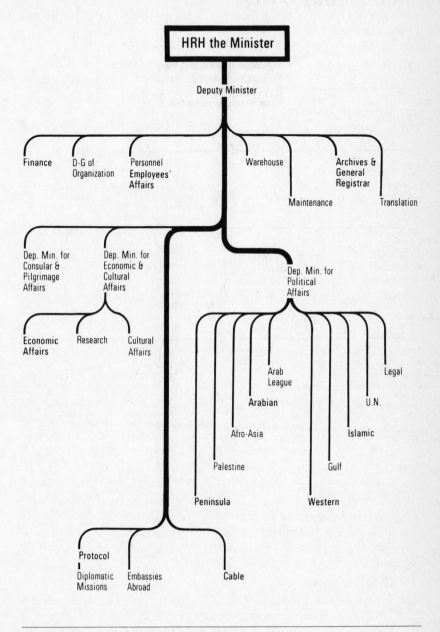

Source : Obtained by author from the Ministry of Foreign Affairs. Author's translation.

IVc Ministry of Labor & Social Affairs (A)

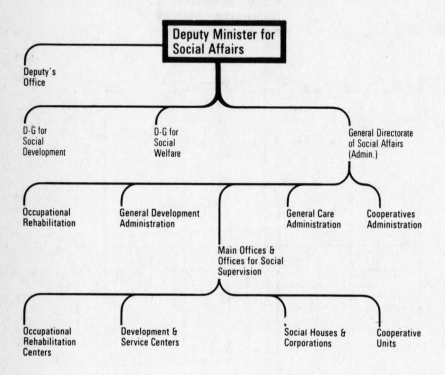

IVd Ministry of Labor & Social Affairs (B)

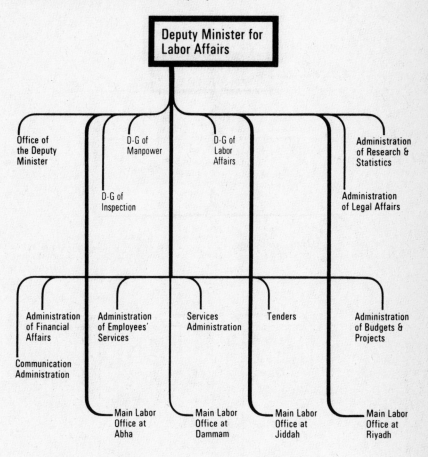

IVe Ministry of Labor & Social Affairs (C)

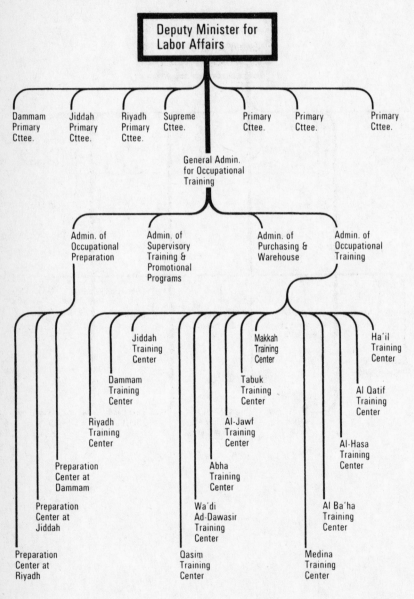

IVf **Ministry of Labor & Social Affairs (D)**

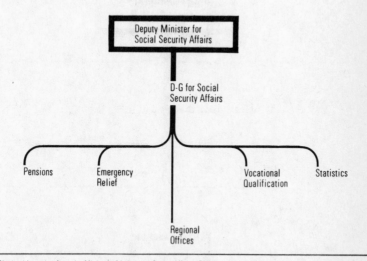

Source: Obtained by author from the Ministry of Labor and Social Affairs, Riyadh in June 1975. This Ministry is now divided into three major units, the Deputy Ministry of Social Affairs, that of Labor, and that of Social Security Affairs. The former is illustrated in one chart (page 101), the second is shown in two charts (above and page 102), and the third in one chart (page 104).

IVg Ministry of Education

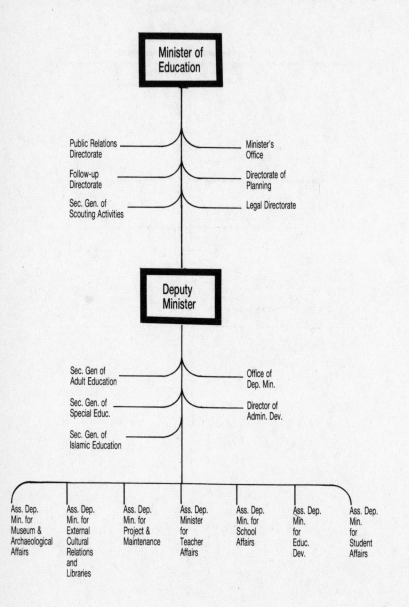

IVh Ministry of Higher Education

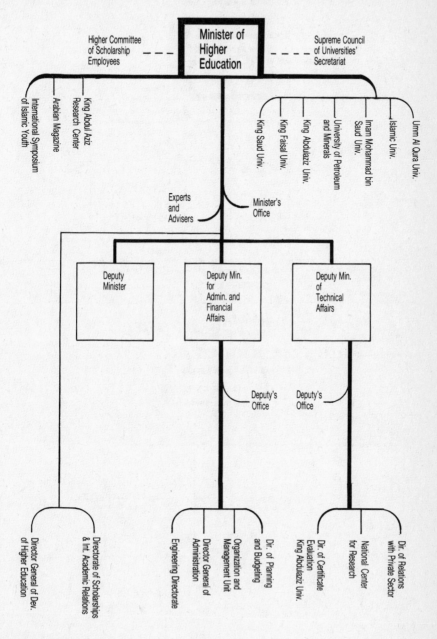

IVi Ministry of Communications

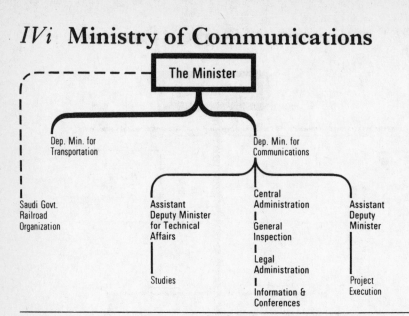

Note: The October 1975 Cabinet established a new Ministry of Posts, Telecommunications and Telephones, thus curtailing the scope of this Ministry.

Source: Obtained by author from the Ministry of Communications, Riyadh in June 1975. Author's translation

IVj Ministry of Telegraphs, Posts and Telephones

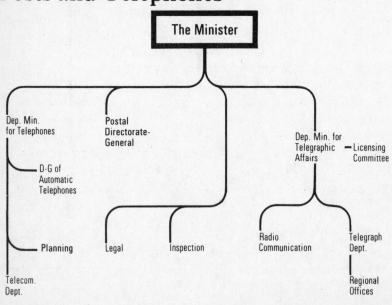

IVk Ministry of Agriculture and Water

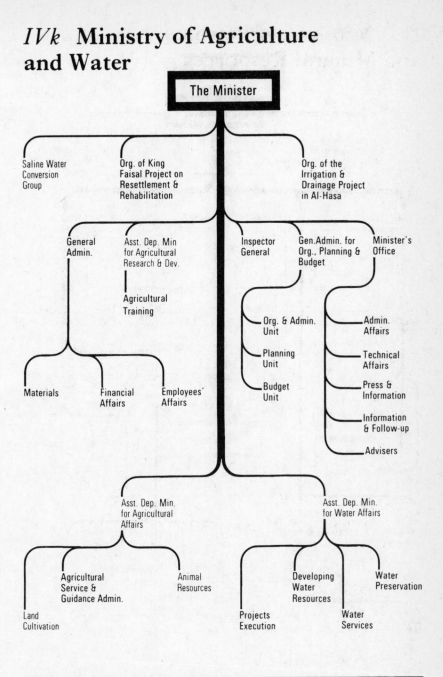

The Minister

Saline Water Conversion Group

Org. of King Faisal Project on Resettlement & Rehabilitation

Org. of the Irrigation & Drainage Project in Al-Hasa

General Admin.

Asst. Dep. Min for Agricultural Research & Dev.

Inspector General

Gen. Admin. for Org., Planning & Budget

Minister's Office

Agricultural Training

Org. & Admin. Unit

Admin. Affairs

Planning Unit

Technical Affairs

Budget Unit

Press & Information

Materials

Financial Affairs

Employees' Affairs

Information & Follow-up

Advisers

Asst. Dep. Min. for Agricultural Affairs

Asst. Dep. Min. for Water Affairs

Agricultural Service & Guidance Admin.

Animal Resources

Developing Water Resources

Water Preservation

Land Cultivation

Projects Execution

Water Services

Source: Obtained by the author from the Ministry of Agriculture, Riyadh in May 1975   Author's translation.

IVl Ministry of Petroleum and Mineral Resources

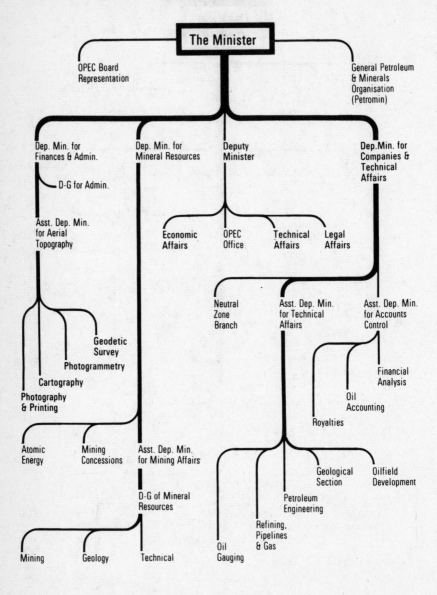

IVm Ministry of Health

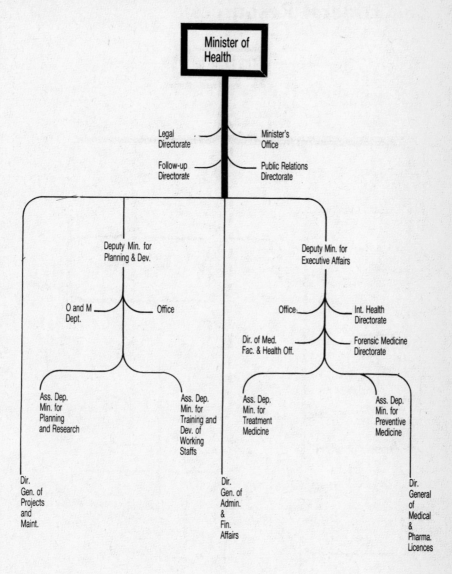

Minister of Health

Legal Directorate

Minister's Office

Follow-up Directorate

Public Relations Directorate

Deputy Min. for Planning & Dev.

Deputy Min. for Executive Affairs

O and M Dept.

Office

Office

Int. Health Directorate

Dir. of Med. Fac. & Health Off.

Forensic Medicine Directorate

Ass. Dep. Min. for Planning and Research

Ass. Dep. Min. for Training and Dev. of Working Staffs

Ass. Dep. Min. for Treatment Medicine

Ass. Dep. Min. for Preventive Medicine

Dir. Gen. of Projects and Maint.

Dir. Gen. of Admin. & Fin. Affairs

Dir. General of Medical & Pharma. Licences

IVn Ministry of Industry and Electricity

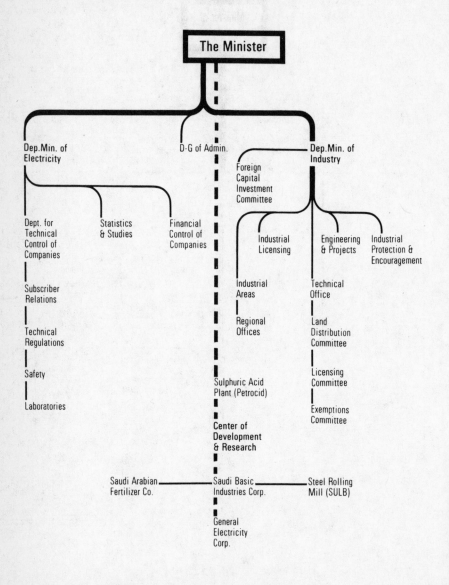

The Minister

Dep.Min. of Electricity

D-G of Admin.

Dep.Min. of Industry

Foreign Capital Investment Committee

Dept. for Technical Control of Companies

Statistics & Studies

Financial Control of Companies

Industrial Licensing

Engineering & Projects

Industrial Protection & Encouragement

Subscriber Relations

Industrial Areas

Technical Office

Technical Regulations

Regional Offices

Land Distribution Committee

Safety

Licensing Committee

Laboratories

Sulphuric Acid Plant (Petrocid)

Exemptions Committee

Center of Development & Research

Saudi Arabian Fertilizer Co.

Saudi Basic Industries Corp.

Steel Rolling Mill (SULB)

General Electricity Corp.

Note : The Ministry was formed out of the former Ministry of Commerce and Industry in October 1975.

IVo **Ministry of Commerce**

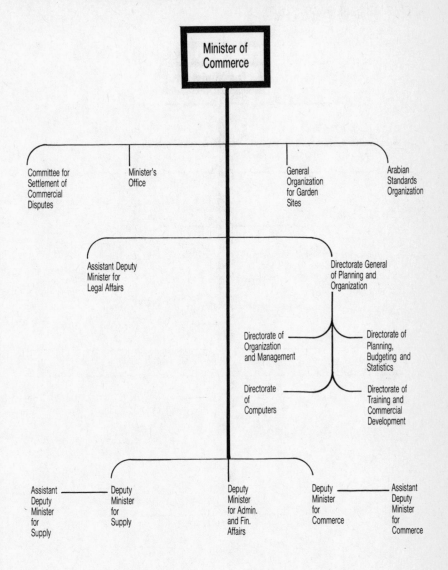

IVp Ministry of Pilgrimage and Endowments

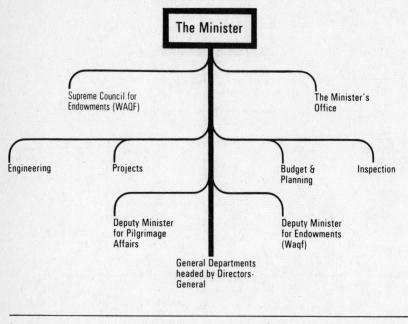

Source: Obtained by the author from the Ministry of Pilgrimage and Endowments, Riyadh in April 1975   Author's translation.

IVq **Ministry of Justice**

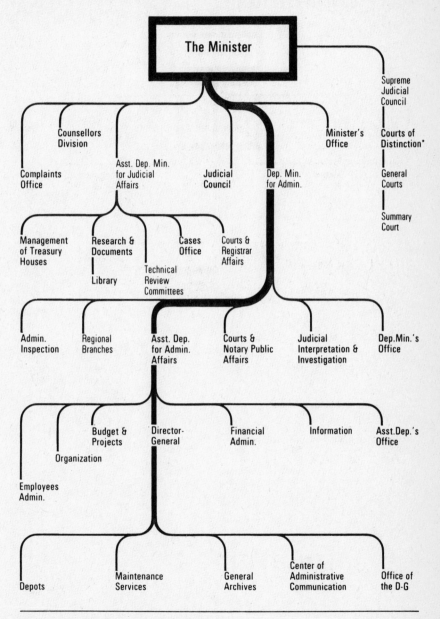

*Parallels the Supreme Appellate Courts in the United States.

Source : Obtained by the author from the Ministry of Justice, Riyadh in May 1975   Author's translation.

IVr **Ministry of Information**

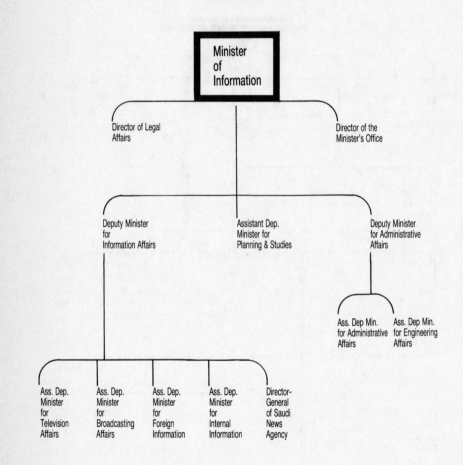

IVs **Ministry of Interior**

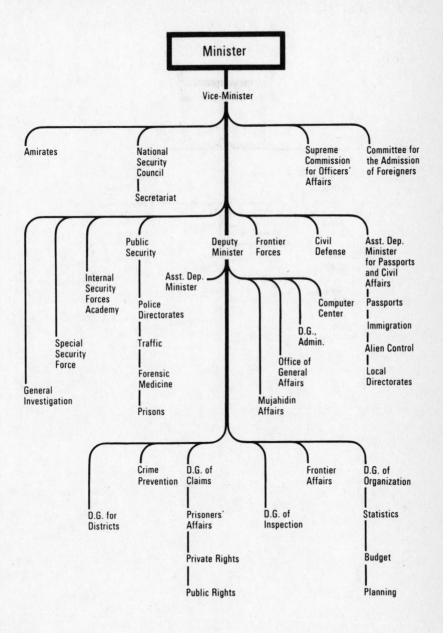

IVt **Ministry of Public Works & Housing**

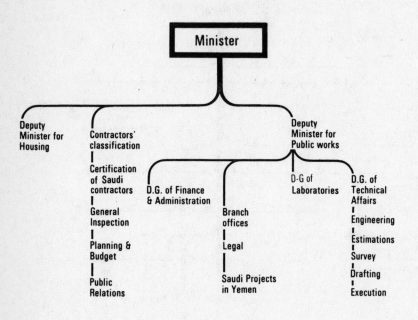

IVu Ministry of Municipal & Rural Affairs

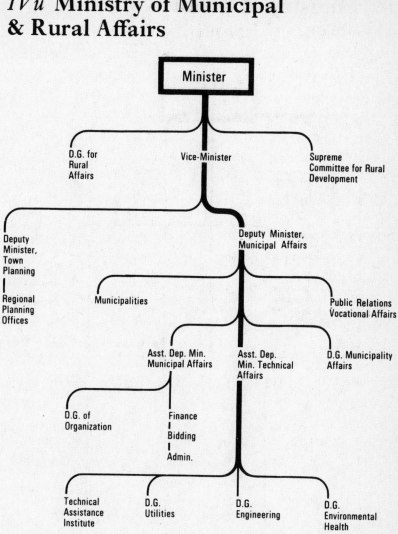

IVv Ministry of Finance and National Economy

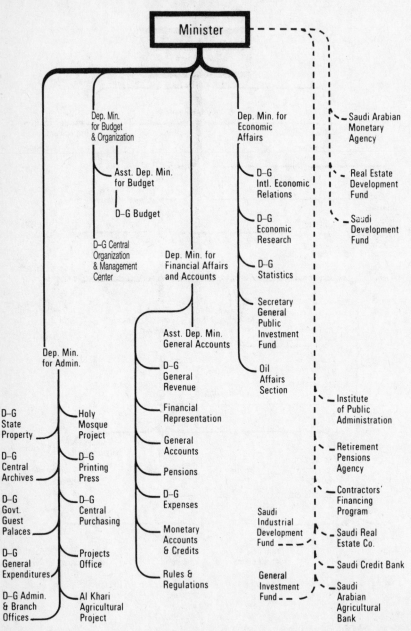

IVw Civil Service Bureau

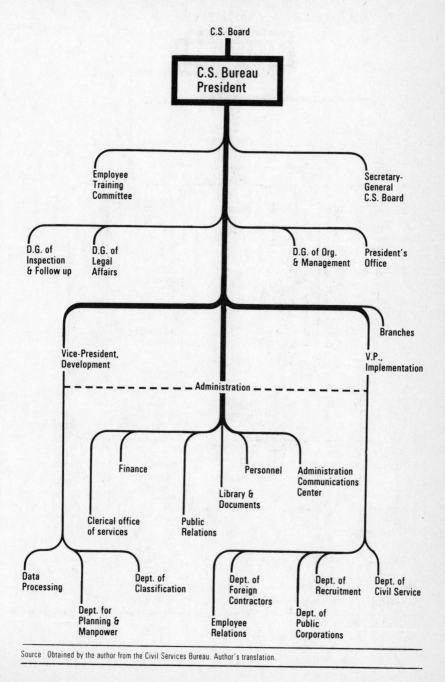

Source: Obtained by the author from the Civil Services Bureau. Author's translation.

IVx Audit Bureau

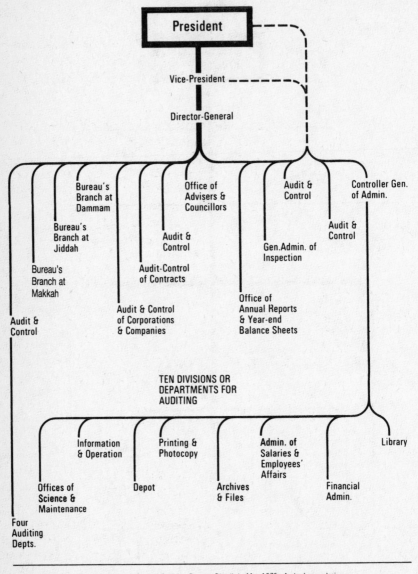

Source: Obtained by the author from the General Auditing Bureau, Riyadh in May 1975. Author's translation.

IVy Investigation and Control Board

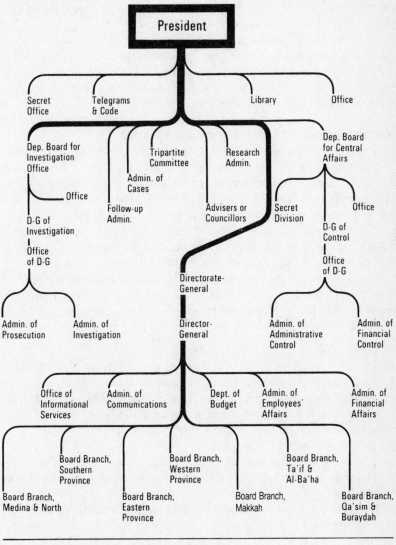

Source: Obtained by the author in Riyadh, June 1975   Author's translation.

The first of these independent agencies, the Civil Service Bureau, is charged with the affairs of the Government's civil servants. The second agency is in charge of auditing the Government's various ministries and departments at all levels. The third body, in case of Government employee misconduct, handles the legal aspects of the investigation and decides whether or not he should be disciplined. If the accusations are dismissed, the investigation process ends at this stage. On the other hand, if the person accused is proven guilty, the case is transferred to the fourth organization for disciplinary action. The organization charts of the first three independent organizations are shown on pages 127–9.

Institute of Public Administration – Riyadh[21]
One of the essential needs of a developing nation is the capacity to deal swiftly and efficiently with its administrative problems. A prerequisite for this is the proper administrative training of the country's civil servants at all levels. This is best accomplished by the systematic administrative training of existing Government employees rather than by wholesale replacement. Indeed, in the case of Saudi Arabia, replacement would have been almost impossible at the time the country started its reform programs, unless most Government employees were to be expatriates.

The Government agency responsible for administrative reforms in the Kingdom is the Institute of Public Administration (IPA) in Riyadh, founded by Royal Decree in 1961.[22]

The Institute of Public Administration is a governmental entity whose functions are as follows:

1 To raise the degree of efficiency among the government's employees.
2 To prepare those employees in a practical and scientific manner, to shoulder their responsibilities and exercise their authority in a fashion which will lead to higher administrative standards and the solidifying of the foundation of the country's national economy.
3 To organize training courses.
4 To participate in the administrative organization of government.
5 To render advice in all administrative problems submitted by various ministries.
6 To conduct and encourage research in the field of administrative affairs.
7 To strengthen cultural relations in the realm of public administration.

The IPA is governed by a board of directors composed of the following:

1 Minister of Finance and National Economy (President).
2 Deputy Minister of Finance and National Economy (Vice-President). and the following members:

3 Deputy Minister of Education.
4 Deputy Director of Riyadh University.
5 Director General of the Civil Service Bureau's Administration.
6 Director General of the IPA.

It is entrusted with formulating the general policy of the Institute and supervising its execution. The Institute is autonomous and possesses the necessary authority for the achievement of its objectives. The board may also issue whatever regulations and instructions may be necessary to guarantee the efficient execution of the Institute's work. This unusual autonomy is suggested by the composition of the board whose president is the Minister of Finance.

The Institute offers training programs for government employees at various levels. These training programs, by 1978, included the following:

In-Service Training Programs
A *Programs for developing high level executive skill carried on by the Higher Programs Unit*
B *Administration Programs*
1 Public Administration
2 Intermediate Administration
3 Administration and Organization
4 Administration of Employees' Affairs
5 School Administration
C *Financial Programs*
1 Intermediate Financial Affairs
2 Preliminary Financial Affairs
3 Budgetary Administrative
4 Depots Program (Warehouse)
D *Secretarial Programs and Clerical Works*
1 Higher Secretarial
2 Clerical Works
3 Arabic Typewriting
4 English Secretarial Work and Typewriting
5 Clerical Employee Affairs Works
E *Statistics*
1 Intermediate Statistics
2 Primary Statistics
F *Libraries*
1 Librarians
G *Development*
1 Planning and Development
H *English Language*
I *Special Programs*

IVz Organization Chart of the Institute of Public Administration

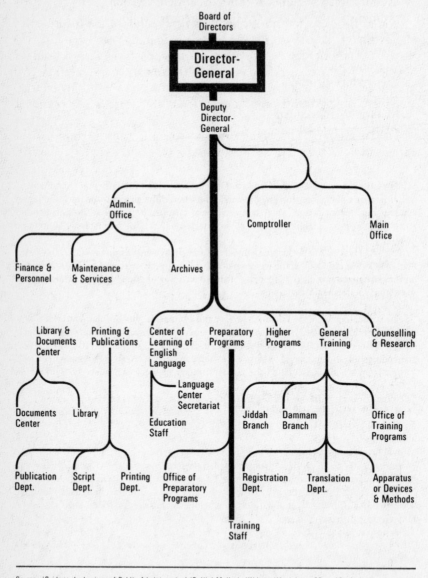

Source : 'Guide to the Institute of Public Administration' (Da'liel Ma'had al'I'dara al'Am'a), no. 22, p. 18. Author's translation.

Preparatory Programs – pre-entry service programs carried on by the Administration of Preparatory Programs
1 Systems Studies
2 Administrative Studies – "Employee Affairs Major"
3 Administrative Studies – "High Secretarial Major"
4 Financial Studies
5 Statistical Studies
6 Customs Studies
7 Preparatory Printing
8 Hospital Programs and Health Administration
9 Material Management
10 Passports and Nationality

---

[1] The capitalized version of "Constitution" refers to the fundamental document of Saudi Arabia's polity, i.e. the Holy *Quran*. This should not be confused with the lower case version, "constitution", which is the official term used to refer to the constitutive terms of reference establishing and governing the Council of Ministers. See note 9, below.

[2] Al Sa'yed Hassan Kutbi (former Minister of Pilgrimage and Endowments), "How the Free World Should Look at the Religion of Islam," a speech delivered in South Korea in his official capacity, n.d., p. 7. (A copy of the speech was obtained by the author in May 1975 from the former Minister.)

[3] *Ibid.* p.15.

[4] Seminar dealing with the Islamic *Shari'ah* and Human Rights in Islam, attended by a group of highly regarded *Ulama* of Saudi Arabia and a group of prominent Western jurists, sponsored by the Ministry of Justice of Saudi Arabia at Riyadh, 1972. The proceedings in the following pages were translated from Arabic to English by the Author from a booklet issued by the Saudi Ministry of Information on the Seminar in 1972.

[5] Seminar dealing with the Islamic *Shari'ah* and Human Rights in Islam.

[6] Charles W. Harrington, "The Saudi Arabian Council of Ministers," *The Middle East Journal*, 12 (1958): 1.

[7] *Ibid.* p. 5.

[8] Royal Decree dated October 9, 1953 (1 Safar, 1373 AH).

[9] *Constitution of the Council of Ministers and Constitution of the Divisions of the Council of Ministers* (published in *Umm al-Qura* [Government Official Gazette], No. 1508, 26 March 1954 [21 Rajab, 1373 AH], Dammam, Saudi Arabia, Language Services Section, Local Government Relations Department, Arabian American Oil Company, May 1954), pp. 1–4.

[10] See above, p. 92.

[11] *Constitution of the Council of Ministers and Constitution of the Divisions of the Council of Ministers*, p. 6.

[12] *Ibid.*, pp. 2–4.

[13] Harrington, "The Saudi Arabian Council of Ministers," p. 12.

[14] 1954 Constitution of the Council of Ministers.

[15] Soliman A. Solaim, *Constitutional and Judicial Organization in Saudi Arabia*, unpublished Ph.D. dissertation, Johns Hopkins University, 1970, p. 55.

[16] These four divisions of the Council of Ministers were established in compliance with Articles 19 and 20 of the constitution of the Council of Ministers.

"Two points may call for clarification. The first is that although the fifth part of the Constitution of the Council of Ministers is titled 'Divisions of the Council of Ministers', Article 19 states that the Council 'Shall have a Cabinet consisting of the following divisions. . . .' These divisions are those of the Cabinet [De'wan] of the Council and not of the Council itself as formed according to Article 2 of the first Part of the Constitution.

'[Article 2/Part I of the Constitution of the Council of Ministers shall consist of:

A His Majesty's active Ministers who are appointed by a Royal Order.

B His Majesty's Advisers who are appointed by a Royal Order to be active members in the Council of Ministers as Ministers of His Majesty.

C Those whose attendance at the Council of Ministers is desired by His Majesty the King].'

"The awkward wording of the title of the fifth part of the constitution of the Council of Ministers is noticeable.

"The second part is that the Cabinet of the Council of Ministers should be completely distinguished from the Cabinet of the President of the Council of Ministers. The latter is not bound by the constitution of the Divisions of the Council of Ministers and it serves purely as an office for the president. . . . [The Cabinet of the President] consists mainly of two divisions: Political and Administrative Affairs. Both are headed by Deputy Ministers of State and subdivided into several Directorates General. It consists also of branches relating to different activities of the government."

From: Solaim, *Constitutional and Judicial Organization in Saudi Arabia*, pp. 58–59.

For further information on the constitution of the Divisions of the Council of Ministers, consult the above source, pp. 59–65.

[17] A reference must be made to the fact that the constitution of 1954 was drafted and approved with the objective that the King would simultaneously be the President of the Council whereas the new constitution of 1958 was promulgated at the time when the presidency of the Council had been assumed by Crown Prince Faisal. This situation gave a new status to the decisions of the Council of Ministers. Retrospectively, under the 1954 constitution, all the Council's decisions were subject to the King's sanction whereas the constitution of 1958 provided for a new formula – that is, a distinction between those decisions that could be finalized by the mere approval of the Council and those that could be approved and sanctioned only through a Royal Decree (e.g., international agreements and concessions).

[18] Royal Order No. A/236, dated October 13, 1975 (Sh'awal 8, 1395 AH).

[19] *Al-Riyadh*, No. 3164, October 24, 1975, 1–3.

[20] Through interviews in Riyadh, Saudi Arabia, during May and June of 1975, the Author obtained current organizational charts of the various ministries and independent government agencies in Saudi Arabia prior to the new cabinet of October 13, 1975, and in accordance with each of these bodies' budget of 1975–1976 (1395–1396 AH). These were revised in 1985. All the charts are the Author's translation.

[21] Most of the following data on the IPA have been drawn from: Institute of Public Administration (*Da'lil Ma'Had Al'Idara Al'Am'A* (*Guide to the Institute of Public Administration*), IPA Publication No. 22 (Riyadh: Al-Ga'Zira Printing Corporation, 1975), pp. 15–23. (F.F. translation.)

[22] Royal Decree No. 93 dated April 10, 1961 (24/10/1380 AH).

CHAPTER V

Innovation

*Our government does not restrict its international
relations to the Arab and Islamic countries, but extends
itself to all nations and countries that believe in God and
the principles of justice and righteousness.*

HM King Fahd ibn Abdul Aziz

Introduction

TO EXAMINE the Kingdom of Saudi Arabia's development is a challenging
task. The dynamic pursuit of systematic development is a clearly articulated Government objective. The pace of change is rapid and can be
perceived not merely year to year but, indeed, month to month.

The Author was able to make, through interviews conducted in Riyadh,
May–June of 1975, a survey of innovative projects within Saudi Arabia.
The first of these was an examination of the operations and activities of
the United Nations Development Program (UNDP) with headquarters
in Riyadh.

The second part of this chapter will deal with the affairs of the Center
for Training and Applied Research in Community Development and a
study of its various activities as an arbitrary model of one of the large
scale projects conducted in Saudi Arabia. The First, Second, Third and
Fourth Five Year Plans (1970 to 1990) constitute the third, fourth, fifth
and sixth parts of this chapter respectively.

The seventh and final part will examine the various universities of
Saudi Arabia, Saudi students studying abroad and the fields of their study.
A final assessment of the Saudis who have already obtained their higher
degrees will conclude this chapter.

In the realm of development, it is of great importance to emphasize
that the Kingdom's ultimate objective:

is to transform [its] economy from overwhelming dependence on export of crude oil into diversified industrial economy, although the dependence on the export of crude oil will continue for a considerable period of time since oil revenues are the chief means through which the Kingdom can finance its economic and social development programs. [*The Guide to Industrial Investment* in Saudi Arabia further delineates the Kingdom's industrial objectives in the non-oil industrial sector]:

i   to increase the domestic economy's capacity to produce at competitive costs a wide range of products for domestic as well as for export markets.

ii the industrial exploitation of the substantial comparative advantage arising from low cost energy, raw materials, from hydro-carbon related industry, minerals, agricultural, and fishery resources.

iii widening and deepening the Kingdom's access to modern technology.

iv to encourage fuller utilization of capacity in the private manufacturing sector.

v   to secure regional balanced development of industry.

vi to increase productivity through closer approach to optimal size of plants.

vii to reduce dependency on expatriate workers by national skill creation, through the development of general and technical education.

viii to promote interlinkage among industries.[1]

United Nations Development Program (UNDP) – Riyadh[2]

The United Nations Development Program started its activities and operations in 1957 under the name of Technical Assistance Board (TAB) under an agreement between the government of Saudi Arabia and the United Nations. In 1960–1961 another agreement was concluded between His Majesty's government and the United Nations, still under the aegis of the Technical Assistance Board. In 1970, the name of the Technical Assistance Board was changed to United Nations Development Program and its representation in Saudi Arabia became known as the United Nations Development Program Office at Riyadh.

In the Arabian Peninsula there are many programs and projects which are supervised by the New York Office of the UNDP, along with other of the United Nations executive and specialized agencies. These various and affiliated bodies of the United Nations which are operating in projects under the auspices of the United Nations Development Program of the Riyadh office are shown in Table 5.1 on page 137.

All the agencies of the United Nations listed in Table 5.1 operate in Saudi Arabia and the Arabian Gulf area under the auspices of the UNDP at Riyadh.

Generally speaking, projects supervised by the United Nations agencies are initiated by mutual consultation between the government of Saudi Arabia and the United Nations, both guided by the priorities of the Kingdom's relevant Five Year Plan. Currently, concentration is focused on the technical training of Saudi personnel.

These projects are classified into the following categories:

1 Large Scale Projects.
2 Small Scale Projects.

In both categories, large and small, there are projects which are subsidized by the United Nations as well as by the Saudi government,

5.1 United Nations Agencies Operating in Saudi Arabia in 1978

Name of Agency of the United Nations	Regional Office (If any)	Head Office
Food and Agricultural Organization (FAO)	Cairo	Rome
Office of Technical Cooperation (UNOTC)		New York
World Health Organization (WHO)	Alexandria	Geneva
United Nations Industrial Development Organization (UNIDO)		Vienna
International Labor Organization (ILO)		Geneva
International Telecommunication Union (ITU)		Geneva
International Atomic Energy Organization (IAEO)		Vienna
United Nations International Children's Fund (UNICEF)	Beirut	New York
Economic Commission for Western Asia (ECWA)		Beirut
United Nations Educational, Scientific, and Cultural Organization (UNESCO)		Paris
International Bank for Reconstruction and Development (IBRD)		Washington
International Monetary Fund (IMF)		Washington
International Maritime Consultative Organization (IMCO)		London
Universal Postal Union (UPU)		Berne
United Nations Conference on Trade and Development (UNCTAD)		Geneva
International Civil Aviation Organization (ICAO)		Montreal
World Meteorology Organization (WMO)		Geneva

Source: Obtained by author through an interview with Mr. Mostafa Badawi, Programs Assistant in the United Nations Development Program Office at Riyadh, Saudi Arabia, in May 1975. (Designed by F. F.)

while other projects that are called FIT projects (Fund-in-Trust) are individually financed by the government of Saudi Arabia. The financing in the latter is done by the deposit of an agreed sum of money by the Saudi government at the disposal of the United Nations in order that the latter may arrange for such specific projects, sending advisory personnel and conducting studies.

3 Regular Programs: usually short range programs with low financing.
4 Country's Participating Program – UNESCO.
5 Fund-in-Trust for both large and small scale projects.
6 Regional and international–regional projects. Such projects are usually financed by the United Nations along with fellowships, seminars, training courses and symposia. These activities may come under the large scale category and are sometimes directly implemented by the United Nations by sending individuals to conduct surveys, make comprehensive studies, draft plans, or carry out studies in certain fields. Such personnel dispatched by the United Nations are called visitors and consultants. Often their missions are of short duration – seven days to a month.

The United Nations Development Program offers fellowships at two levels. In connection with the large scale projects, these fellowships, called counterpart fellowships, are given to Saudi Arabian nationals for the duration of the project conducted in the Kingdom. In other words, while the project is being executed in Saudi Arabia for two or three years under foreign advice, Saudis are sent abroad (usually to Western Europe, Canada, or the United States of America) for the duration of the project, and are trained in the same field. When the project's time has expired and the foreign advisers leave for their homes, they are replaced by Saudi nationals, thus providing continuity for the project as well as increasing the staff of the Saudi technical advisory group. Counterpart fellowships for small scale projects are financed differently. If a Saudi national is sent abroad under the (IPF) Indicative Planning Figure (Country Program) the United Nations will finance his fellowship. But if he is sent under the Fund-in-Trust (FIT), the Saudi government sponsors his fellowship directly.

Tables 5.2 and 5.3 show large and small scale projects planned or being implemented in Saudi Arabia in 1978.

Center for Training and Applied Research in Community Development – Ad-Dir'iyah[3]
The second part of Chapter Five uses as a model one of the large scale projects executed in Saudi Arabia with the cooperation of the United Nations Development Program. It focuses on the project's objectives, organization and achievements.

Va Organizational Structure of the Center for Training and Applied Research in Community Development

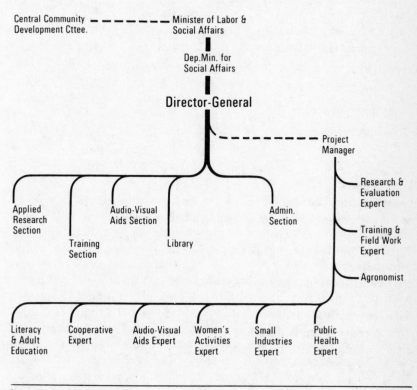

Central Community — — — — — — Minister of Labor &
Development Cttee.   Social Affairs

Dep.Min. for
Social Affairs

Director-General

Project
Manager

Research &
Evaluation
Expert

Applied   Audio-Visual   Admin.
Research   Aids Section   Section
Section

Training &
Field Work
Expert

Training   Library
Section

Agronomist

Literacy   Cooperative   Audio-Visual   Women's   Small   Public
& Adult   Expert   Aids Expert   Activities   Industries   Health
Education   Expert   Expert   Expert

Source: Kingdom of Saudi Arabia, Ministry of Labor and Social Affairs, 'Center for Training and Applied Research in Community Development', p. 16. Author's translation.

The Center for Training and Applied Research in Community Development was inaugurated June 16, 1970, under an agreement between the Saudi government, represented by the Minister of Labor and Social Affairs, and the United Nations Development Program and Technical Cooperation Office (UNDP-TC), represented by the United Nations Resident Representative in Riyadh. The project was launched on July 1, 1970. The major objectives and aims of the Center are:

> To train senior level personnel, field work staff, specialists and technicians as well as local leaders in the different fields of community development.

5.2 United Nations Large Scale Projects in Saudi Arabia in 1978

Large Scale Projects	Locations of Projects in Saudi Arabia	Name of UN Agency* in charge
Center for Training and Applied Research in Community Development	Ad-Dir'iyah Riyadh	UNOTC
Regional and Natural Physical Planning (Town Planning)	Riyadh	UNOTC
Industrial Studies and Development Center	Riyadh	UNIDO
Irrigation Development Wadi Jizan	Jizan	FAO-completed projects, supplemental project
Farm Engineering Center	Riyadh	FAO-completed projects, supplemental project
Tele-Communications and Broadcasting Training Center	Riyadh Jiddah	ITU
Center for Applied Geology	Jiddah	UNESCO
Educational Research Center (completed project)	Riyadh (faculty of education)	
Training in Civil Aviation (including Fund-in-Trust)	Jiddah & Dhahran	ICAO
National Transport Survey (completed project)	Riyadh	IBRD
Road and Ports Fund-in-Trust	Riyadh	UNOTC
Agriculture and Waters Development	Riyadh	117-FIT-FAO

*Key
FAO: Food and Agricultural Organization
FIT: Fund-in-Trust
IBRD: International Bank for Reconstruction and Development
ICAO: International Civil Aviation Organization
ITU: International Telecommunications Union
UNESCO: United Nations Educational, Scientific, and Cultural Organization
UNIDO: United Nations Industrial Development Organization
UNOTC: United Nations Office of Technical Cooperation

Source: Information obtained by author in an interview with Mr. Mostafa Badawi, Programs Assistant in the UNDP, Riyadh, Saudi Arabia in May 1975. (Designed by F. F.)

To advise and assist the Ministry of Labor and Social Affairs and other related ministries in the implementation of procedures conducive to efficient administration, supervision and evaluation of rural development programs.

To strengthen the existing community development centers and assist in the establishment of new ones.

To assist the government in carrying out rural, social and economic development activities in selected areas; these activities will form an

5.3 United Nations Small Scale Projects[1] in Saudi Arabia in 1978

Small Scale Projects	Locations of Projects in Saudi Arabia	Name of UN Agency in charge
Agricultural Training Adviser	Riyadh	FAO
Irrigation Adviser – Senior Irrigation Adviser	Riyadh	FAO
Vocational Preparation	Riyadh	UNICEF
Tele-Communication Planning and Programming Adviser	Riyadh	ITU
Education Research	Riyadh	UNESCO
National Accounts and Economic Statistics Adviser	Riyadh	UNOTC
Standardization Quality	Riyadh	OTC
Meteorology Communication Adviser	Jiddah	WMO
Sanitary Engineering and Municipal Programming Adviser – FIT[2]	Riyadh	WHO
Telephone System (automatic and manual telephone system) FIT	Riyadh	ITU
Industrial Standardization and Quality Control FIT	Riyadh	UNICO-SIS[3]

[1] When the project has only one foreign adviser it is termed "small scale."
[2] Fund-in-Trust.
[3] Special Industrial Service.

Source Information obtained in an interview with Mr Mostafa Badawi, Programs Assistant in the UNDP, Riyadh, Saudi Arabia in May 1975. (Designed by F. F.)

integral part of the training and research elements activities.

To conduct action-oriented research whose results will be utilized in training and community development activities.

To offer specialized seminars and courses in agriculture, health education, literacy and adult education, cooperatives, and social welfare, etc.[4]

The Center's Central Committee established by the Saudi Council of Ministers governs its affairs.[5] The Central Committee consists of the following personnel:

Minister of Labor and Social Affairs	Chairman
Deputy Minister for Social Affairs	Vice-Chairman and Member
Director, Community Development Administration	Member
Director General of the Center	Member and Rapporteur
Director General, Technical Cooperation Administration	Member
Representative of Ministry of Agriculture	Member

Representative of Ministry of Education	Member
Representative of Ministry of Health	Member
Representative of Central Planning Organization	Member

The Central Committee is charged with the following functions: (1) the planning and implementing of community development policy and projects throughout the country; (2) follow-up and appraisal of community development projects; (3) study of problems confronting community development programs, and the submission of recommendations for their solution; (4) acting as coordinator and liaison officer between the ministries concerned and agencies active in community development work; (5) submission of the budget necessary for development programs, specifying the required allocations from every contributing organization prior to each new financial year; (6) supervision of training staff as well as of research in community development; and, finally, (7) preparing periodic reports on the progress of the community development programs.

Training is the first of the Center's tasks, this being one of the most essential requirements for social and economic development. The availability of sufficient highly trained manpower in specialist fields must greatly enhance a country's development. Being aware of this fact, the Center for Training and Applied Research adopted a tri-partite formula for the training of Saudi manpower:

1 Preparation of the necessary number of specialists in fields relevant to social development.
2 Focus on local environmental conditions and utilization of available human and national resources in various processes.
3 Training local leaders and making full use of their status in community development.
  The Center for Training and Applied Research in Community Development plans its programs and functions in the framework of these objectives. Training activities are designed for top personnel engaged in various social and economic schemes in different regions of the Kingdom. Personnel engaged in local community development in the fields of health, education, social affairs and agriculture constitute the main groups who participate in the long and short scale courses planned by the Center.[6]

The methods and techniques of training utilized by the Center are as follows:

1 An integrated approach to socio-economic development of the community.

2 Linkage with development objectives, targets, needs, plans and problems of local communities in the various regions.
3 Cooperation and coordination with various local institutions within the framework of national development plans.
4 Scientific methods in the investigation of the environment and in the identification of needs and problems.
5 Application of modern techniques and even utilization of mass media and audio-visual aids tailored to activities contributing to change of attitudes, technology and new practice.
6 Field work to implement the theoretical framework in rural and the urban communities.
7 Exchange of experiences, ideas and knowledge among trainees, supervisors, officials and experts.
8 Follow-up and evolution of training needs among graduates of the Center. (These approaches or techniques will eventually lead to the enrichment of the basic skills and experience of persons engaged in community development schemes.)[7]

The Center's second objective is the development of social research, as well as social studies, as a basic dimension in the community development process. The Center believes that analysis of existing circumstances and further evolution of the human and material elements at hand, along with the declared need for development, are essential for planning in developing nations. The planning of social programs, aimed at the elimination of existing hindrances to the welfare and progress of society, necessitates the identification of elements influencing communities as well as of social problems that have resulted from change. Social research is described as "the scientific method for collecting, analyzing, and interpreting facts and data needed for community development".[8]

The Center's training programs began on December 19, 1971. The Community Development Program in Saudi Arabia is a multi-purpose and coordinated activity with the ultimate intention of meeting major community needs. Its final goal is to develop human resources by providing opportunities for decision-making and self-reliance, for exercising responsibility and acquiring positive social attitudes. The Saudi government regards this program as an essential factor in its national development plan – the Five Year Plans – for social and economic progress. The community development program is also considered an integral part of the overall national development program of the Kingdom. According to the First Five Year Plan that started in 1970 (1390 AH), "the community development program seeks to coordinate government services with community efforts to maximize the use of local, economic, and social resources for the improvement of the welfare of the country".

An interview with the Chief Adviser and Superviser of the Training Center Community Development Program, Dr. Ali Mahjoub, revealed that the community development program was established under the auspices of the ministries of Education, Health, Agriculture, Labor and Social Affairs.[9] The first community development pilot project in Saudi Arabia was launched in the town of Ad-Dir'iyah in October 1960 with the technical cooperation of the United Nations and its international specialized agencies. One year prior to the establishment of the present center, the Ministry of Labor and Social Affairs was established and the administration of the community development program was transferred to this ministry. A division for the community development program was subsequently established with the collaboration of the Ministries of Education, Health and Agriculture. The Ministry of Labor and Social Affairs has shouldered the responsibility of promoting and supervising the community development project at Ad-Dir'iyah, assisted by the international agencies of the United Nations. By the year 1964, there were seventeen community development centers operating in Saudi Arabia – eleven in rural areas and six in cities. Seventeen additional centers were established during the Second Five Year Plan (1975–1980).[10] The Center's achievements in these training courses are suggested by Table 5.4.

Besides the training courses enumerated in Table 5.4, Table 5.5 shows courses which were in progress in June 1975.

Within these various training programs, there were annually repeated courses.

1 A long term training course in community development for specialists working in the community development centers. Its duration is usually for nine months starting in October of each year and ending in July of the following year.
2 The training course in literacy and adult education for headmasters and teachers of literacy in adult education schools. The duration of this course is usually two months, conducted in July and August of each year.

5.4 Community Development Courses Given by the Center for Training and Applied Research in 1978

Name of Course	Number of Participants	Duration of the Course
Training Course for the Directors of Community Development	17	two weeks
Training Course in Case Work for Social Workers in the Ministry of Labor and Social Affairs	26	four weeks
Training Course for Directors of Social Welfare Institutions	14	four weeks

Name of Course	Number of Participants	Duration of the Course
Training Course for Social Workers in Community Development Centers	18	four weeks
Training Course in Literacy and Adult Education	95	two months
Long Training Course in Community Development	56	eight months
Training Course in Literacy and Adult Education	60	two months
Long Training Course in Community Development	40	nine months
Training Course in Health Education	21	two months
Training Course for Social Security Researchers	36	two months
Training Course in Literacy and Adult Education	60	two months
Long Training Courses for Directors of Social Welfare. Institutional Directors in this course were chosen from University graduates for the first time.	14	nine months
Long Training Course in Community Development	43	nine months
Orientation Course for Specialists in Rural Industries and Vocational Rehabilitation	23	two weeks
Workshop for Potters in Makkah Area	13	three weeks
Training Course for Local Leaders in Medina Area	50	one week
Refresher Course for the Specialists in Community Development	16	one week
Training Course for Local Leaders in Al-Hasa Area (local leaders refers to People's Committees in the Community Development Centers and Administrative Boards of the Cooperative & Voluntary Societies)	28	one week
Refresher Course for Specialists in Community Development in El Jafr Area (in Al-Hasa)	16	one week
Agriculture Expansion Seminar in the Irrigation and Drainage Projects (in Al-Hasa)	50	two weeks
Training Course for Local Leaders in Unayza Area (Qasim area)	20	one week

Name of Course	Number of Participants	Duration of the Course
Training Course for Community Leaders in Howeilan Area (Qasim)	32	one week
Training Course for Specialists in Community Development Centers in Unayza (Qasim) and Howeilan	24	one week
Training Course in Literacy and Adult Education	60	two months
Long Training Course in Community Development	40	nine months
Training Course for Social Security Researchers	50	two months
Training Course for the Female Directors of Women's Activities and Courses in the Western, Eastern and Central Provinces		

Source: Obtained by the author in an interview with Dr. Ali Mahjoub, Chief Adviser and Supervisor of the Training Center at the Center in Ad-Dir'iyah during June 1975. (Designed by F. F.)

5.5 Courses of the Center for Training and Applied Research in June 1975

Number of Courses	Name and Nature of the Course	Duration of the Course
Four	Long Training Courses in Community Development and Social Welfare	nine months each
Four	Short Courses in Literacy and Adult Education	two months each
One	Short Course in Health Education	two months
One	Short Course in Social Security	two months
Three	Short Courses for One Month each for Directors and Social Workers in Community Development Centers	two months
One	Training Course for the Potters in Makkah Area	three weeks
Four	Training Courses for Local Leaders	one week each
Four	Training Courses for Specialists in Community Development Centers	one week each
One	Training Course for Agricultural Specialists in the Irrigation and Drainage Project at Al-Hasa Area	two weeks

Source: Obtained by the author in an interview with Dr. Ali Mahjoub at the Center in Ad-Dir'iyah during June 1975. (Designed by F. F.)

The Ad-Dir'iyah Center trained only Saudi nationals with specialties in various aspects of community development. Training courses conducted outside the Ad-Dir'iyah Center included both Saudis and non-Saudis. Moreover, they included both males and females working as specialists in various community development centers. A survey of participants trained in the community development centers in Medina, Al-Hasa and Qasim areas showed that of fifty-four who had taken part in various training programs twenty had been female.

In the Center's second activity, *i.e.* applied research, it concluded several descriptive and evaluative studies of training programs and trainees. The purpose of such evaluations was to obtain the reactions of the trainees to the courses of study, the materials used, the duration of the courses and the means and methods employed in conducting these courses. The trainees' suggestions were welcomed and thoroughly studied. The Center completed the following studies:

Techniques of evaluating training programs.
Facts about trainees attending the third training program organized by the Center.
Evaluation of the third training program by trainees attending the program.
Facts about trainees attending the fourth training program.
Evaluation of the fourth training program by trainees.
Facts about trainees attending the fifth training program.
Evaluation of the fifth training program by trainees.
Facts about trainees attending the sixth training program.
A general survey of "Hurymia" village.
Several other studies were conducted by the section (in applied research and evaluation of the Center) at the request of the Ministry of Labor and Social Affairs.[11]

The Organization of the Center is shown in Chart Va, on page 139.
Among successfully completed projects implemented under the supervision and cooperation of the United Nations Development Program at Riyadh are:

1 Faculty of Engineering, which is currently one of the faculties of the University of Riyadh.
2 Faculty of Education, also currently a faculty of the University of Riyadh.
3 A Farm Engineering Center in Riyadh.
4 The Wadi Jizam Irrigation Project.
5 The Qatif Experimental Farm.

The First Five Year Plan (1970–1975) (1390–1395 AH)
It is not the Author's intention to analyze in general the various aspects of

the First Five Year Plan and the progress it accomplished; rather, the contention in the present part of this chapter is to introduce and discuss the Kingdom's Five Year Plan as one of the most significant and innovative events occurring in the Kingdom. The five year planning phenomenon started in Saudi Arabia in 1970 (1390 AH) with the country's First Five Year Plan to the end of the fiscal year of 1975 (1395 AH). The beginning of the new fiscal year of 1975–1976 (1395–1396 AH) marked the official inauguration of the country's Second Five Year Plan to 1980 (1400 AH). The purpose in this part of the chapter is to summarize and discuss the achievements of the First, Second and Third Five Year Plans and to introduce the guiding principles and goals of the Fourth Five Year Plan. Only the most important aspects of the First Five Year Plan will be analyzed. The magnitude of the other Five Year Plans will necessitate similar abbreviated treatment.

A report prepared by the Central Planning Organization[12] (CPO) and submitted to His Majesty, the King, on the findings and achievements reached during the Kingdom's First Five Year Plan outlined the basic goals of the Plan:

> The general objectives of economic and social development policy for
> Saudi Arabia were to maintain its religious and moral values, and to raise
> the living standard and welfare of its people, while providing for
> material security and maintaining economic and social stability. These
> objectives were to be achieved by:
> 1 Increasing the rate of growth of gross domestic product (GDP).
> 2 Developing human resources so that the several elements of society
>   will be able to contribute more effectively to production and participate
>   fully in the process of development, and,
> 3 Diversifying sources of national income and reducing dependence on
>   oil through increasing the share of other productive sectors in gross
>   domestic product.
> Furthermore the purpose of the plan is to provide a rational and orderly
> approach to achieving the nation's development objectives. The plan was
> not intended to be a rigid, restrictive set of rules and regulations but a
> means of bringing increased rationality into public sector programs by
> establishing priorities and integrating activities to avoid bottlenecks and
> ensure coordination.[13]

By examining the reported progress during the opening years of the First Five Year Plan, the CPO reported the establishment of a new classification system and salary scale for both civil servants and non-cadre employees in 1971 by a Royal Decree and in harmony with the Plan's aims for more institutional and administrative reforms. Furthermore, a public investment fund was established during the fiscal year of 1971–1972 (1391–1392 AH) with an initial budget of SR 350 million, with further additions of SR 250 million in 1972–1973 (1392–1393 AH) and

SR 600 million in 1973–1974 (1393–1394 AH).[14] The final target of the fund was to reach SR 2,000 million. The basic objective of this public investment fund was to finance investments in production projects of a commercial nature. The fund's affairs were entrusted to a board of directors consisting of the President of the Central Planning Organization, the Minister of Finance, the Governor of Saudi Arabian Monetary Agency (SAMA) and two members chosen from the Council of Ministers. The immediate intention behind the establishment of this fund was to use financial backing of the Government to encourage and promote commercial projects needed in the country's development plan.

Vocational training, student enrollment and school construction expanded considerably in accordance with the Plan's gradual acceleration of these fields. In a developing nation, it is believed, development and progress are not overnight creations, rather they are the result of sound, long-range planning and the rigorous efforts of personnel in charge of planning affairs. The concentration on education, both vocational and academic, should undoubtedly fill the urgent needs for technically educated manpower who are expected to shoulder properly the responsibilities of continued progress.

Another improvement, in the Kingdom's telecommunication network, was made with the establishment of new television stations, the study for the eventual introduction of color television and the expansion made in the automatic telephone program from 134,700 lines to 172,200. Postal service improvement began in the fiscal year 1972–1973 (1392–1393 AH) aiming at the construction of new and well-equipped complexes in the major cities (a very impressive complex was completed in 1975 at Makkah). Also, improvements in training and operations, urgently needed to meet the ever-increasing task confronting the postal service, were made with the ultimate goal of the total mechanization of postal operations.

Further progress was made in the realm of social services, which included institutional care, social security, community development and service centers. The concern of the social welfare program is reflected in providing care for orphans, the aged, handicapped persons and delinquents. Through 1971–1972 (1391–1392 AH) the government was operating ten social centers, seven for boys and three for girls. These centers provided care – food, clothing, lodging, education, and training – for 682 boys and 177 girls between the ages of six and eighteen.

In 1972 (1392 AH) the Council of Ministers approved the establishment of an orphanage at Makkah to provide care for foreign children.[15] Four resident homes for the aged and handicapped throughout the Kingdom caring for 92 persons as of 1972 (1392 AH) were founded and preparations were on the way to establish a fifth in the Asir area by 1973 (1393 AH).

A social security program was initiated in the fiscal year 1962–1963 (1382–1383 AH) to include financial disbursements for almost 77,412 persons with an allocation of SR 16.6 million. By the 1970–1971 (1390–1391 AH) fiscal year, social security payments reached SR 47.6 million covering 225,642 beneficiaries. Pension disbursements increased from 1970 through 1974 by fifty-one per cent while the number of persons covered increased by 53.7 per cent.[16]

Impressive progress was made in health services of the Kingdom. Total budget appropriations for the overall improvement of health services increased from SR 259.8 million in the fiscal year 1969–1970 (1389–1390 AH) to SR 659.0 million in 1972–1973 (1392–1393 AH) and to SR 1,085.9 million for 1973–1974 (1393–1394 AH). In terms of manpower operating in the medical sphere, there were, in 1971, 1,138 physicians and 5,078 para-medical personnel providing public and private medical services within the Kingdom.[17] New allocations for 450 more physicians and an additional 1500 para-medical personnel were approved for the 1972–1973 (1392–1393 AH) fiscal year.[18]

Another crucial advance was being made in the development of the country's water resources. Desalination facilities at Jiddah were reported complete, while two more desalination plants at Khobar and Khafji were finished by 1973–1974 (1392–1394 AH). Construction of two smaller desalination plants was to begin at Um-Laj and Jubail during the same year. Development of twenty-four water supply systems throughout the Kingdom already in progress and the construction of seventeen more was commissioned to start by 1972–1973 (1392–1393 AH).[19] Needless to say, the development and preservation of water resources in Saudi Arabia is of vital importance to the country's developmental planning and the well-being of its citizens. A great effort has been made to meet the ever-increasing demands on the water supply on which depends much of the country's development.

Exhaustive efforts were being made in town planning to further the surveys and studies under way which would eventually lead to detailed and sound planning for cities and adjacent areas. The final goal was gradual integration of such plans within the Second Five Year Plan.

In the area of transportation and communications, the plan's target was met on time, and in many instances, in advance of schedule. Over 500 kilometers of the 1,000 kilometer[20] target for main and secondary roads were completed in 1970–1971 (1390–1391 AH), and a total of 20 new projects, representing over 900 kilometers of new roads, had been authorized in the 1972–1973 (1392–1393 AH) budget.[21] Construction of the Jiddah port was completed in 1972 (1392 AH), and the expansion of Dammam port facilities, which began in the first year of the Plan, was in progress and would meet with scheduled plans. Moreover, the national

airports development plan proceeded well as new airports were completed at Medina, Ta'if, Tabuk and Khamis Mushayt. The Medina Air
Terminal was completed by 1974 (1394 AH) while work on the Khamis
Mushayt Air Terminal was begun in 1973 (1392–1393 AH). Saudia, the
Kingdom's national airline, was making progress and by 1972 (1392 AH)
it was operating a fleet of nine jet and eleven piston engine aircraft. The
latter were eventually to be phased out upon the completion of the
country's airports program. In 1975 (1395 AH) Saudia concluded a contract with McDonnell-Douglas Corporation for the purchase of five to
seven Tri-Star commercial jets. Delivery started in July 1975 (1395
AH).

Finally, the Plan's

> policy of intensifying production on developed land was being pursued
> through the programs of the Agricultural Extension Services, the
> Agricultural Research Centers, and the Agricultural Credit Bank. . . . The
> policy of expanding arable land is being accomplished through the large
> irrigation projects at Al-Hasa and Wadi Jizan, the settlement project at
> Haradh, and the Fallow Land Distribution Program.[22]

The achievement of the Kingdom's First Five Year Plan

> is modestly described as "mixed", in the sense that not every program
> was fully implemented. Nevertheless, [the] achievement was great.
> Water supply projects were carried out for six major cities. Five
> desalination plants were built on the Red Sea and two on the Arabian
> Gulf Coast. . . . Principal towns and cities were linked by a network of
> 6,800 miles of paved roads. Twenty domestic airports were served by
> Saudia Airline. . . . [Moreover] during the First Plan the construction
> industry doubled its activity . . . education system [in addition] was
> established on a strong base . . . health and social security services
> expanded steadily. On the other hand, housing did not keep pace with
> urban growth, and development of a national telecommunications system
> did not meet demand.[23]

Perhaps the most significant outcome of the First Five Year Plan was
the planning experience gained by the Central Planning Organization.
Undoubtedly, "the Saudi planners are no beginners at the game. They are
now [with the beginning of the Kingdom's Second Five Year Plan] ready
to tackle a job nine times bigger than that of the First Plan."[24]

The Second Five Year Plan 1975–1980 (1395–1400 AH)[25]

The following pages will examine the major objectives and policies of the
Kingdom's Second Five Year Plan, effective for the period 1975–1980
(1395–1400 AH), with an overall allocation of $140,997 million.[26] Table
5.6 provides a breakdown of the financial appropriations of the plan in
both Saudi and United States currency.

Two fundamental guidelines were carefully delineated in the country's Second Five Year Plan. The first was the construction of large factories, *e.g.* petrochemical, petroleum refinery, steel and iron, glass, aluminum complexes. The recommendation was to build these factories on the western and eastern coasts of the Kingdom, specifically in the towns of Jubail and Yanbu. These towns have now become the country's major industrial areas, exporting petroleum and petrochemical products throughout the world. Secondly, there was great emphasis on the maximum utilization of the Kingdom's mineral resources. Feasibility explorations proved the existence of large deposits of these resources which are internationally marketable and were considered to be a major source for certain mineral industries. The Government granted certain concessions to international specialized companies for the exploration of mineral resources in various parts of the country.

5.6 Financial Appropriations[1] of the Second Five Year Plan (1975–1980) (1395–1400 AH)

Appropriations	Saudi Riyals (in millions)	US Dollars (in millions)
Economic Resource Development	92,135	26,063.00
Human Resources Development	80,124	22,665.91
Social Development	33,213	9,395.47
Physical and Infrastructure Development	112,945	31,995.75
Administration	38,179	10,800.28
Defense	78,196	22,120.50
External Assistance, Emergency Funds, Food Subsidies, Transfers to General Reserve	63,478	17,957.00
Total	498,270	140,997.91

[1] At constant 1974–1975 prices
Source: **The Wall Street Journal**, October 6, 1975, p. 10

The Second Five Year Plan put much emphasis on educational and training programs in the Kingdom. Free universal education was expected to "inculcate the spirit of honest work". Thomas Jefferson's early and righteous assertion and belief in the effectiveness and importance of education for the development of nations is clearly manifested through the advanced and sophisticated technical status the United States has attained. Pages 178–194 summarize the country's vigorous and ambitious efforts in the field of education.

From a survey of data about the Saudi Second Five Year Plan in 1978, three goals could be identified. The Kingdom was striving for the diversification of its economic base by establishing new industries which would enable it in the distant future to lessen its reliance on petroleum as the major source of the country's revenues. Secondly, the plan focused on improving and enlarging its manpower base to carry out more effectively the nation's development. There was heavy emphasis on vocational and technical training; it provided for the establishment of new vocational schools which would graduate, through the five years of the plan 2,800 students.[27] The plan asserted that:

> the enormous education program intended by the Government is one (essential) way of increasing the efficiency of the work force at all levels. At the same time, it is planned to increase reliance on non-Saudi labor. The Saudi work force will increase from 1,236,000 to 1,518,000, while non-Saudis will more than double from 314,000 to 812,000 by the end of the present plan.[28]

The third major objective of the plan was to develop non-petroleum industries throughout the country. For that purpose and to achieve overall industrial integration in the Kingdom, the plan provided for the establishment of various industries such as canning, minerals, water supply, cement, glass, lumber, fisheries, marble, cotton weaving, leather and synthetics.[29]

The Kingdom's oil reserves were considered ample to sustain any foreseeable level of production required, either for revenues to finance the Plan, or to meet the needs of the extensive hydrocarbon-based industrial complexes which were being planned for the next decade. Nevertheless, economic planning for the optimum utilization of these depletable resources was essential to ensure that the long-run objective of economic diversification and reduced dependence on oil could be achieved.

Petromin, the Saudi National Oil Company (a government corporation) had allocations for projects which were the largest in the Second Five Year Plan; *i.e.* ten per cent of the total financial allocation of the plan. This is attributed to the fact that Petromin was considered

> the cornerstone of the Kingdom's strategic industries and within the next few years will place the country among the leading industrial nations. The total sum allocated for Petromin projects during the plan is SR 50 billion. . . . Among its projects are two pipelines for gas and petroleum extending from the Eastern province to the Western province, with a natural gas collecting plant in the former province, an aluminum smelter, two oil refineries, three petro-chemical complexes and an ammonia fertilizer plant which will make the city of Jubail the most important industrial town in the Middle East and perhaps in Asia.[30]

Agricultural projects were also given heavy emphasis in the Plan.

During the First Five Year Plan, a sharp disparity between domestic food production and consumption was noted. Stress was therefore placed on increased productivity in agriculture; the target at the end of the Second Plan was to produce fifty per cent of the total wheat domestically consumed. The annual wheat production of approximately 4,200 tons was to be increased to 250,000 tons annually by the end of the Second Plan.

Desalination projects were given great attention. The target of the Second Plan was to increase the capacity of existing desalination plants, due to the expectedly high demand for water both for industrial and household use. It was expected that Riyadh would need up to three times as much water. In 1975, Riyadh consumed 58 million gallons daily and total daily consumption was expected to reach 130 million gallons during the plan period. Jiddah's consumption (57 million gallons daily) was expected to reach 142 million gallons during the Second Five Year Plan. New desalination plants were to be established in Hakl, Umm Lij, Rabigh, Al Lith, Al Qunfudhah, and Jubail and they, besides producing water, would aid in increasing electricity output for certain parts of the Kingdom, as well as helping to provide needed electricity to neighboring factories.

In the field of education, the greatest emphasis was manifested in the concern of the Saudi planners to expand and increase the quality of education at all levels. At the elementary level, the goal was universal education through the year 1980 for boys and girls. Enrollment of boys would increase 677,500 a year, through the Plan's period, from a 1975 figure of 401,300; the girls, 353,400 from 214,600 annually. At the secondary level, the target was to increase boys' enrollment from 99,300 to 179,200; and girls, from 46,200 to 100,700. The tremendous increase in enrollment at these two levels of education would require the further construction of approximately 2,000 new schools and enlargement of the present schools during the Second Five Year Plan, 1975–1980 (1395–1400 AH).

At the university level, the objective was to increase the current enrollment figure of 14,500 to 49,000 by the end of the Plan period. This would be accomplished through the then six universities in Saudi Arabia which, along with the new Umm al-Qura University, are described in the final part of this chapter.

Goals of public and personal health in Saudi Arabia were uncommonly ambitious; health services for both the Saudis and non-Saudis resident in Saudi Arabia would be increased by increasing the number of out-patient treatment clinics from 215 to 452. The number of hospital beds was to increase from 4,000 to 11,400. The number of physicians per patient would increase to six for each ten thousand persons.[31]

Information projects, as well, have been the focus of the Saudi planners.

To suit and cope with the present information needs of the country, the Plan's objective was to increase television broadcasting to cover ninety per cent of the total area of the Kingdom as well as the western parts of neighboring countries of the Arabian Gulf area, United Arab Emirates, Qatar, and Bahrain. Daily television broadcasting would be doubled from five hours to ten. The establishment of new rediffusion stations was planned for Do'ba, Al-Gurayat, Jiddah and Jizan, and twenty medium wave broadcasting stations would be constructed throughout the Kingdom. All existing and new information projects must be guided by the Kingdom's overall commitment to enhance and develop a better understanding of Islam and to apply the principles of Islam in all domestic and international activities.

In communications, the construction of 13,000 kilometers of main roads as well as the construction of 10,000 kilometers of rural roads was planned for the Plan period. This would double road mileage in the country, making Saudi Arabia among the leading nations of the Middle East in respect of quality and mileage of roads.

Twenty new piers would be constructed at Jiddah port, sixteen new piers at Dammam, three at Yanbu, and two at Jizan. In addition, a new seaport was to be established near the Port of Yanbu to export petroleum and gas products across the Red Sea.

Telephone service would be expanded from 93,400 to 666,535 lines and Telex lines from 450 to 1,500. The establishment of two permanent ground Telstar stations at Riyadh and Jiddah were included in the Second Plan, along with the transfer of the two temporary stations from Riyadh and Jiddah to Tabuk and Abha. This would mean eventually twenty telephone sets for every hundred citizens in major cities and five telephone sets for each hundred persons in smaller cities with the ultimate goal of further expansion to reach the level found in the United States.[32]

A final analysis of Saudi Arabia's two Five Year Plans seems appropriate at this stage. First, the financial allocations of the two plans reveal that "total financial allocation for the [First Five Year] Plan amount[ed] to SR 41.3 thousand million"[33] while the financial allocation of the country's Second Five Year Plan amounted to SR 498,270 billion.[34]

These allocations reflect the tremendous increase in the country's Second Five Year Plan over that of the first. In other words, the allocation of the First Five Year Plan amounted to about thirty-four per cent of the total allocations of the Second Plan.

Secondly, examination of categories of the two plans indicates that major categories of the country's First Five Year Plan were in the fields of administration, defense, education, vocational training and cultural affairs, health and social affairs, public utilities and urban development, transport and communications, industry, agriculture, and, finally, trade and services.[35] But the Second Five Year Plan's main emphases were: economic resource development, human resource development, social development, physical infrastructure development, administration, defense, external assistance, emergency funds, and, finally, food subsidies. A survey of these categories of the two Five Year Plans[36] leads us to comment on these areas of emphasis. The objectives and nature of the country's First Five Year Plan were general in scope, and experimental in nature. The Kingdom's developmental needs in its different areas were almost even in terms of their priorities. The stress was on improving existing conditions in the various development fields, e.g. agriculture, communication, education, vocational training. By contrast the Second Five Year Plan resembled a rocket launched from an existing launching pad, namely the First Five Year Plan. *The Wall Street Journal* stated it thus:

> the most important feature of the First Plan was the experience gained by the Central Planning Organization and the Ministries in this field [that is, the field of planning]. The Saudi planners are no longer beginners at the game. They are now ready to tackle a job nine times bigger than that of the First Plan.[37]

The emphasis of the country's Second Five Year Plan was focused on the vital objective of diversifying the Saudi economic base by developing the agricultural and industrial sectors. A comparison of the financial appropriations of the two Plans devoted to the objective of diversifying the Kingdom's economic and agricultural structure reveals the predicament of the Saudi planners *vis-à-vis* their Second Five Year Plan. While financial allocations of the First Five Year Plan for industry, agriculture, education, vocational training and cultural affairs reached the US $2.78 billion mark,[38] financial allocations in the Second Five Year Plan devoted to these same purposes were $31.4 billion. This is an increase of 112 per cent over the First Five Year Plan allocations.

Finally, being aware of its international responsibility,

> the Saudi Arabian government takes very seriously the responsibility of wealth, not only in seeking to use it creatively at home . . ., but also in assisting less fortunate [LDCs] of the "Third World". [As new allocations in the Second Five Year Plan were appropriated for international aid]. . . . it seems fair to assume that the "assistance" element in the [appropriations item of the Second Plan] must be over SR 20 billions. This can be deduced from the budget for the current fiscal year, which is the first year of the Plan. Funds are provided for SR 4.25 billions to be disbursed directly as loans or grants . . . to developing countries.[39]

5.7 Total Allocation of the Planned Projects for Saudi Arabia during the Second Five Year Plan

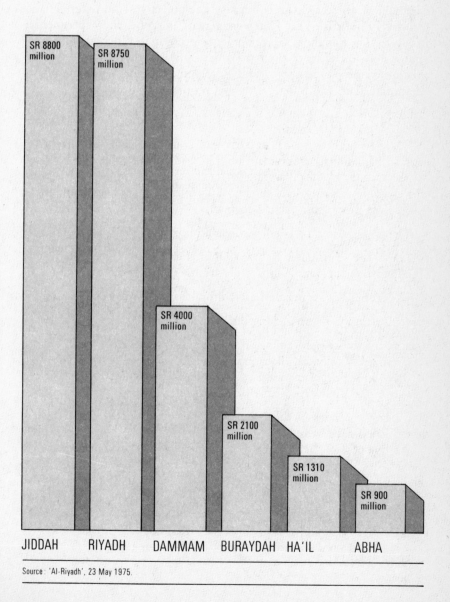

Source: 'Al-Riyadh', 23 May 1975.

This foreign aid appropriation by Saudi Arabia amounts to $1.3 billion annually, that is, 5.75 per cent of its $22.6 billion total revenues in 1974.[40] Table 5.7 shows the total appropriations for development projects in major cities in the country which have been executed during the Second Five Year Plan.

The Third Five Year Plan 1980–1985 (1400–1404 AH)[40A]

Examination of the First Five Year Plan (1970–75) reveals that the scope of that plan was wholly comprehensive in nature, *i.e.* it was an exploration – theoretical and empirical – of the planning phenomenon in Saudi Arabia and of all the various aspects of its development. It must be admitted that the plan was not implemented *in toto*. Yet, the biggest achievement of that plan was the experience gained by Saudis in the field of developmental planning.

The Second Five Year Plan (1975–80), compared with its predecessor, was a phenomenal achievement both in volume and value.

As indicated by the pillargram 5.7 on page 157, the thrust of the Second Plan was towards the establishment of the infrastructure and the industrial sources of the Saudi national economy.

The Third Five Year Plan (1980–1985) is distinguished by its deter-mination to consolidate past achievements and to continue progress in a planned and controlled fashion. Diversification of the economy into productive sectors (agriculture, industry and mining) is considered essen-tial for future economic prosperity. At the same time, human resources are firmly identified as the Kingdom's most valuable asset. The desire to ensure stability by broadening the economic base, by developing Saudi manpower and thus, in both economic and social terms, increasing the Kingdom's independence and self-sufficiency permeates the thinking behind the Plan. The Third Five Year Plan emerges as a rational development of the previous Plan and the Government's experience of implementing it. There are no abrupt changes of policy, rather an increasing sharpness in the definition of the basic objectives, as defined in the Second Five Year Plan.

It is not possible here to give more than the briefest of summaries of the Third Five Year Plan and such a summary cannot, in any way, do justice to the comprehensive scope of the plan or the integration of the economic and social philosophy which underlies it. It is nevertheless useful in giving a broad indication of how the Government of Saudi Arabia is responding to the challenges of a society which has developed at an unprecedented rate.

The Third Five Year Plan (1980–1985) set three fundamental objectives.

1   *structural changes in the economy*
to conserve the natural resources of oil and gas in order to increase the long-term potential for value-added development; to fix levels of crude oil production to generate sufficient revenue, together with revenue from monetary reserves, to cover the financial requirements for the development plan.

to diversify the economy, in particular into the sectors of agriculture, industry and mining, concentrating investment in these productive activities.

to continue development of the physical infrastructure of the Kingdom but at a reduced rate in relation to other sectors of the economy to permit maximum investment in agriculture, industry and mining.

2   *increased participation and social welfare in development*
encouragement of all Saudi citizens to make a contribution to the development of the nation; to give all regions of the country the opportunity to develop their full potential; to assist Saudi society with the problems associated with rapid economic growth; to control inflation and reduce subsidies while, at the same time, protecting lower income groups; to expand and improve the social services.

3   *increased economic and administrative efficiency*
to increase the present and long-term efficiency of the economy itself, the management of the economy and government administration.

Objectives for Administrative Development
to introduce, where necessary, basic changes in government administration; to attain optimum utilization and performance of manpower; to ensure that all managerial and senior administrative positions are held by Saudi citizens.

Objectives for Manpower Development
to increase the total numbers of available manpower; to increase the productivity of manpower in all sectors; to deploy manpower in those sectors with the greatest potential for growth; to reduce dependence on foreign manpower.

Objectives for the Preservation of National Fixed Capital
to preserve national fixed capital and to ensure that sufficient manpower and financial resources are available to operate the infrastructure to full capacity.

Objectives for Fiscal Management
to achieve the planned growth rate for the various sectors and to prevent the rate of inflation from exceeding tolerable levels.

One or two of the objectives of the Third Five Year Plan are particularly worthy of comment. It is government policy that diversification of the economy (which is a primary objective of the Plan) should be undertaken largely by the private sector. The government's role will be to set priorities for investment; to provide information and research on which the private sector can sensibly base investment decisions; and to supply the necessary infrastructural support for the development by the private sector of productive enterprises. Clearly, it is the government's wish that an

5.8 Total Government Expenditure on Development* (1400–1405 AH, corresponding to 1980–1985 AD)

Function of Expenditure	SR Billion Current Prices
Economic Resource Development	261.8
Human Resource Development	129.6
Social Development	61.2
Physical Infrastructure	249.1
Subtotal: Development	701.7
Administration	31.4
Emergency Reserves, Subsidies	49.6
Total Civilian Expenditure	782.7

* Total excludes: transfer payments; non-civilian sectors; foreign aid.
Source: Third Development Plan.

Abdul Aziz Al-Saud, the first king of Saudi Arabia, left a unified country when he died in 1953. Saudi Arabia was indeed his workmanship— born of his vision, military skill, statesmanship, and faith in God.

I

*It was Dir'iyah, near
Riyadh, that served as
the central town of the
Emirate which from
time to time dominated
the Najd from the 18th
century. But it was well-
watered Riyadh that
Abdul Aziz chose as his
capital. A plan of the
city is seen (right)
showing its extent at the
time of its capture by the
young Abdul Aziz in
1902, when he stormed
the Musmak fortress
(marked by the figure 2).
Riyadh's population
today numbers over one
million.*

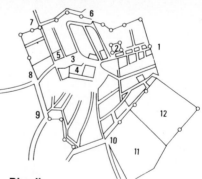

Riyadh
in 1902

1	THUMAYRI GATE	7	ZUHAYRI GATE
2	MUSMAK FORTRESS	8	BADIYYAH GATE
3	MAIN SUQ	9	MURAYQIB GATE
4	QASR OF KING ABDUL AZIZ	10	DAKHANAH GATE
5	GREAT MOSQUE	11/12	NEW QUARTER
6	SUWAYLIM GATE		

Under the remarkable
leadership of King
Faisal ibn Abdul Aziz,
Saudi Arabia moved
to a position of authority
in the world. By his
death in 1975, he had
created a structure of
modern statehood.

III

The start of the reign of King Khalid ibn Abdul Aziz (above) in 1975, coincided with the launching of the Second Five Year Plan, which represented an immense stride forward by the Kingdom. King Khalid died in 1982.

IV

King Fahd ibn Abdul Aziz with his son, Prince Abdul Aziz.

V

Crown Prince Abdullah ibn Abdul Aziz, Deputy Prime Minister and Head of the National Guard.

H.R.H. Prince Sultan ibn Abdul Aziz, Second Deputy Prime Minister, Minister of Defence and Aviation, Inspector General.

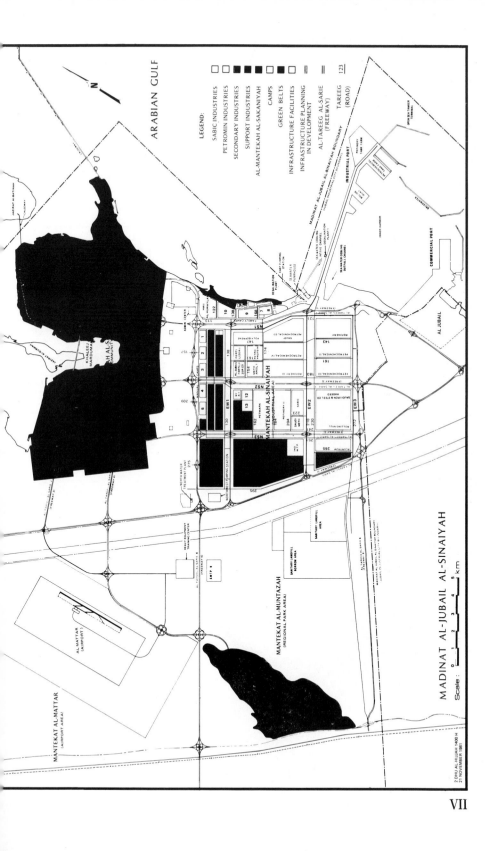

ARABIAN GULF

LEGEND:

☐	SABIC INDUSTRIES
☐	PETROMIN INDUSTRIES
■	SECONDARY INDUSTRIES
■	SUPPORT INDUSTRIES
■	AL-MANTEKAH AL-SAKANIYAH CAMPS
■	GREEN BELTS
■	INFRASTRUCTURE FACILITIES
☐	INFRASTRUCTURE PLANNING IN DEVELOPMENT
═	AL-TAREEG AL-SARIE (FREEWAY)
═	TAREEG (ROAD)
123	

MADINAT AL-JUBAIL AL-SINAIYAH

Scale : 0 1 2 3 4 5 km

MANTEKAT AL-MATTAR
(AIRPORT AREA)

MANTEKAH AL-MUNTAZAH
(REGIONAL PARK AREA)

2 DHU AL-HIJJAH 1400 H
21 NOVEMBER 1981

VII

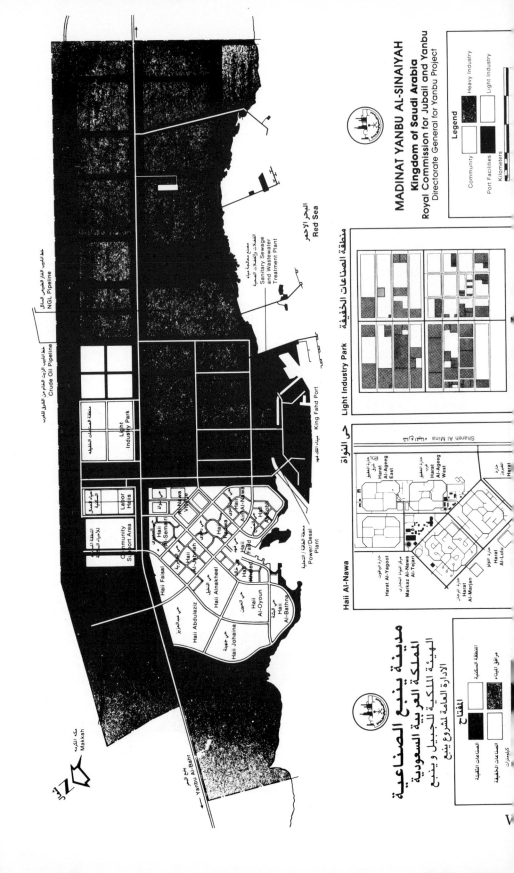

MADINAT YANBU AL-SINAIYAH

Kingdom of Saudi Arabia

Royal Commission for Jubail and Yanbu
Directorate General for Yanbu Project

Legend

- Community
- Port Facilities
- Heavy Industry
- Light Industry

Kilometers

منطقة الصناعات الخفيفة **Light Industry Park**

حي النواة **Haii Al-Nawa**

Sharen Al Mina شارع الميناء

Harat Al-Ageeg East حارة العقيق شرق

Harat Al-Ageeg West حارة العقيق غرب

Harat حارة

Harat Al-Yagoot حارة الياقوت

Markaz Al-Nawa Al-Tejari مركز النواة التجاري

Harat Al-Nawa حارة النواة

Harat Al-Marjan حارة المرجان

Harat Al-Lulu حارة اللؤلؤ

مدينة ينبع الصناعية
المملكة العربية السعودية
الهيئة الملكية للجبيل و ينبع
الإدارة العامة لمشروع ينبع

المنطقة السكنية
مرافق الميناء
الصناعات الثقيلة
الصناعات الخفيفة

خط الأنابيب الغاز الطبيعي السائل **NGL Pipeline**

خط الأنابيب الزيت الخام من الشرق للغرب **Crude Oil Pipeline**

البحر الأحمر **Red Sea**

المصنع معالجة مياه الصرف الصحي **Sanitary Sewage and Wastewater Treatment Plant**

Light Industry Park منطقة الصناعات الخفيفة

Labor Helis حيس العمال

Community Support Area المنطقة للخدمة العامة

Haii Al-Semeri حي السمري
Al-Nawa Village
Hawa
Hall Al-Nawa
Hall
Haii Faisal حي فيصل
Haii Al-Jimah
Haii Alnakheel حي النخيل
Haii Abdulaziz حي عبدالعزيز
Haii Johaina حي جهينة
Haii Al-Oyoun حي العيون
Haii Al-Bathna حي البطحاء
Fajid
Hall

بيناء الملك فهد **King Fahd Port**

محطة الطاقة التحلية **Power/Desal Plant**

مكة **Makkah**

ينبع البحر **Yanbu Al-Bahr**

N
شمال

increasing number of Saudi citizens should become directly involved in and committed to this phase of the Kingdom's development. It will lead to a diminution in the importance of the role of the agent (the Saudi citizen who represents foreign companies) and will increase the importance of Saudi companies in the development of local industrial and agricultural projects.

Manpower development is given the highest national priority. Education at the primary, intermediate, secondary and university level will be geared to the needs of the society. Above intermediate level, there will be streaming of the students to ensure that sufficient students remain in formal education and that the Kingdom's requirements for skilled technicians are taken into account. The private sector will be encouraged to expand training programs and government loans will be made dependent upon the provision of a full training scheme for Saudi citizens in the project. At the same time, Saudi citizens will be encouraged, through incentives, to enrol in training courses for technical and skilled jobs. Surplus manpower, currently employed in areas with limited economic potential will be encouraged to move to work in high growth sectors of the economy. A special effort will be made, through government sponsored research, to devise plans for the most effective use of manpower in general.

Both the policy of requiring the Saudi private sector to play a crucial role in diversifying the Saudi economy and the emphasis on the training and use of Saudi manpower indicate the Government's awareness of the need to involve Saudi citizens as much as possible in the future development of their own society.

The Strategy of the Fourth Five Year Plan 1985–1990 (1405–1410 AH)

The Author thought it would be most beneficial to include, at this point, the following document which gives a brief summation of the objectives and strategy of the Fourth Five Year Plan.

This document was prepared and published by the Ministry of Planning on the occasion of the official launching of the Fourth Five Year Plan on 29 Jamad Al-Thani, 1405 AH (corresponding to 20 March, 1985).

To maintain high standards of product supply and consumer protection.

To grow in accordance with the requirements and needs of the national economy and to encourage private capital into domestic investment.

To develop a set of approved Saudi standards and specifications to be appropriate for the requirements of commercial and industrial sectors within the Kingdom.

To enhance compliance with approved Saudi standards particularly in the national industrial sector.

To improve the health, safety, and living conditions of the citizens of the Kingdom through the provision of meteorology and environmental protection services in the Kingdom.

To protect the environment of the Kingdom and its natural resources, from pollution, desertification and environmental deterioration.

To provide precise and reliable statistical data to support planning operations.

To continue improving and providing support to computer data processing.

Principal achievements envisaged for Services Sectors
The emphasis of the commercial service programs is on ensuring business regulations keep pace with development needs, extending the consumer protection activities and assisting the business community in investment and export promotion initiatives. The financial sector will also be a leading growth sector. Considerable development of the Kingdom's financial structure is to be encouraged, the need for a formal stock exchange examined, and longer term lending by the commercial banks stimulated. Government services will concentrate on expanding their capacities and strengthening the enforcement of regulations.

The government credit institutions will provide the following loans during the Fourth Development Plan.

Institution	*Fourth Plan Total* SR Million
Saudi Arabian Agricultural Bank	10,150
Saudi Credit Bank	1,250
Saudi Industrial Development Fund	7,500
Real Estate Development Fund	21,000
Specialist Funding Programs	1,500
Public Investment Fund	18,700
Total	60,100

The Fourth Five Year Plan 1985–1990 (1405–1410 AH)

1   Main Features of the Development Plans in Saudi Arabia
Socio-economic planning started in Saudi Arabia at the beginning of 1390 AH, during which the First Development Plan was prepared. Most of its programs concentrated on construction of basic infrastructure, public utilities and the development of manpower. The Second Development Plan provided the first major thrust to development. It concentrated on the provision of modern infrastructure, the development of hydrocarbon

based industries, manpower and the diversification of non-oil economy. The Third Development Plan emphasized diversification and focused on the producing sectors such as agriculture, industry and mining, and on the completion of the associated infrastructure.

Fourth Plan Themes
Although the objectives of the Fourth Plan are mostly continuations of the principles and policies of the Third Plan there are four broad themes which characterize it and differentiate it from its predecessors. These are:

1 a greater concern with the efficiency of operations and usage of the Kingdom's resources and facilities and with the discovery and development of renewable alternatives;

2 a stronger focus of the diversification strategy on development of the producing activities, particularly manufacturing, agriculture and finance;

3 a commitment to reduce the number of unskilled and manual foreign workers in the Kingdom by more than half a million;

4 a clear and definite emphasis on promoting the private sector's involvement in economic development.

2 Elements of the 4DP

2.1 Objectives
In its resolution No. 36 dated 24.2.1404 AH, the Council of Ministers specified eleven objectives for the Fourth Plan as follows:

1 To safeguard Islamic values . . . duly observing, disseminating and confirming Allah's *Shari'ah.*

2 To defend the faith and the nation; and to uphold the security and social stability of the Realm.

3 To form productive citizen-workers by providing them with the tributaries conducive thereunto – ensuring their livelihood and rewarding them on the basis of their work.

4 To develop human resources thus ensuring a constant supply of manpower and upgrading and improving its efficiency to serve all sectors.

5 To raise cultural standards to keep pace with the Kingdom's development.

6 To reduce dependence on the production and export of crude oil as the main source of national income.

7 To continue with the real structural changes in the Kingdom's economy through continuous transformation to produce a diversified economic base, with due emphasis on industry and agriculture.

8 To develop mineral resources and to encourage discovery and utilization thereof.

9 To concentrate on qualitative development through improving and further developing the performance of the utilities and facilities already established during the three development plan periods.

10 To complete the infrastructural projects necessary to achieve overall development.

11 To achieve economic and social integration between Arab Gulf Cooperation Council countries.

2.2 Basic Strategic Principles

In its previously mentioned resolution, the Council of Ministers specified eight basic strategic principles to achieve the objectives mentioned in the said resolution. They are as follows:

1 Emphasis should be laid on improving the economic productive standards of the services, utilities and products which the Government provides for citizens – both directly (such as education and security services); and indirectly (such as electricity, transport and basic commodities).

2 Adopt a policy giving the private sector the opportunity to undertake many of the economic tasks of the Government, while the Government would not engage in any economic activity undertaken by the private sector.

3 Rationalize the system of direct and indirect subsidies on many goods and services provided by the state.

4 The consideration of economies should predominate in many government investment and expenditure decisions.

5 Continue the development of Saudi manpower, through the evaluation of education and training programs and curricula as well as by the further development or modification of these in conformity with the Islamic *Shari'ah*, the changing needs of society, and the requirements of the developing process.

6 Attention should be given to the development of Saudi society; to the provision of social welfare and health care for all; and to the support given to society's participation in the implementation of the programs of the plan as well as reaping the benefits of development.

7 In order to carry out the second objective the defense and security authorities shall plan their strategy in order to ensure the defense of the nation, and shall submit that strategy to the National Security Council preparatory to presenting it for consideration to the Council of Ministers.

8 Adopt a fiscal policy which keeps the level of expenditure in line with the Government's revenues through the Fourth Plan period.

These basic strategic principles include a total of 61 detailed policies which as a whole form a comprehensive policy framework to provide a base for Government expenditure and development operations. Most of the policies have a close relationship with each sector, and have been summarized in the following sections. Some of these policies are more applicable to the Government agencies and some to the private sector.

Reducing production costs of public services and utilities.

Ensuring that services are appropriate and not excessive, *e.g.* by limiting specifications for construction or operation of projects to what is actually required.

Utilizing technology in all public service sectors through mechanization and the use of advanced technology.

Judging the economic feasibility of projects (of all types) by including operational and maintenance costs (including management costs) and not only capital costs.

Developing appropriate administrative organizations to serve the new needs of the community.

Giving the private sector the opportunity to operate, manage, maintain and renovate many of the utilities currently operated by Government provided that this results in lower costs, better performance, and employment opportunities for Saudi citizens.

Re-considering some of the prevailing methods, policies and regulations so as to allow the private sector to operate more freely and more flexibly and to assist it in becoming more creative and developed.

Reducing subsidy rates in ways that will rationalize consumption without significantly affecting low income consumers.

All Government departments which administer public services should make economic efficiency a fundamental objective by adopting two basic principles. First, the cost of producing such services to the Saudi community should be reduced, and second, the price of such services should not be less than production costs, except in rare areas and with the proviso that the prices should be periodically reviewed.

3 *The Economic Context of the Fourth Plan*

The Fourth Plan has been prepared at a time of new economic conditions which have been gradually developing since the end of the Second Plan. These are:

1 Completion of the greater part of the basic infrastructure.

2 Considerable progress made in the diversification of the economy.

3 Increased capabilities and efficiency of Saudi manpower.

4 More efficient government administration.

5 Greater maturity and business skills of the private sector.

6   Lower levels of oil revenues.

7   Increased oil production by non-OPEC countries.

8   The world economy began its recovery from the longest economic recession period in its recent history.

4 *Planning Approach to the 4DP*

The Fourth Development Plan introduces a new planning methodology – the program approach. It is derived directly from the 8th basic strategic principle. As well as stipulating fiscal balance, this principle includes a policy directing that all authorized projects must comply with development objectives and principles as summarized above.

The "Program Approach" has introduced certain new emphases in planning government expenditure: on whole programs rather than on individual projects, on structure of expenditure rather than the component items; on responsibility for priorities and proportions rather than detailed commitments.

The program based method has also introduced other major changes in the planning process and in the allocation of government expenditure for the plan. It provides increased flexibility for the government agencies to select projects within the specific allocations for the program; taking into consideration the objective of co-ordinating regional development.

5 *The Role of the Private Sector during the 4DP*

The 4DP introduces a major change in the respective roles of the government and the private sector. Many of the key goals and objectives of the plan will be achieved through the private sector. In particular great reliance is placed on the private sector to continue the strategy of economic diversification through the development of agriculture, industry and mining, and to improve the efficiency and productivity of existing economic units.

To facilitate this, financial provision has been made within the total 4DP expenditure to support and encourage the private sector to increase its contribution to development.

6 *Civilian Expenditure during the 4DP*

In light of the Kingdom's recent experience the importance of Saudi Arabia's strategy of diversification away from oil has been underlined. Government expenditure in the 4DP will reinforce this strategy.

The total government expenditure in the 4DP has been determined at SR 1000 billion (in current prices). Of this SR 500 billion is to be devoted to development expenditure. The largest share of development expenditure 27.1% (SR 135.3 bn) will be allocated to human resources development, economic resources will receive 26.1% (SR 130.7 bn), health and social services 17.9% (SR 89.7 bn), transport and telecommunications 15.4% (SR 76.9 bn) and municipalities and housing 13.5% (SR 67.4 bn).

The amount allocated for the economic and human resources and health and social services will be more than the actual spending on these sectors during the 3DP. The percentage increase ranges between 28.9% for health and social services and 8.6% for economic resources. However, the basic infrastructure allocation will be lower. The reasons for this are first, conformity with the strategic principle that emphasizes development of the producing sectors, second, most of the infrastructure projects are already completed and third, it is expected that project cost will be reduced through the implementation of programs concerned with the modification of construction specifications, reducing the scope of projects and through higher competition in the market.

The number of projects to be implemented over the plan period total 3226 of which 1444 are new, and 1782 under construction and scheduled to be completed during the 4DP period.

7 Development Sectors and Support Sectors

The development sectors include natural resources, producing sectors, human resources, social development and basic infrastructure.

Also included are other sectors such as services which although not classified as development sectors support the development sectors.

7.1 Natural Resources

Natural resources include water, energy (oil, gas and solar energy) and minerals.

Main Objectives of the Natural Resources Sector

To meet the present and future needs of society.

To limit the development of water resources and conserve and rationalize the use of water.

To conserve and manage hydrocarbon resources and so achieve maximum benefits in the long run.

Develop solar energy as one of the alternative sources of energy in the Kingdom.

Investigate and explore mineral resources to determine occurrences in the Kingdom.

Explore and evaluate promising mineral deposits, and develop them if economically feasible.

Encourage both the public and private sectors to develop and utilize mineral resources.

Main Achievements Envisaged in Natural Resources

Desalination capacity will be increased by 364.4 thousand cubic meters of water per day, and by 603 megawatts of electric power generation. By 1409/10 the total capacity will be 1.8 million cubic meters of water per day and 3,748 megawatts of electricity capacity. Other programs include the implementation of national and regional water plans, regular assessment of water and agricultural policy, definition of maximum pumprates, and the establishment of a new tariff system. Greater emphasis is to be given to developing reclaimed water and surface water for direct use and for recharging aquifiers. New supply networks will be constructed to improve access to water by small towns and rural areas.

Establishment of 675 water projects of various sizes in a number of towns and villages throughout the Kingdom. These will include the drilling of 750 wells; the erection of 60 new dams and the installation of 480 pumping units all over the Kingdom.

Completion of the gas gathering and distribution system. Development of four major refineries, bulk storage plants and petroleum pipelines and also the implementation of a new project for hydrogen production through solar energy.

Production of geological maps for the Arabian Shield and phanerozoic rocks.

Exploration of 30 gold deposits, 5 silver deposits, 20 copper deposits, 12 tin-tungsten deposits, 12 niobium and 3 crome-nickel deposits.

The Saudi-Sudanese Joint Commission will implement pioneer mining projects in Atlantic Deep 2.

5.9 Government Expenditure on Natural Resources Sector: 4DP

	SR million	%
Water	31,789	58
Energy	18,821	34
Mining	4,427	8
Total	55,037	100

7.2   Producing Sectors

The non-oil producing sectors include: agriculture, industry, electricity, construction, and The Royal Commission for Jubail and Yanbu.

Main Objectives of the Producing Sectors:

To realize an acceptable increase in agricultural production using least possible costs and critical water resources.

The improvement of efficiency in the producing and marketing of agriculture products and attracting the private sector to invest in the agricultural sector.

To contribute to the Kingdom's growth and process of diversification through the continuation of the industrialization programs.

The development and utilization of hydrocarbons and mineral resources to increase the added value of these resources.

The provision of reliable electricity services for all population growth centers.

The conservation of energy and rationalization of electricity consumption.

The improvement of productivity of electric power utilities.

Supporting and encouraging Saudi construction industry.

Increasing the productivity and capabilities of Saudi contractors.

Reducing construction and associated maintenance costs.

The provision of necessary infrastructure for industry and residential communities.

Increasing private sector investment.

Main Achievements Envisaged for Producing Sectors

Projects include: the surveying and classification of 1,250,000 hectares of land, improvement of the irrigation network to cover more than 5 thousand hectares, cultivation of 8 thousand hectares of pasture, protection of 2.5 million hectares of cultivated land. Veterinary services will be established at Saudi ports for 37.5 million animals, and the production of 600 thousand tonnes of crops and 800 thousand tonnes of fertilizers will be subsidized. Disbursements of SR 350 million of subsidies will be made for the production of dates and palm offshoots. Distribution of 300 thousand tonnes of various improved seeds and 250 thousand improved fruit seedlings will be made.

As part of SABIC's activities five major projects are scheduled to come on stream during the Fourth Plan. These are the production of Methyl Tertiary Butylether (500,000 tons/yr), Butadiene (128,000 tons/yr), Butene-1 (80,000 tons/yr), Vinyl chloride monomer (300,000 tons/yr), Polyvinyl chloride (200,000 tons/yr).

Other SABIC projects under evaluation are polypropylene, propane dehydrogenation, downstream propylene derivatives, compound fertilizers, additional ammonia capacity, single cell protein and a rolled steel mill with a 1 million tonnes annual capacity.

Programs for other manufacturing are broader and more supportive of private sector initiatives. New industrial cities will be completed in Medina, Asir, Makkah, Hail, Tabuk, Jizan and Najran. A comprehensive industrial extension service and a new Small Industry Loan Facility are being evaluated. Greater emphasis is to be given to project identification and investment promotion and a program aimed at promoting manufactured exports is to be introduced that will include an export insurance and supplementary credit scheme. A pre-investment service is planned which will assist potential investors in the selection of projects and guide them in the procedures for applying for assistance.

The capacity of grain silos will be increased from 955 thousand tonnes/year to 1855 thousand tonnes/year, the capacity of flour mills from 748 thousand tonnes/year to 979 thousand tonnes/year and fodder from 336 thousand tonnes/year to 480 thousand tonnes/year.

The electric power networks will be expanded to serve about 828 thousand new customers, in so doing the long standing goal of full electrification of the Kingdom will be realized.

Encouragement will be given to construction companies to diversify into new activities, especially servicing and maintenance, through the implementation of the 30% rule and open tendering.

5.10 Government Expenditure on the Producing Sectors: 4DP

	SR million	%
Electricity	41,932	48
Royal Commission for Jubail and Yanbu	30,000	35
Agriculture	10,810	12
Industry	4,241	5
Classification of Contractors	—	—
Total Expenditure	87,054	100

7.3 Services Sector

The service sector includes: commercial services, banking and finance, environmental pollution control, specifications and standards, and statistical information services.

Main Objectives of Services Sector

To increase the contribution of the private sector in the activities currently undertaken by the government.

To increase the export of Saudi industrial products, and improve trade relations with other countries particularly with the G.C.C.

Government Expenditure on Services Sector
Although most of the finance for this sector will be provided by the private sector, the government will contribute SR 64,821 million during the Fourth Plan of which 86% will be in the form of loans from the Specialized Credit Institutions.

5.11 **Government Expenditure on Services Sector: 4DP**

Sector	SR millions	%
Commercial Services	825	1
Banking and Finance	60,100	93
Meteorology and Environment Protection	2,831	4
Standards and Specifications	507	1
Information and Statistical Data	558	1
Total Expenditure on Services Sector	64,821	100

7.4 Social and Cultural Development

This sector includes social, cultural, health services, information, judicial, religious affairs, youth and sports development.

Major Objectives for Social and Cultural Development Sector

1. To safeguard Islamic values – duly observing, disseminating and confirming Allah's *Shari'ah*, God's Divine Law.
2. To continue providing integrated health services, particularly primary health care and increase coordination and operating efficiency. Special consideration will be given to preventive services, and to mother and child care.
3. To expand integrated social development in coordination with other agencies which provide such services, and to encourage the participation of local community in social development.
4. To improve and upgrade cultural levels, guide and orient the members of the community to match the development process in the Kingdom, strengthening family relations in order to develop the Youth, and to sponsor sports activities.

Major Achievements expected for Social and Cultural Development Sectors

About 45 hospitals will be established providing an additional 8,944 beds and increasing the total number of hospitals by 1409/10 (1989/90 AD) to approximately 138 with 27,857 beds. Moreover numerous primary health care centers will be established throughout the Kingdom by 1409/10 (1989/90 AD) the total number will reach about 2,187 against 1,306 in 1404/1405 (1984/5 AD). In addition about 100 maternal and diagnostic centers will be established in different areas of the Kingdom.

Approximately 50 classes for handicraft training will be established as well as 50 benevolent societies of which 20 will be concerned with women. There will be an expansion in pensions and also in social support to accommodate about 95,000 cases. Also 20 new social security offices will be opened.

The surrounding areas of the Holy Mosque at Makkah will be expanded to accommodate about 1.5 million pilgrims. The Prophet's honourable congregational Mosque at Medina will be expanded and renovated. Services provided to the pilgrims will be improved.

5.12 Government Expenditure on Social and Cultural Development Sectors: 4DP

Sector	SR million	%
Health	62,239	57
Judicial and Religious Sectors	18,501	17
Cultural, Information and Youth Welfare	13,617	13
Social Services	14,280	13
Total Social and Cultural Development	108,637	100

7.5 Human Resources

The human resources development sector includes general education for boys and girls, higher education, technical education and vocational training, education and training in other government sectors, private sector manpower development, training programs and science and technology.

Main Objectives

1 Improving the efficiency and quality of education, and the elimination of the incidence of illiteracy among Saudi adults.

2 Ensuring that Education is in conformity with Islamic values and Allah's *Shari'ah* (God's Divine Law).

3 Provision of competent manpower required to achieve the objectives of national development.

4 Developing and improving internal training, on-the-job training programs, increasing coordination among training programs under the Government supervision, achieving Saudization goals in both the public and private sectors, provision of competent cadre for the public sector and the identification of employment opportunities for women in a manner which would not be contrary to Muslim faith.

5 Taking necessary action required for the implementation of proper strategies to increase Saudization rate and productive efficiency.

6 Facilitation of the application of Science and Technology in support of the objectives of long-term development in the Kingdom.

Expected Main Achievements of Human Resources
The number of male students in various levels of General Education will increase from 914,000 in 1404/1405 (1984/5 AD) to 1,168,000 in 1409/1410 (1989/90 AD). The number of female students in General Education will increase from 655,000 in 1404/1405 to 937,000 in 1409/1410. The number of total students will increase from 1,569,000 at the beginning of 4DP to 2,105,000 at the end of 4DP.

The number of male students in higher education will increase from 51,000 in 1404/05 to more than 69,000 in 1409/10. The number of female students in higher education will increase from 28,000 in 1404/05 to more than 39,000 in 1409/10. The total number of students will increase from approximately 80,000 at the beginning of 4DP to more than 108,000 by the end.

The number of male graduates from secondary level will increase from a 3DP total of 70,076 to approximately 109,500 during the 4DP. The number of female graduates at secondary level will increase from a 3DP total of approximately 62,208 to 105,500 during the 4DP. The total number of graduates at secondary level will increase from a 3DP total of 132,284 to approximately 215,000 during the 4DP.

The number of male graduates from higher education will increase from a 3DP total of 28,000 to approximately 38,000 during the 4DP. The number of female graduates will increase from a 3DP total of 13,000 to approximately 22,000 during the 4DP. The total number of graduates from higher education will increase from a 3DP total of 41,000 to approximately 60,000 during the 4DP.

The number of enrollments at technical education schools will increase from 12,000 in 1404/1405 to 16,000 in 1409/1410, and the number of graduates from technical education will increase from approximately 5,239 to 18,942 by 1405/1406. The number of enrollments at vocational training centers will also increase from approximately 11,000 in 1404/05 to 17,000 in 1409/10, and the number of graduates of vocational training will increase from 37,576 to 43,255 during the 4DP.

5.13 Government Expenditure on Human Resources: 4DP

	SR million	%
General Education	85,232	62
Higher Education	40,291	30
Technical Education and Vocational Training	6,586	5
Institute of Public Administration	1,053	1
Manpower Development*	1,195	1
Sciences and Technology	1,816	1
Total Expenditure on Human Resources	136,173	100

* Civil Service Bureau, Deputy Minister of Labor and Manpower Council.

7.6   Physical Infrastructure
The Physical Infrastructure Sector includes Transport facilities, Postal Services, Telecommunications, Housing, Municipal and Public Works Services.

8   Labor Force and GDP in 4DP

8.1   Labor Force
The plan target is to increase productivity by 4 per cent per annum. As a result the total civilian labor force will decline by approximately 1% per year leading to a reduction in employment of 855,000 compared to employment in 1404/05 (1984/5 AD). Simultaneously the target growth in non-oil economy of 2.9 per cent per annum will create new employment opportunities for 630,000.

   Moreover the numbers of Saudis in the workforce will increase by 374,700 during the 4DP. As a result there will be an overall reduction in non Saudi manpower of 600,000.

8.2   GDP
It is expected as a result of following the strategy approved by the Council of Ministers that GDP will grow at an annual average rate of 4% p.a. The absolute value will increase from SR 284.1 billion in 1404/05 to SR 354.9

billion in 1409/10 (constant 1399/1400 prices). The oil sector will grow at 5.6% p.a. and non-oil sector at the rate of 2.9% p.a.

The most important sectors expected to contribute to this growth are Industry which is expected to grow at 15.5% per year, Finance and Business Services (9% per year), Agriculture (6% per year).

Growth in other sectors will be lower: Construction 2.8% p.a., Commercial Services 2.5% per annum, Oil and Gas 3.8% per annum. In Real Estate and Government there will be no growth. Nonetheless although these growth rates are lower they do approximate to those achieved in the 3DP and remain high by world standards.

Main Objectives of Physical Infrastructure

Expansion as necessary to cope with the gradual increase in demand on transport services.

Greater equality in the provision of physical infrastructure and municipal services throughout the Kingdom, increased efficiency of operation and improvements in services in villages and urban areas.

Improving the quality of housing and efficient utilization of the existing housing stock.

Supporting private sector housing construction through Real Estate Development Fund.

Expansion of and improvements to the Postal Services and Telecommunications particularly in areas where coverage is yet to be fully completed.

Expected Main Achievements of Physical Infrastructure

The first stage of the new international airport at Dhahran will be completed by the end of 1410 (1990 AD). New roads will be constructed to bring the total length of road network to 116,000 km: which will comprise 20,000 km main roads, 15,000 km secondary and feeder roads and 81,000 km of rural roads.

The Postal Service will be expanded to cover a further 1200 villages, and the local telephone networks will be enlarged to give 250,000 new subscribers access to installed exchange capacity. Network switching capacity will be increased to 300,000 lines.

The following Municipal projects will be implemented: 185 water projects, 78 sewage, 11 water drainage, 57 flood protection, 47 markets, 152 public utilities, 341 urban streets, 42 Governmental buildings, 6 environmental improvements, 24 planning studies, 11 training, 215 other Municipal projects.

5.14 Government Expenditure on Physical Infrastructure

	SR million	%
Transport	54,851	36
Postal Services and Telecommunication	28,581	19
Municipal and Public Works	63,500	42
Housing	3,828	3
Total of Physical Infrastructure	150,760	100

From these objectives the eight basic strategic principles are deduced:

1   the improvement of economic productive standards of services, utilities and products which the Government provides for its citizens – both directly (such as education and security services); and indirectly (such as electricity, transport and basic commodities).

2   the adoption of a policy giving the private sector the opportunity to undertake many of the tasks of the Government.

3   the rationalization of the system of direct and indirect subsidies on many goods and services provided by the State.

4 · giving predominance to economies in the government's investment and expenditure decisions.

5   the continued development of Saudi manpower through the evaluation of educational and training programmes and curricula as well as by the further development or modification of these in conformity with the Islamic *Shari'ah*; the changing needs of society; and the requirements of the developmental process.

6   further development of Saudi society; the provision of social and health welfare for all; support for society's participation in the implementation of the programmes of the Plan as well as reaping the benefits of development.

7   the preparation by defense and security authorities of their strategy to ensure the defense of the nation.

8   the adoption of fiscal policies which keep the level of expenditure in line with the Government's revenues throughout the Fourth Plan period.

In economic terms, the keynote of the Fourth Five Year Plan would seem to be consolidation. With the fall in oil prices and the reduction in oil production, Saudi Arabian revenues have dropped substantially. The development program remains ambitious but the will to expand is tempered by the constraints of the budget and the need for tighter fiscal control.

In many ways, this general policy of consolidation makes sense, regardless of financial considerations. The extraordinary program which has taken Saudi Arabia from an undeveloped country twenty years ago to a society with a modern infrastructure and the potential to develop a diversified economy has been successful. A few statistics, comparing 1972 with 1982, will serve to indicate the scale of achievement:

5.15 Developments 1972–1982: Key Statistics

	1972	1982
Length of paved roads (kms)	8,614	23,794
Volume of import cargo unloaded by ports (thousand weight tons)	2,286	36,360
Saudia (Saudi Arabian Airlines) revenue passenger distance (million kms)	971	12,278
Number of Telephones operating (thousands)	57	633
Number of Schools (year end)	3,659	12,574
Number of Teachers (year end)	27,627	94,213
Number of Students (year end)		
– pre-school	7,000	36,000
– elementary education	475,000	998,000
– intermediate education	84,000	274,000
– secondary education	23,000	116,000
– higher education	9,000	63,000
– training abroad	2,000	18,000
– teacher training	15,000	20,000
– technical education	1,000	9,000
– adult education	46,000	146,000
– other	7,000	11,000
TOTAL	669,000	1,691,000
Number of Hospitals	51	70*
Number of Hospital Beds	8,132	13,066*
Number of Doctors	1,081	4,618*

* figures given are for 1981; 1982 not available.
Source: Achievements of the Development Plans 1970–1982

This selection of statistics gives a broad indication of the scale of development attempted and achieved over the last decade. In many key areas, expansion must be calculated not in tens but in hundreds of percentage points.

Development has been particularly determined in the educational field. In 1983–1984, there were more than 14,000 schools in the Kingdom, serving a pupil population of more than 2 million. Of these more than three quarters of a million were girls.

UNIVERSITY EDUCATION
Existing universities in Saudi Arabia will be the major concern of this part of the work. Saudi Arabian universities will be dealt with in order of their establishment. The final part of this chapter will examine both the quantity and quality of education now being offered to Saudi citizens.

King Saud University – 1957[41]
Established in 1957, the King Saud University (originally called the University of Riyadh), is constituted of eleven faculties including Agriculture, Arts, Commerce, Education (also in Abha), Engineering, Medicine, Pharmacy, and Sciences. The faculties confer Bachelor of Arts degrees or have diploma programs. It also has faculties of Dentistry and Nursing. Faculties authorized to confer higher degrees are as follows.

1 The Faculty of Arts confers Master of Arts degrees in Geography and History, starting with the academic year 1973–1974 (1393–1394 AH). Starting with academic year 1975–1976, the same faculty has offered a Master of Arts program in Arabic Language. Since 1975, this faculty also has offered a one-year program leading to a diploma in Information. It now gives a Bachelor of Arts degree in Information.
2 The Faculty of Education offers the one-year diploma programs in the following fields: (a) Educational Administration, usually offered to the Directors (Principals) of the general high schools; (b) diploma in Education. There are several higher education programs currently under study which will be taught by the Faculty of Education in the near future. These programs are: (a) Master of Arts in Educational Psychology; (b) Bachelor of Science in Fine Arts; (c) Bachelor of Science in Physical Education; (d) Educational Techniques diploma (one-year program).

Islamic University in Medina – 1961
The Islamic University in Medina is analogous to the Al-Azhar University of Cairo. It is essentially a school of Islamic Theology. Although the Al-Azhar of Cairo in recent years has expanded its field to secular programs of study such as Medicine and Engineering, this has not been the case at the Islamic University at Medina. The Islamic University consists of the following faculties which confer Bachelor of Arts degrees only: *Da'wa* (Preaching), *Shari'ah* (Theology) and *Quranic* Studies (activities

started in 1975). Enrollment in the faculties of *Shari'ah* and *Da'wa* for the academic year of 1971–1972 was 467 non-Saudi students from Arabian and Islamic countries out of the total number of 568.[42] By 1978 the total student body had risen to an estimated 2,500.

King Abdul Aziz University in Jiddah and Makkah – 1967

Established, initially, as a private university, King Abdul Aziz University was converted to a state university in 1971. It consists of the following faculties: Arts, Education (in Makkah), Economy and Management, Engineering, Medicine, Science, and *Shari'ah* (Theology) (in Makkah).

All these faculties confer Bachelor of Arts and Bachelor of Science degrees in the various fields of their specialties. The Faculty of Medicine was inaugurated in 1975. At the level of higher education, both the faculties of education and *Shari'ah* confer Master of Arts degrees.

Imam Muhammad Ibn Sa'ud Islamic University in Riyadh – 1974

The university was inaugurated by Royal Decree in 1974.[43] Currently the university is made up of an institute and several faculties. The High Judicial Institute was originally established in 1965 (1385 AH) for the purpose of graduating qualified *Shari'ah* judges. The period of study is for three years, after which a student receives a Master's degree in Judicial Affairs and Jurisprudence. The Faculty of *Shari'ah* (Theology) was established earlier in 1953 (1373 AH) for the purpose of meeting the demand for qualified *Ulama* and preachers throughout the country. It confers a Licentiate degree (equivalent of a Bachelor of Arts degree) after four years of study. The Faculty of Arabic Language and Social Science was originally established as the Faculty of Social Sciences in 1970 (1390 AH) and was expanded in 1974 by adding the Arabic Language major and a program in Library Science. The period of study is four years after which the student receives the equivalent of a Bachelor of Arts degree.

At the present time, there are several proposals being considered for the purpose of expanding the educational activities of the university. At the High Judicial Institute, there are plans to initiate doctoral study. The Faculty of *Shari'ah* is considering establishing another three majors in the fields of Essentials of Jurisprudence, Interpretation and *Hadith*, and Preaching and Guidance. The Faculty of Arabic Language and Social Sciences is considering the establishment of new programs in the field of higher education.[44]

King Faisal University in Dammam and Hofuf – 1975

The idea of establishing a university in the Eastern Province was originated by King Faisal in 1974 (1394 AH). The then Crown Prince Fahd's efforts brought into existence King Faisal University which was inaugurated during the academic year 1975–1976 (1395–1396 AH) with two campuses. The first campus is in Hofuf in Al-Hasa and is constituted of the faculties of Agriculture, and Veterinary Medicine and Animal Resources. The second campus is located in Dammam and is comprised of the faculties of Medicine and Medical Sciences, established with the educational cooperation of Harvard University (an agreement for that cooperation had been concluded with King Faisal University and Harvard University): and a faculty of Engineering.[45]

Higher Education

The University of Petroleum and Minerals in Dhahran in the Eastern Province (see also Chapter 2)

The University of Petroleum and Minerals was founded as a College in 1963 with less than one hundred students. By 1974, it had increased student enrollment to 1500. The following year the College was elevated to University status and its student intake continued to increase. In 1983/84, more than 3,800 students were enrolled at UPM.

UPM is an autonomous institution, under the authority of the Ministry of Petroleum and Minerals, established to provide graduate manpower for the petroleum and mineral industries of the Kingdom.

UPM now includes a research institute with six divisions:

Petroleum and Gas Technology
Energy Resources
Geology and Minerals
Water and the Environment
Meteorology Standards and Materials
Economic and Industrial Research

UPM can now claim to be a University with internationally acknowledged and respected standards of academic and technical excellence in the fields of petroleum and mineral technology.

Umm al-Qura University

Umm al-Qura University, which was established in the course of the Third Development Plan, apart from its colleges of Education and Engineering and Applied Sciences, is primarily concerned with the study and teaching of Islam and Islamic culture. In 1983/84, the University had more than nine thousand students (of which almost 3,000 were women) and its student enrollment is expected to increase to 15,000 by 1989/90. It contains five research centers:

Center for Scientific Research and Islamic Heritage Renaissance
Educational and Psychological Research Center, Makkah
Islamic Studies Center
Haj Research Center
International Islamic Education Center

5.16 Enrollments and Faculty Strength in Five Principal Saudi Universities in the early 1970s

University	Student Enrollment	Faculty Strength	Academic Year of Survey	Student Enrollment 1977–8 estimate
King Abdul Aziz	1,976	176	1971–1972	14,000
Imam Muhammad Ibn Sa'ud Islamic University	2,224	94	1971–1972	3,500
Islamic University	568	29	1971–1972	2,500
King Saud University	7,823	975	1971–1972	12,000
University of Petroleum and Minerals	1,475	295	1973–1974	2,200
King Faisal University	—	—	—	550
Total	14,066	1,569	—	34,750

Source: (except for last column) Kingdom of Saudi Arabia, Ministry of Education, Statistics Research and Educational Documents Unit (Statistical Unit). Educational Statistics, 1971–1974. 5th issue pp. 288–289

5.17 Student Enrollment in Saudi Arabian Universities – actual 1983/84 and forecast 1989/90

University	1983/84	1989/90
King Saud	22,166	20,000
King Abdulaziz	18,905	20,000
University of Petroleum and Minerals	3,814	5,000
King Faisal	2,610	10,000
Imam Muhammad	10,807	10,000
Islamic Medina	3,233	5,000
Umm-al Qura	9,348	15,000
Girls' Colleges	11,730	35,000
New Universities	—	15,000
Community Colleges	—	15,000
Technical Colleges	—	10,000
TOTAL	82,613	160,000

Source: Ministry of Higher Education

5.18 Breakdown of Total Female Student Enrollment – 1983/84

King Saud	4,835
King Abdulaziz	5,695
King Faisal	1,000
Imam Muhammad Ibn Saud	1,455
Umm al-Qura	3,778
Girls' Colleges	11,730
TOTAL	28,501

Source: Ministry of Higher Education

With the objective of preparing women for fuller participation in the social, economic and cultural life of the country, the Third Development Plan made provision for faculties to cater for a substantially increased number of female students. One of the most important achievements of the Third Development Plan has been the fast expansion of women's education with actual attainment exceeding targets in all areas.

5.19 University Teaching Staff – actual 1984/85 and forecast 1989/90

	1984/85	1989/90
Saudi	4,000	10,000
Non-Saudi	5,000	8,000
TOTAL	9,000	18,000

Source: Ministry of Higher Education

5.20 Comparison of Proportion of Students at Bachelor level in Different Disciplines – actual 1979/80; and forecast 1989/90

	1979/80	1989/90
Humanities	44.2%	34.4%
Social Sciences	15.9%	15.6%
Science	5.8%	9.4%
Education	14.7%	18.7%
Engineering	12.2%	12.5%
Medicine	4.7%	6.3%
Agriculture	2.5%	3.1%
TOTAL	100.0%	100.0%

Source: Ministry of Higher Education

Along with the University of Petroleum and Minerals in Dhahran, there are seven universities operating throughout Saudi Arabia providing for the well-trained manpower needed for the nation's development. Table 5.16 shows student enrollment as well as faculty strength in five Saudi Universities in the early 1970s. Tables 5.17 to 5.20 give actual figures for

5.21 Disciplines of Saudi Students Pursuing University Undergraduate and Graduate Education Abroad in 1975 (30/4/1395 AH)

Discipline	Number	Discipline	Number
Accounting	38	Electrical Engineering	53
Adult Education	1	Electronics Engineering	93
Agriculture	11	Engineering	408
Agricultural Engineering	5	English	192
Air Conditioning	4	Field Crops	2
Animal Production	1	Fine Arts	19
Anthropology	1	Food Industry	1
Applied Mechanics	1	Forestry	1
Arabic Language	3	French Language	12
Arabic Language and Criticism	3	General Electricity	6
Arabic Literature	10	General Study	2
Archaeology	2	Geography	39
Arts	149	Geological Engineering	1
Arts and Sociology	2	Geology	33
Audio Methods	1	Geo-Physics Engineering	2
Aviation Engineering	15	Guidance and Design	1
Biology	11	High School Studies	2
Botany	20	History	30
Business Administration	144	Hospital Management	45
Cartography	2	Hotel Management	1
Chemical Engineering	4	Human and Public Relations	2
Chemistry and Physics	5	Hydrology	6
Chemical Industry	3	Industrial Engineering	12
Cinema and Television	5	Industrial Management	2
Cinema and Television Direction	5	Industrial Relations	1
Civil Engineering	137	Information	17
Commerce	87	International Relations	5
Computer Science	24	Islamic Studies	10
Construction Engineering	66	Labor Relations	1
Criminology	3	Law	122
Curriculum	5	Library Science	25
Dairy Science	2	Local Government	2
Decore (Mechanical) Drawing	12	Local Government Management	12
Desalination Major	3	Management Engineering	4
Eastern Studies	1	Management Organization	2
Economics	171	Marketing	2
Economic Development	1	Maritime Engineering	22
Education	51	Maritime Navigation	12
Educational Documentation	1	Mathematics	43
Education Management	12	Mechanics	8
Educational Planning	1	Mechanical Engineering	11
Medicine	1,086	Rocks and Minerals	1

Discipline	Number	Discipline	Number
Mining Engineering	1	Science	28
Music	1	Science of Poisons	1
Nuclear Engineering	3	Secondary School Management	2
Nutrition	11	Social Work	4
Oceanography	1	Space Engineering	1
Pharmacy	21	Sociology	33
Physical Education	7	Statistics	13
Physics	43	Structural Design	6
Physics and Mathematics	1	Technical Education	10
Police Management	2	Telecommunication Engineering	134
Police Science	4	Television Management	19
Political Science	42	Theatrical Arts	6
Ports Engineering	3	Topography	7
Postal Science	15	Town Planning	5
Poultry	1	Traffic Engineering	1
Preparation and Organization	8	Training	16
Psychology	27	Undecided Majors	1,127
Public Finance	5	Urban Planning	1
Public Health	10	Weather Forecasting	1
Public Management	66	Welding and Dedenting	4
Public Utilities	3	X-ray Engineering	5
Religion	6	Zoology	21
Remaining Engineering Fields	11	Total	5,108

Source: Kingdom of Saudi Arabia Ministry of Education Directorate General for Relations and External Scholarship, Bayan Bi Altalata Al-Daresson Fi Alkharij Muaza'en Masab Al Tahhassosai their Distribution and the level of Study. June 1975 (30/4/1395 AH). Typewritten statistics obtained by author in Ryadh, June 1975. (F.F. translation).

NB: In 1984, there were more than 13,000 Saudi students pursuing university courses overseas. In terms of subject, the main emphasis was on science. It is worth remarking that scholarships for first degree courses overseas have now been curtailed, since there are now adequate university places for Bachelor degrees available in the Kingdom.

1983–1984 and forecasts for 1989–1990. Table 5.17 shows student enrollment broken down by university. Table 5.18 gives a breakdown of total female enrollment in Saudi Universities. Table 5.19 gives the figures of Saudi and non-Saudi university teaching staff in Saudi Arabia. Table 5.20 gives a breakdown of Saudi undergraduate students according to subject.

Tables 5.21 and 5.22 show the number of Saudi students who were pursuing their education abroad in 1975 and their fields of study. The data obtained for these tables are presented here in English for the first time. Table 5.23 shows the number of Saudi citizens who had already earned their doctoral degrees in the various disciplines of science by the end of 1974. The source and dates of these degrees is also shown in Table 5.24.

5.22 Countries in which Saudi Students Were Pursuing University Undergraduate and Graduate Education Abroad in 1975 (30/4/1395 AH)

Country of Study	Number	Per Cent of Total (5,108)
Austria	53	1.04
Belgium ⎫		
France ⎪		
Holland ⎬	58	1.14
Spain ⎭		
Egypt	1,244	24.35
Germany, Federal Republic of,	122	2.39
Iran	10	.2
Iraq	22	.43
Italy	47	.92
Jordan	11	.22
Kuwait	16	.31
Lebanon	784	14.64
Morocco	2	.04
Pakistan	212	4.15
Sudan	4	.08
Switzerland	21	.11
Syria	6	.41
Tunisia	2	.04
Turkey	4	.08
United Kingdom	487	9.53
United States of America	2,003	39.21

Source: See Table 5.21, p. 184.

5.23 Ph.D. (or Equivalent) Degrees Obtained by Saudi Citizens Abroad from 1927 through 1974

Discipline	1927 to 1960	1961–62	1962–63	1963–64	1964–65	1965–66	1966–67	1967–68	1968–69	1969–70	1970–71	1971–72	1972–73	1973–74	1974	TOTAL
Accounting	1															1
Accounting & Management									1							1
Agriculture														1		1
Agriculture Economy									3							3
Analytical Chemistry					1											1
Anthropology												1	1			2

Discipline	1927 to 1960	1961–62	1962–63	1963–64	1964–65	1965–66	1966–67	1967–68	1968–69	1969–70	1970–71	1971–72	1972–73	1973–74	1974	TOTAL
Applied Botany	1															1
Applied Geology			1													1
Applied Mathematics													1			1
Applied Mechanics											1					1
Arabic Literature	1					1	5	2	1	1	1	1				13
Arid Land														1		1
Arts Law														1		1
Botanical Physiology													1			1
Botanical Science											1			4		5
Business Administration									1					1		2
Business Administration and Marketing											1					1
Chemical Engineering		1														1
Chemical Geology												1				1
Chemistry												2	2	3	1	8
Chemistry and Biology											1					1
Chemistry and Pharmacology									1							1
Chemistry and Pharmacy										1						1
Civil Engineering											1	2		1		4
Communication Engineering		1														1
Constructural Engineering									1			1				2
Economics		1							1	1	1	3	2	2		11
Education	1										1	1	2	3	2	10
Education Management													1	2		3
Educational Planning											1					1
Educational Psychology										1						1
English Language											1					1
English Literature						1								1		2
Food Technology										1						1
General Chemistry											1			3		4
General Engineering										1						1
General Geological Science					1								1			2
General Theory Structure and Composition													1			1
General Zoology													1	2		3
Geography										1			1	1		3
Geology										1	1	2	1	1	1	7

Discipline	1927 to 1960	1961–62	1962–63	1963–64	1964–65	1965–66	1966–67	1967–68	1968–69	1969–70	1970–71	1971–72	1972–73	1973–74	1974	TOTAL
Governments														1		1
Heat Engineering									1							1
History	1						1		1	1		1	1	3	1	10
History – Geography									1							1
History of Modern Saudi Arabia										1						1
Horticulture														1		1
Industrial Education												1				1
Industrial Engineering														1		1
Industrial Petroleum Management				1												1
Information											1					1
Inorganic Chemistry							1				1	1		1		4
International Law										1						1
International Relations										3		1	1			5
Islamic History										1		1	1			3
Islamic Law										1						1
Islamic Shari'ah										1			1			2
Islamic Studies													1			1
Islamic Studies and Art										1						1
Law						1				1			1			3
Law and Political Science										2						2
Library Science														1		1
Linguistics														1		1
Mathematical Science														1		1
Mathematics												1	1			2
Medicine	1		1	1	1	1	1	1	1				1	1		10
Medicine and Anatomy									1							1
Medicine and Orthopedic Surgery				1												1
Medicine and Surgery								1	1							2
Medicine and Urology											1					1
Mineral Mining														1		1
Money and Banking								1								1
Pharmaceutical Science											1					1
Pharmacy													1			1
Philosophy												1				1

Discipline	1927 to 1960	1961–62	1962–63	1963–64	1964–65	1965–66	1966–67	1967–68	1968–69	1969–70	1970–71	1971–72	1972–73	1973–74	1974	TOTAL
Physical Chemistry	1													1		2
Physics								1					1	1		3
Physics and Chemistry											1					1
Physics Science														3		3
Political Geography											1					1
Political History												1				1
Political Science		1									1					2
Political Science and International Relations												1				1
Private Law								1								1
Psychology													1			1
Public Administration	1									1		1	1		1	5
Public Health											1					1
Public Management Education														1		1
Radiological Chemistry												1				1
Roads and Bridges Engineering										1						1
Sociology & Science						1	1	1	1							4
Sociology														1		1
Topographical Engineering														1		1
Traffic Management													1			1
Veterinarian Medicine												1				1
Zoological Chemistry												1				1
Annual Totals	7	3	2	5	4	8	7	10	18	30	25	17	24	48	3	

GRAND TOTAL 211

Source: Da'lel Ra'sael Al-Doctora & Majester Lil Mouatinen Al Saudien 1348–1394 AH (Guide to Doctoral and Master's Degrees of Saudi citizens, 1927–1974). Ministry of Education, Division of Documentary Education, Riyadh, May, 1975, pp. 1–7. (Tables are the Author's design and translation)

Before examining the material presented in Tables 5.17 to 5.24, it is important to mention that the figures in Tables 5.23 and 5.24 prepared by the Division of Educational Documentation of the Saudi Ministry of Education include only degrees of which notification has been received. Some Saudi citizens who have already been awarded doctoral degrees may not yet have reported the receipt of their degrees. While these tables do not show the total numbers of Saudi doctoral graduates they do, on the other hand, illustrate the progress achieved at the doctoral level by Saudi citizens through 1974. It was estimated in 1977 that the number of Saudi

5.24 Source of Ph.D. Degrees Obtained by Saudi Citizens Abroad from 1927 through 1974

Country	1927 to 1960	1961–62	1962–63	1963–64	1964–65	1965–66	1966–67	1967–68	1968–69	1969–70	1970–71	1971–72	1972–73	1973–74	1974	TOTAL
Austria									1	2						3
Britain	1	1		2	2	6	3	3	5	6	11	6	17	20	3	86
Egypt						1				2	1		1	1		6
France						1		1	1							3
Germany, Federal Republic of									1	1	1	1		1		5
Iran					1				1							2
Italy	1			1					1			1				4
Lebanon	1				1	1			1	1						5
United States of America	3	1	1	1	1	1	3	7	10	13	15	7	10	23	1	97
Total	6	2	1	4	5	10	6	11	21	25	28	15	28	45	4	

GRAND TOTAL 211

Source: See Table 5.23, p. 186.

Ph.D. holders was more then three hundred.[46] By 1984, there were six hundred Saudi citizens holding a doctorate.

Surveying the total educational system of Saudi Arabia, it must be remembered that it had its real start only in 1949–1950 with the personal support of the then Prince Faisal and the encouragement of Prince Fahd ibn Abdul Aziz, who later became Minister of Education and President of the Saudi Higher Council of Education, the highest educational authority in the Kingdom, and is now the King.

Further, it should be noted that the Saudi educational system is merely thirty-five years old. The statement of C. Arnold Anderson is applicable to the educational policies initiated and adopted in Saudi Arabia:

> In formulating educational policy, every society must compromise among three goals: (1) efficiency in allocating training to individuals most likely to profit from it; (2) equity in opening opportunities for education impartially to various groups; and (3) free choice of educational careers to maximize motivation and flexibility.[47]

"Compromise" suggests that efficiency, equity and freedom of choice are, in that sequence, the three important elements necessary for a sound educational system. If these three elements cannot be attained in equal proportions, priority must be given to the criterion of efficiency. In most developing nations, the financial realities and sometimes poor judgment, make it impossible for their educational systems to effectively balance these three elements. For example, the Egyptian educational system, in implementing equity and freedom of choice for students, sacrificed efficiency. This result was of course not intentional on the part of the Egyptian policy makers, but was unavoidable. Inadequate financial resources and the crippling factor of over-population compounded the disparity between intention and achievement.

Some other countries, which neither lack the financial resources nor are over-populated, deprive their students of an important element of the Anderson formula, *i.e.* the freedom of choice. Indeed the freedom of choice of an educational career is vital and essential since it "maximizes motivation and flexibility". Currently, Libya is one of the developing nations which has adopted such a policy, with the rationale of producing specialists in the various fields of education. Such a result can be automatically achieved when the demand for well-trained manpower in almost all the fields of education in a developing nation like Libya absorbs all the available output of educated manpower.

Although Saudi Arabia's educational policy makers may not have been aware of the Anderson formula of efficiency, equity and freedom of choice, they are built into the Saudi educational system at all levels. Saudi Arabia's abundant financial resources enable the country to pursue such a policy with ease and effect. For example, the efficiency element sometimes necessitates the hiring of educational personnel from distant countries, *e.g.* the United States of America, and despite the heavy financial requirements involved in such a case, the Saudi policy makers do encourage it as it is to the country's ultimate benefit and for the fulfillment of its educational goals. The equity element is also achieved by having a free educational system open to all citizens at all levels. Yet at certain levels such as the university, in order to maintain a high standard, a student must possess specified academic qualifications for admission. This policy is sound as it will keep the university as a serious institution of higher learning, rather than allow it to be used as a boarding house for uninterested students. In Egypt, when universities began, during the 1960s, admitting students according to an equity criterion based on political motivations (the ideology of socialism), an enormous surplus in university graduates resulted. University graduates often waited two years after graduation only to be appointed to Government positions which rarely did justice to their educational qualifications. This situation has not changed much despite the introduction of rigid entrance requirements to Egyptian universities. Surpluses of unwanted and unemployed university graduates still represent a major problem facing Egypt today. This result undermines efforts of Egyptian educational policy makers who find it extremely difficult, even dangerous, to alter the *status quo*.

Saudi educational policy makers, viewing the Saudi educational system from another perspective, were able to cope with an important problem prevailing in other countries, namely the cultural gap resulting from the great emphasis on secular education on the one hand and the neglect of religious education on the other. The strong Islamic culture of the country enabled the Saudi Arabian educational system to avoid the persistent problem of the modernization of the educational system at the expense of religion. Secularized schools in Saudi Arabia have not created a religious and cultural gap. In Egypt, for example, religious courses at the high school and university levels are weak and inadequate. In the high school senior year, religion is taught with the understanding that the student will not have to take a final examination. As a result, religious courses are severely undermined and neglected by students. At the university level, no religious courses are offered except to students of Al-Azhar University.

In Saudi Arabia, by contrast, religious courses are taught at the high school level with full seriousness and are accorded high status. At the university level, reasonable religious courses are taught along with other secular courses in all years, and are required of all students. Islam, being a way of life, is accessible to educated and uneducated people alike. The assumption is that religion finds its way to their souls and, once this is achieved, psychological stability is attained. Consequently, the pursuit of all activities is rendered much easier and can be approached with full concentration. Even after reaching the highest levels of education in various fields, a true Muslim invariably remains faithful to his religion.

The Saudi Arabian educational system does, however, rely on foreign sources for improving its quality. The need for outside help from experienced personnel to instruct at all levels of education until self-sufficiency is attained is essential. At the same time, Saudi students are being sent abroad to advanced countries to attain the highest levels of education. Table 5.22 shows the Saudi students pursuing their education abroad are doing so in countries known for the excellence of their educational systems. These students pursuing their education in various countries are providing the country

> with alternative educational models [which] may widen . . . [its range] of effective choice and increase the likelihood that indigenous educational institutions may develop along lines more closely adapted to national needs than is possible for any post-classical echo of over-valued metropolitan practice. Diversity may also foster a climate of tolerance, flexibility, and responsiveness to innovation.[48]

The number of Saudi students pursuing higher education abroad compares favorably with the situation of Iraq and Egypt. In 1959–1961

Egyptian students receiving education in foreign countries totalled 3,739, while the Iraqis reached a 1,862 goal, a combined total for both countries of 5,601.[49] The combined population of Iraq and Egypt at that time was almost thirty million.

Although we are comparing 1961 with 1975, so far as can be determined the number of Egyptian–Iraqi students studying abroad has not drastically increased since 1961. The number of Saudi students pursuing their education abroad as of mid-1975, reached 5,108 (Table 5.21). Given a population of 6.5 million the percentage is 0.85 per cent for Saudi Arabia. Egypt with a population of forty million has a percentage of 0.1 per cent, while Iraq with a total of twelve million has a 0.2 percentage. It is likely that this 1975 figure of Saudi students receiving education abroad will have doubled by the turn of the century.

Before analyzing Table 5.23 showing the number of Saudi citizens who have already obtained their doctoral degrees, the limitation described above on page 189 must be kept in mind.

There is still another way of judging Saudi Arabia's educational accomplishment (at the doctoral level) in a comparative context. Using the period of 1966–1974 as a basis for comparison, the number of United States citizens obtaining their doctoral degree during that time[50] totalled 210,772.[51] For the same period, the number of Saudi citizens who reported receiving their doctoral degrees was 187. Comparing these figures on a percentage basis, we find that out of the United States population of 214 million, approximately one thousand individuals out of each million earned a doctoral degree from 1964 through 1974. As for Saudi Arabia, with a population of about six to seven million, approximately twenty-five persons out of each million received a doctoral degree for the same period of time. Examination of the figures for 1974 alone reveals that during that year 26,585 United States citizens earned a doctoral degree while forty-eight Saudi Arabians received their doctoral degrees. Thus, 125 persons out of each million in the United States earned a doctoral degree, while seven Saudi citizens out of each million received a doctorate.

Such a comparison between Saudi Arabia, a developing nation with an educational system only thirty-five years old, and the United States, an advanced nation two hundred years old, is not without meaning. Considering all the differences between Saudi Arabia and the United States (*e.g.*, population, age, advancement), the results reflect favorably on the Saudi Arabian effort.

Perhaps the fact that most, if not all, of the educational systems of Middle Eastern countries were copied from previous colonial experiences hindered these countries' educational policies, since adjustment compatible with their indigenous needs required lengthy and tortuous attitudinal and institutional change. The situation in Saudi Arabia was different; the Saudi educational system had an initial advantage and its *de novo* start gave the Saudi policy makers an excellent opportunity to gear the system's needs to the country's requirements with advice from the most advanced educational systems of the world.

Note on Industrial Development

Part of the Government's strategy to reduce dependence on the production of crude oil as the primary source of national income has been encouragement of the development of a wide range of industries in the Kingdom. Statistics published by the Ministry of Industry and Electricity bear witness to the success of this strategy. The chart below shows the number of factories which have been set to work in the years 1977–1982.

5.25 **Development of Licensed Factories classified according to years from the end of year 1397 to the end of year 1402 AH**

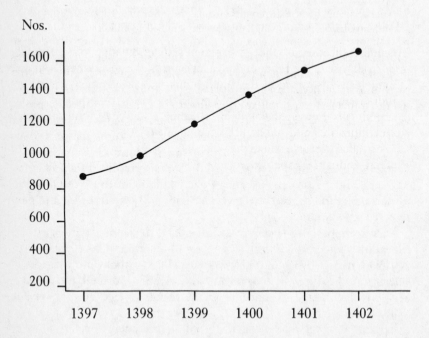

In the period 1977–1982, the major sectors for industrial development have been:

5.26

	No. of Factories	No. of Workers	Capital in SR 000
Chemical Industries	112	8,276	34,486,882
Construction Materials	73	4,690	4,438,775
Metal Industries	130	8,450	3,596,552
Foodstuffs, Drinks and Tobacco	97	4,971	2,479,936

Source: Industrial Statistical Bulletin for the year 1402 AH, Industrial Affairs Agency

The expansion of these and other sectors continues apace. In its Statistical Summary for 1984, the Saudi Arabian Monetary Agency comments:

> In the industrial sector, three petrochemical plants in Jubail were inaugurated; the Yanbu refinery was completed and Rabegh refinery was nearing completion. A total of 130 industrial enterprises in the private sector started production during the year. More industries are expected to come on stream soon. During the first six months of 1984, the government approved 135 new industrial projects involving a total investment SR 2.4 billion.

A good indication of the government's determination to expand the industrial base of the economy and a measure of the government's success are the loans disbursed by the Saudi Industrial Development Fund. The Saudi Industrial Development Fund (SIDF) is a government agency charged with the responsibility of providing a source of funds to private sector industries and public utility companies.

The following table shows the scale of the SIDF's involvement in Saudi Arabia's industrial expansion over the seven years 1977/78 to 1983/84:

5.27 Loans disbursed by SIDF (SR millions)

Fiscal Year	Industry	Electricity Gas and Water	Total
1977/78	1,268	3,883	5,151
1978/79	1,117	5,729	6,846
1979/80	1,307	5,184	6,491
1980/81	1,172	5,489	6,661
1981/82	797	4,551	5,348
1982/83	878	4,238	5,116
1983/84	1,056	4,169	5,225

In the first ten years of its existence (1974–1984), the SIDF approved 906 loan applications to finance 788 projects with cumulative loan commitments of SR 11.2 billion. By 1984, total disbursements had reached a cumulative total of SR 8.6 billion (about 77% of total loan commitment).

The SIDF's loans cover a wide range of industrial sectors, including construction materials; industrial products and equipment; transport and automotive products; and consumer products.

In the electricity sector, the SIDF has played an even more crucial role. In the years 1974 to 1984, the SIDF has disbursed loans of SR 36.3 billion to this sector, facilitating the expansion of power generation facilities throughout the Kingdom. The capacity of the electric companies rose from 1,080 megawatts in 1975 to 9,000 megawatts in 1982.

Behind all these figures lies the sustained strategy of reducing Saudi Arabia's dependence on oil. It is a daunting task. Saudi Arabia possesses some 25% of the non-Communist world's oil reserves. Inevitably, its economy must remain oil-based in the foreseeable future. Nevertheless, by judicious use of the oil revenues, the government of Saudi Arabia is expanding the industrial and other economic sectors and reducing the degree of dependence. The expansion of non-oil activities brings with it the acute need to make best use of man-power at all levels. Saudi Arabia has a small population relative to the size of the economy. Much of the economic expansion of the last ten years has necessitated the use of ex-patriate labour. Saudi Arabia's government's determination to reduce reliance on foreign labour, especially in the areas of technology and science, is clearly evinced in the government's investment in and strategy for education.

By 1985, total nominal capacity generated by turbine had risen to 14,578 Mw (actual capacity 11,853 Mw). A further 1,708 Mw in the Eastern Province and 950 Mw in the Western Province was contributed by desalination plants (Source: Electricity Corporation, Riyah 1408 AH/ 1985 AD).

SABIC

The Saudi Arabian Basic Industries Corporation (SABIC) is an example, *par excellence*, of the practical results of the Kingdom's blend of long-range planning, long-term major investment and the judicious use of public and private sources of finance.

SABIC was established by Royal Decree in 1976 – its task to set up and operate hydrocarbon and mineral-based industries in the Kingdom of Saudi Arabia. The Public Investment Fund provides long-term loans to SABIC on highly concessional terms. The balance of SABIC's capital requirements come from SABIC's joint venture partners. In addition, SABIC can make use of normal commercial loans. With these

sources of finance, SABIC is able to undertake industrial projects considerably in excess of its own authorized capital of SR 10 billion.

The main features of the first phase of the industrial program
launched by SABIC are:

5 ethylene-based petrochemical complexes with a total annual capacity of 1.6
million tons of ethylene

2 chemical-grade methanol plants with a total annual capacity of 1.25 million
tons

1 urea plant with an annual capacity of half a million tons

1 iron and steel plant at Jubail with an annual capacity of 800,000 tons

expansion of the Jiddah Steel Rolling Mill to produce 140,000 tons per annum

Project implementation began in 1979. In that year, SABIC concluded
four joint venture agreements with foreign companies. In the following
year, the joint venture Saudi Yanbu Petrochemical Company was set up
with the objective of producing 450,000 tons of ethylene per annum. At the
same time another joint venture, the Jubail Petrochemical Company was
established to produce 260,000 tons of low density polyethylene. Later in
1980, the Saudi Petrochemical Company was set up with the objective of
producing 656,000 tons of ethylene in Jubail and new joint venture
operations followed in 1981.

In 1981 the Jiddah Steel Rolling Mill began production, to be followed
by the Jubail Iron and Steel Plant in 1982.

SABIC's major role in the development of petrochemical and mineral-
based industries in Saudi Arabia is clear. Less obvious but perhaps more
important is the function SABIC fulfils in providing a mechanism for the
aquisition by Saudi citizens of the managerial, professional and technological skills required to control and expand a modern industrialized
economy.

The challenges which SABIC faces (not all of them technical) are far
from over.

By 1985, the year in which exports of Saudi Arabian petrochemicals to
Europe have been scheduled to begin, the governments of Europe,
persuaded by the lobbying of the European petrochemical companies,
have set extremely small duty-free quotas for Saudi Arabian petrochemical imports. The effect is that any substantial quantities of Saudi Arabian
petrochemicals exported to Europe will be handicapped by duties of up to
20%.

For Saudi Arabia, this act of protectionism is doubly disappointing.
First, the development of a petrochemical industry is of central importance to the Kingdom's plans to reduce economic dependence on the export
of crude oil. The setting up of what are, in effect, tariffs against Saudi

petrochemicals in the large European market is unhelpful. Secondly, Saudi Arabia believes in a free market and free trade. It has shown this belief in allowing almost all imports into the Kingdom duty-free. It is sad that those who have enjoyed the benefits of free trade in Saudi Arabia for so long adopt a protectionist stance as soon as they are faced by competition from the products of Saudi industry, which represent a mere 4–5% of petrochemical production world-wide.

There must also be disappointment that Europe has not taken a longer term view in this matter. In an issue of *The Economist* in January, 1985, an article on this subject included the following comment:

> European protectionism has so far left Saudi faith in the free market undented. Nearly all imports enter Saudi Arabia duty-free – despite the temptation to use tariffs to protect fledgling local industries. If the Europeans succeed in blocking Saudi petrochemicals from their markets, the Saudis have high hopes of selling the stuff to others.

It will not, in the long run, help European economies to compete in world markets if they rely for their petrochemicals on the product of an expensive, tariff-protected petrochemical industry.

SABIC's Industrial Policy[1]

SABIC's policy and strategies are directly derived from its planned objectives. Having been established as one of the principal vehicles for diversifying the Saudi economy, SABIC's strategies were drawn along three basic lines of action.

The first is to make use of the comparative advantages of local industrial production by utilizing and adding value to available natural resources . . . Hence, the setting up of basic industries that are based upon hydrocarbon and mineral resources.

The second is to construct related downstream and supporting industries, thus contributing to the expansion of the Kingdom's industrial base, and at the same time providing investment opportunities for private capital either directly in SABIC's industries or in related industries and services.

The third line of action is to participate in training and building Saudi technical and managerial capabilities in industrial planning, implementation, operation, maintenance and development.

Now, with SABIC's projects moving from the construction and implementation phase to that of actual production, there have emerged the elements of efficient, safe and profitable operation of industries – together with the most important requirement for the continued development of SABIC as a successful commercial enterprise, and as a corporate vehicle for marketing its products.

[1] This note on SABIC's Industrial Policy was supplied by the management of SABIC.

5.28 SABIC Project Descriptions

Project Name	Location	Feedstock	Product	Capacity (in MTPA)
Saudi Iron & Steel Co. (HADEED)	Al-Jubail	Iron Ores Limestone Natural Gas Scrap Iron	Rods and Bars	800,000
Jiddah Steel Rolling Mill Co. (SULB)	Jiddah	Steel Billets	Rods and Bars	140,000
Saudi Methanol Co. (ARRAZI)	Al-Jubail	Methane	Chemical Grade Methanol	600,000
Al-Jubail Fertilizer Co. (SAMAD)	Al-Jubail	Methane	Urea	500,000
Saudi Yanbu Petrochemical Co. (YANPET)	Yanbu	Ethane	Ethylene Ethylene Glycol LLDPE HDPE	455,000 200,000 205,000 90,000
Al-Jubail Petrochemical Co. (KEMYA)	Al-Jubail	Ethylene	LLDPE	260,000
Saudi Petrochemical Co. (SADAF)	Al-Jubail	Ethane Salt Benzene	Ethylene Ethylene Dichloride Styrene Ethanol Caustic Soda	656,000 454,000 295,000 281,000 377,000
National Methanol Co. (IBN SINA)	Al-Jubail	Methane	Chemical Grade Methanol	650,000
Arabian Petrochemical Co. (PETROKEMYA)	Al-Jubail	Ethane	Ethylene	500,000
Eastern Petrochemical Co. (SHARQ)	Al-Jubail	Ethylene	LLDPE Ethylene Glycol	130,000 300,000
National Industrial Gases Co. (GAS)	Al-Jubail	Air	Nitrogen Oxygen	146,000 438,000
National Plastic Co. (IBN HAY YAN)	Al-Jubail	Ethylene Ethylene Dichloride	Vinyl Chloride Monomer Polyvinyl Chloride	300,000 200,000

In this direction, SABIC is careful to enter the petrochemical markets as a world wide producer worthy of its name:

Seeking the best and most appropriate qualities in its products;

Pursuing serious, fair and honest competition in its business dealings; and

Endeavouring in a gentlemanly way, and within its direct interests, to work for the benefit of both the consumer and world industry as a whole.

Saudi Arabian Aid to the Developing World

Throughout its own development, Saudi Arabia has been mindful of its responsibilities in the community of nations, especially in the Arab world and amongst the less developed countries. Blessed with its vast reserves of oil and minerals, Saudi Arabia has willingly accepted the Muslim obligation to share its wealth with those less favored. Although a relatively young country, Saudi Arabia has quickly understood the reality of inter-dependence, one nation with another. The Middle East is particularly involved with the industrialized nations of the West, supplying much of these countries' energy requirements and importing much of the West's technology. But there is also an interdependence, both moral and economic, between rich nations and poor.

Financial assistance from the Kingdom of Saudi Arabia has come to form a significant share of total development aid reaching Third World countries,

said Mohammad Aba Alkhail, Minister of Finance and National Economy.

In the distribution of overseas aid the Saudi Fund for Development (SFD) plays a key role. The SFD was established by Royal Decree in 1974 in order to finance, with soft loans, development projects in Third World countries. The Fund's capital base has been systematically increased over the years in response to the growing needs of the developing countries. Its initial capitalization was SR 10 billion. It was raised to SR 15 billion in 1980 and to SR 25 billion in 1981.

In the Fiscal Year 1982/83, the SFD's commitments exceeded SR 2 billion. Twenty-three projects were approved in 14 countries in Africa and Asia. The countries of Africa were Botswana, Comoros Islands, Gabon, Mali, Mauritania, Morocco, Senegal, Tunisia, Zambia; the countries of Asia were Indonesia, Malaysia, Pakistan, Turkey, the Arab Republic of Yemen. In addition the SFD joined the Government of Malta in financing a desalination plant.

5.29 Regional Allocations: 1402/03 AH (1982/83)

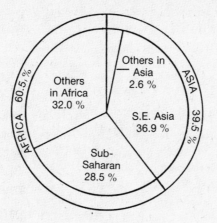

5.30 Loan Agreements Signed: Africa, Asia and Other Regions: 1402/03 AH (1982/83)

Region	Amount SR million	No. of Projects
Africa	1,029.73	13
Asia	456.60	5
Others	41.00	1
Total	1,527.33	19

5.31 Regional Allocations: Africa & Asia: 1402/03 AH (1982/83)

Region	Amount Committed		No. of Projects		No. of Countries in Each Region	Average Size of Loan (SR million)
	Total SR Million	As % of Total	Total	As % of Total		
Africa	1,263.40	60.5	13	56.5	8	97.2
Asia	825.90	39.5	10	43.5	6	82.6
Total	2,089.30	100.0	23	100.0	14	90.8

5.32 Allocations to Countries in Africa: 1402/03 AH (1982/83)

Country	Amount Committed SR million	No. of Projects
Algeria	380.00	3
Cameroun	60.00	1
Comoros	10.00	1
Guinea-Bissau	29.00	1
Ivory Coast	120.40	1
Morocco	278.00	4
Sierra Leone	86.00	1
Sudan	300.00	1
Total	1,263.40	13

5.33 Allocations to Countries in Asia: 1402/03 AH (1982/83)

Country	Amount Committed SR million	No. of Projects
Bangladesh	117.00	2
China (Taiwan)	103.50	1
India	275.20	2
Malaysia	189.20	2
Nepal	86.00	1
Oman	55.00	2
Total	825.90	10

Source: SFD Annual Report 1402/03 AH (1982/83)

The list of countries receiving development loans in one year alone indicates the breadth of Saudi Arabia's view of its responsibilities. But the benefits of such aid goes even further than the list of countries suggests. Unlike the often conditional loans of industrialized nations, Saudi Arabia does not expect its loans to be recycled back to its own economy. In the main, Saudi Arabia has neither the technology nor the capital goods to fulfil the needs of the developing countries. The recipients of SFD loans are therefore free to spend the money on technology and equipment from any country at market prices. Thus the industrialized nations, as well as the Third World, benefits from SFD aid.

---

[1] Kingdom of Saudi Arabia, Industrial Studies and Development Center, *Guide to Industrial Investment in Saudi Arabia*, 4th ed. (Jiddah: Dar al Asfahan & Co. [Al Asfahan Publishing Co.], 1974 [1394 AH]), p. 29.

[2] Data on the activities of the United Nations Development Program (UNDP) at Riyadh, Saudi Arabia, were obtained by the author through three interviews in May, 1975: the first, with Dr. Fredrick Thomas, the Deputy Regional Representative of the UNDP for Saudi Arabia and the Gulf area (Qatar, Oman, Bahrain, and United Arab Emirates); the second and third interviews with Mr. Mostafa Bedawi, Programs Assistant at the UNDP. Tables and arrangement of materials were designed by the Author.

[3] Most of the materials of this part of Chapter V were obtained by the Author in an interview with Dr. Ali Mahjoub, Chief Adviser and Supervisor of the Training Center, in Ad-Dir'iyah, Saudi Arabia in June, 1975.

[4] Kingdom of Saudi Arabia, Ministry of Labor and Social Affairs and UNDP, *Center for Training and Applied Research in Community Development* (Riyadh: 1975), p. 4.

[5] Resolution No. 384 of the Saudi Council of Ministers, 1971 (26–27/5/1391 AH).

[6] Kingdom of Saudi Arabia, *Center for Training and Applied Research in Community Development*, pp. 7–8.

[7] *Ibid.*

[8] *Ibid*, p. 9.

[9] Interview with Dr. Ali Mahjoub, Chief Adviser and Superviser of Training Center, Ad-Dir'iyah, Saudi Arabia, in June, 1975.

[10] June, 1975.

[11] Kingdom of Saudi Arabia, *Center for Training and Applied Research in Community Development*, p. 14.

[12] Since 1975, elevated to the Ministry of Planning.

[13] Kingdom of Saudi Arabia, Central Planning Organization, *Report of the Central Planning Organization 1394 AH/1974* (Jiddah: Banawi Printers, 1974), p. 17.

[14] SR stands for Saudi Riyal, the Kingdom's currency. The 1975 rate of exchange was 1 US dollar = 3.5 (1978: approx 3.45).

[15] *Report of the Central Planning Organization*, p. 74.

[16] *Ibid.*

[17] *Ibid*, p. 67.

[18] Reflecting the Kingdom's continued efforts for the well-being of its citizens is the fact that when medical treatment needed for a certain type of illness is not available in the Kingdom, patients may be sent abroad at the government's expense, where the critically needed medical knowledge is available.

[19] *Report of the Central Planning Organization*, p. 18.

[20] One mile equals 1.6093 kilometers.

[21] *Report of the Central Planning Organization*, p. 18.

[22] *Ibid.*, p. 19.

[23] *The Wall Street Journal*, October 6, 1975, p. 10.

[24] *Ibid.*

[25] The data of this part of the chapter dealing with the Second Five Year Plan was up-dated from the Document issued by the Ministry of Planning.

[26] Since the Second Five Year Plan's objectives are mentioned in Chapter III above, p. 80 ff, they will not be repeated here.

[27] *Al-Riyadh*, May 23, 1975, p. 3. (F.F. translation.)

[28] *The Wall Street Journal*, October 6, 1975, p.10.

[29] *Al-Riyadh*, May 23, 1975, p.3 (F.F. translation.)

[30] *Ibid.*, p. 1.

[31] *Ibid.*, p. 3.

[32] *Ibid.*, p. 3.

[33] Kingdom of Saudi Arabia, Central Planning Organization, *Development Plan 1390 AH (1970)* (Dammam: Al-Mutawa Press Co., 1970), p. 30.

[34] *The Wall Street Journal*, October 6, 1975, p. 10.

[35] *Development Plan, 1390 AH (1970)*, p. 43.

[36] *The Wall Street Journal*, October 6, 1975, p. 10.

[37] *Ibid.*

[38] *Development Plan, 1390 AH (1970)*, p. 43.

[39] *The Wall Street Journal*, October 6, 1975, p. 10.

[40] In 1973, United States total foreign aid represented 0.6 per cent of its annual budget for the same year. The budget outlay for 1973 was $246.5 billion. (*Budget of the United States, Fiscal Year 1973*, p. 15). United States international development assistance for 1973 totaled $1.5 billion (US Government Printing Office, *The Budget of the United States Government, Fiscal Year 1973*, p. 15).

[40A] The Deputy Minister of Planning declined to provide the author with basic guidelines of the Third Five Year Plan, stating that the Third Plan was still under study (March 1979).

[41] Data on the University of Riyadh were partly obtained by the Author through an interview with Dr. Salah Hou'tar, Director of the Department of Studies and Information, University of Riyadh, in June, 1975.

[42] Kingdom of Saudi Arabia, Ministry of Education, Statistics, Research and Educational Documents Unit, Statistical Unit, *Educational Statistics Yearbook 1971–1972*, 6th issue (Riyadh: National Offset Printing Press, 1971–1972), p. 301.

[43] Royal Decree No. 52, dated 1974 (Sh'aban 23, 1394 AH).

[44] Materials on Imam Muhammad Ibn Sa'ud Islamic University were obtained and translated by the Author from the University's Department of Public Relations at Riyadh, in May, 1975.

[45] Information on King Faisal University was obtained through an interview with Dr. Abdul Rahman Aal-Al Sheikh, Vice-President of the University (currently Minister of Agriculture), at Riyadh, in June, 1975.

[46] Ministry of Education, Dept. of Statistics and Research, February, 1978.

[47] Arnold C. Anderson, "Economic Development and Post-Primary Education," in Don C. Piper and Taylor Cole, eds., *Post-Primary Education and Political and Economic Development* (Durham, N.C.: Duke University Press, 1964), p. 365.

[48] James S. Coleman, "Introduction to Part III," in James S. Coleman, ed., *Education and Political Development* (Princeton, N.J.: Princeton University Press, 1965), p. 365.

[49] *Ibid*, p. 363.

[50] This figure does not include doctorates received by women. The number of Saudi females who received their doctoral degrees from 1966 through 1974 was only five, compared to a total of 6,415 United States female graduates. Since education to the doctoral level is officially accepted but not yet widely spread in Saudi Arabia, analysis of only doctorates awarded to men makes this a truer comparison.

[51] Commission on Human Resources, National Research Council, *Summary Report 1974 Doctorate Recipients from United States Universities* (Washington, DC: National Academy of Sciences, 1975), p. 4.

CHAPTER VI
General Summary

As CAN be seen from the literature analyzed in the Appendix, we have carefully studied seventy-four books dealing with the major theme of political development along with nine major journals and three leading series of scholarly works; *i.e.*, the SAGE, the SSRC-CCP (Princeton) and the ASPA-CAG (Duke) series. We find that Saudi Arabia, at any rate up to the mid 1970s, was treated hardly at all either comprehensively or in a peripheral manner.

Furthermore, when Saudi Arabia has been treated, such treatment has frequently manifested the bias and ignorance of scholars who neither can read Arabic nor have ever been to the country. It is the belief of the Author that when the Kingdom of Saudi Arabia has been mentioned it has usually been treated with considerable distortion, and with some bias as well as obvious ignorance. The exception, as is pointed out in the Appendix, was *The Economist*, a British weekly journal which has had a long interest in the affairs of the Middle East, in part because of business connections or transactions and in part because of the British colonial experience in Egypt, Jordan, Iraq and the Trucial States of the Gulf (now the United Arab Emirates). It should be reiterated that *The Economist* is a British journal; no comparable American journal devoted this much attention to Saudi Arabia. The major works on political development in the United States paid virtually no attention to the Kingdom. Some reasons for such a shortcoming can perhaps be adduced. It can be said that the exclusive use of Arabic poses a language difficulty. On the other hand, other countries where a language difficulty prevails, mainly Japan and Iran, have been written about more than Saudi Arabia. While language is partially an answer, it is not the complete answer. Also, it can be said that Saudi Arabia is a somewhat more difficult country to study than other countries since only recently (since 1958) has it begun modernization. Documents are rather difficult to get; universities are not as old as in other nations; and generally western research and western scholarly tradition, as contrasted with the Arabic and Islamic traditions which are highly developed, start almost *de novo*.[1] While this does not offer a complete explanation, it does offer a partial reason for this state of affairs. Having said this, however, it cannot be denied that Saudi Arabia has only been organized as a Kingdom since 1932 and that only recently has it assumed a prominent role in world affairs. Its very existence as a remarkable system of government based on the Holy *Quran* rather than on a secular constitution should have excited the curiosity of a large number of western scholars even if those scholars had not been to that part of the world. Even if they did not know Arabic, the least that could have been done was to make mention of Saudi Arabia and indicate its existence as a very significant and unique kind of political system worth studying. Indeed, in other countries where a language barrier exists, scholars have organized themselves with interpreters and translators. Besides using this kind of assistance, they have had access to documents and materials and made important contributions to the analysis of these countries. Yet this has not been done for Saudi Arabia. We wonder, therefore, what are the real reasons for the Kingdom of Saudi Arabia not having been treated adequately (indeed, even marginally) in the literature of development.

The most critical characteristic revealed by the study of the culture and history of Saudi Arabia is the newness of its political organization as a national state. It must be emphasized that it was only three generations ago during the reign of King Abdul Aziz Al Sa'ud that the Kingdom was organized in what can be regarded as a modern form. Even during the reign of Ibn Saud, the political system was handicapped by financial poverty. Petroleum deposits, after all, were not discovered until 1936 and the wealth derived from petroleum production did not surface until the immediate years following the Second World War, specifically from 1948 through the 1950s. A sense of international political power and influence in the world community were not manifest until the establishment of OPEC in 1960. Even then, this sense of power in the global arena was really dormant until OAPEC was forced to launch its embargo in the aftermath of the Ramadan War of 1973.

The other critical observation which emerges from Chapter Five is the totally Islamic nature of Saudi Arabia. In this respect it is in marked contrast to other important Muslim countries such as Egypt and Turkey. It is also in contrast to other countries with substantial Muslim communities such as India and Lebanon. For some of these countries, notably Egypt and Iran, significant and deeply rooted civilizations existed before Islam, *e.g.* the Pharaonic culture of Egypt (2000 BC) and the culture of the Achaemenid Empire under Cyrus the Great (559–529 BC) and Darius I (522–485 BC) of Iran. But the social organization of the whole Arabian Peninsula was extremely simple, nomadic and *bedouin* prior to the advent of Islam. It is largely for this reason that we find that Saudi Arabian culture, civilization and politics are exactly coterminous with Islam itself. Only when this is understood can the essence of the Saudi polity be appreciated.

Just as the summary of Chapter One reveals that the quintessence of the Saudi polity is Islam, so Chapter Two demonstrates that the critical fact in the Saudi economy is petroleum. Without Islam, Saudi Arabia would not exist as a unique polity; without petroleum Saudi Arabia would either not exist as an effective regional and global force or would be one of the poor nations of the world. As it is, because of petroleum it is one of the world's wealthiest nations. The manner in which this wealth is handled is in itself a mark of the Saudi character and the nature of the modernization process in that country. If the wealth were squandered in the manner of great empires of old, this would show a betrayal of the Islamic and *Quranic* character to which the Saudi nation is committed. We find, on the contrary, that a general ethos of relative austerity pervades the system. There is a highly developed sense of social responsibility in the form of welfare programs. It should especially be noted that there have been extremely cordial relations between the whole Aramco enterprise and the Saudi people and government. Today a casual visitor to Saudi Arabia would notice the atmosphere of mutual respect and cordiality which characterizes the relations between Americans and Saudi officials. This is in marked contrast to comparable relations existing between Americans and indigenous governments of other nations, *e.g.* in Latin America and Asian countries.

The gradual manner in which the Saudi government seeks to control more of its petroleum assets is worthy of notice. Forced expropriation as occurred in Iran and in some Latin American countries has not occurred in Saudi Arabia. Chapter Two has shown in one of its tables that the increasing control of petroleum production by the Saudi government is being accomplished at a planned rate and negotiated very carefully over a protracted period of time. There has been no major outcry against this by either Aramco or the United States government. This suggests a degree of maturity and responsibility on the part of the Saudi government, building on the cordial relations which have existed between the two countries since 1936.

The social organization of Saudi Arabia is relatively simple as contrasted to such complex societies as those of, for example, India, Lebanon or China. Its relative simplicity rests on the fact that it is sparsely populated and the population is concentrated in a few areas. No linguistic divisions exist at all, either in terms of script, language or dialect. The various tribal divisions are not based on ethnicity but rather on an earlier pattern of social organization, and hence the problem of poly-communality noted by Ralph Braibanti and others is virtually non-existent. Indeed, it can be said that probably Saudi Arabia along with Japan, South Korea, Norway, Sweden and Denmark, is one of the most culturally homogeneous nations in the world. This is not to deny the existence of minor regional differences, but these are so minor as to be scarcely worthy of note.

Policy-making in the Kingdom does not follow the practice of such constitutional monarchies as that in the United Kingdom nor does it follow the completely autocratic patterns of earlier pre-constitutional monarchies of various western countries. Rather it is a system which is truly unique. There is a strong and widespread consensual base in the making of policy. This consensual base consists of three parts. The first of these is the Royal Family itself, all of whom are the descendants of King Abdul Aziz, the founder of modern Saudi Arabia. The second part of this consensual base is the *Ulama*, religious leaders of the Wahhabi movement closely linked to the Royal Family by ties of blood. The third part are the tribal and *bedouin* chieftains who are considered on important matters related to their communities and whose influence is not without significance. The relatively smooth operation of this consensual base is evidenced by the fact that the transition of power on the death of King Faisal to King Khalid in March 1975 was achieved in a matter of minutes, much to the surprise of many Western observers whose comprehension of the Saudi system is minimal.

In most political systems, the existence of minority communities is of some significance. As has already been pointed out, no minority community exists within the social organization of Saudi Arabia. On the other hand, there is a rough equivalent in the existence of a large foreign community in the country which, even though part of it is Muslim, is not really an integral part of the social fabric of the nation. This foreign community, generally educated and technically competent, is of considerable significance in bringing about needed development in the country. The way this community is handled and the possible impact of this community on the social practices of the Kingdom is worthy of careful analysis in the future.

The written scholarship on Islamic law in both Arabic and English is enormously voluminous. All Muslim nations of the world have struggled with the problem of incorporating and applying the *Quranic* laws into their own positive laws. In Chapter Three we have merely touched on some of the problems involved in Saudi Arabia. In one respect, the problems in the Kingdom are minimal as compared to other Muslim countries, simply because they (*e.g.* Malaysia, Egypt, Kuwait and Turkey) have avowedly secular constitutions. Further, other Muslim countries are divided into various sects such as in Iran, Lebanon and Pakistan. In Saudi Arabia, on the other hand, since there is no attempt at a secular constitution and since virtually the entire populace belongs to Islam, these problems are minimal. Further, the fact that Saudi Arabia is the birthplace of Islam and contains the most sacred cities in the religion and is the object of pilgrimage of one and a quarter million Muslims each year makes it an Islamic polity in which there is virtually no debate as to whether to be Islamic or not.

The Council of Ministers is one of the principal policy-making bodies in the Saudi political system. Of the twenty-three ministers appointed by King Khalid in October 1975, eleven could be described (to use the term often found in development literature) as "modernizing technocrats". Of these eleven, eight had doctoral degrees earned abroad. Significantly, of these eight, five ministers were between the ages of thirty-four and thirty-seven and had had their doctoral degrees not more than five years. Three of the eleven ministers mentioned above had Master's degrees. Five ministers (not included in the above category of eleven) were Royal Princes who had had extensive administrative and political experience and training or experience abroad. Thus, these five could also be said to be "modernizing technocrats". The remaining seven ministers were distinguished statesmen, representative either of the highly important *Ulama*, or other strata of society. The Council of Ministers functions in a fairly sophisticated and regular fashion, as clearly indicated by its constitution which is a sophisticated document governing its procedure and functions.

The Institute of Public Administration (IPA), established in 1961, is comparable to such institutes organized in other developing countries. It has been a main source of change in the administrative system. While it has received external advice from the Ford Foundation and other sources, it is somewhat more of a Saudi Institute than similar institutions in other countries.

Chapter Four reveals, at least, the beginning of an institutional base for Saudi government. This institutional base appears to be adequate to sustain the ever-increasing responsibilities of government. In short, we are not dealing with a primitive system nor essentially with a nomadic system (which is a common though erroneous impression in the West). Rather, we are dealing with a system which has emerged gradually over a period of roughly five decades without any violent revolutionary change. We are dealing with a system which is entirely proud of its own heritage, both religious and social, and which appears to have no intention of drastically modifying that heritage.

Since much of contemporary analysis of development deals with the problem of the indigenization of its values, the Saudi Arabian case is an outstanding example of how these values can be truly indigenized.

The exogenous institutional sources of innovation in Saudi Arabia are somewhat different than they are in other developing countries. Clearly, foreign assistance by the United States and other Western countries in the form of financial support does not exist. Some advisory services are important, though they are probably not of the same order of magnitude as for other countries. The earliest source of innovation was Aramco which was first established in 1936 in Dhahran. As Aramco trained technicians they gradually penetrated into other geographical areas of the Kingdom as well. The University of Petroleum and Mineral Resources in Dhahran, formerly affiliated to the Ministry of Petroleum and Mineral Resources, has also been a principal source for generating technical and scientific skills. The University is financed entirely by the Saudi government, but with advisory services of outstanding technical universities in the United States. It rapidly became one of the outstanding universities in its field not only in the Middle East but also in the world. As was suggested in an earlier part, the diffusion of innovation through petroleum technology has been facilitated by the cordial reciprocal relations existing between the United States and the Saudis generally.

The influence of the United Nations Development Program (UNDP) is another important source of innovation, but does not loom as large proportionately as it does in some other countries. UNDP activities in Saudi Arabia are illustrated by the various tables at the beginning of Chapter Five.

Another and most significant source of innovation has been the Central Planning Organization, established in 1964 with advisory services since 1967 by the Stanford Research Institute, and now known as the Ministry of Planning. The four Five Year Plans prepared by the Ministry of Planning compare favorably with five year plans of other developing countries. Indeed, it can be said that they are somewhat better than those of other countries. This appears so because they are more attuned to the actual needs of Saudi Arabia, and they are much less ideologically oriented to fads and obsessions. Finally, the problem of abject poverty which faces most of the developing countries is non-existent.

In the final analysis, change and innovation are generated only by persons. In this respect, the results of the Saudi educational policy are singularly impressive. The proportion of students now in the process of receiving advanced degrees is quite remarkable. The distribution of these students in terms of their specialties and in terms of studying in various universities and countries is equally impressive.

The far-sighted policy of the Saudi government for its students abroad with generous allowances for living and tuition with annual trips back to Saudi Arabia has resulted in a situation in which there is no brain drain at all. According to statistics of the Ministry of Education, every Saudi who was trained abroad has returned to the Kingdom and has immediately found an appropriate position consonant with his field of specialty in the country's service. In this respect, it is not without significance that five ministers appointed to the Council of Ministers in 1978 were in their middle thirties and obtained their doctorates abroad as recently as five years before their appointment as ministers. This situation cannot be found in other developing countries and this fact alone is testimony of the sound educational policy of the Kingdom.

It is not easy to review, in its totality, the development of the Kingdom of Saudi Arabia over the last several decades. Inevitably, there are gaps in such a survey and, as the development of this unique country continues, no work of this type can hope to be, even as it goes to press, entirely up to date.

It is, nevertheless, the author's hope that the reader will receive a clear impression not merely of the scale of the progress that has been achieved but, more important, the principles which have guided all developments.

There have always been those who have prophesied ill-fortune for the Kingdom of Saudi Arabia. In the early days, when the oil wealth of the Kingdom was first discovered and its exploitation begun, many forecast that the desert Kingdom would find the transition from poverty to affluence socially and morally destructive. As the vast oil revenues began to flow, so materialism would assert itself, eroding the religious foundation of the country's structure. The wealth would be squandered by the few, either through profligate extravagance or through the inability of those who governed to control the vast budgets that oil generated. How could a simple desert people, rooted in a puritanical form of Islam, deal successfully with the challenges of the modern world which the West's demand for oil would pose? Even if those who governed sought to distribute the benefits of the oil wealth throughout the Kingdom, how could they succeed without the infrastructure which other countries had taken centuries to develop. How would an under-populated, under-educated nation responds to the demands of high technology? Would they not simply be the victims of the technocrats they imported to help them?

This book addresses itself to these questions and, in the answers it supplies, the reader will find the true measure of the achievement of the Kingdom of Saudi Arabia over the last thirty years. With a seriousness of purpose, with intelligence and determination, and with the abiding vision of justice and the dignity of every individual which is inherent in Islam, the Kingdom of Saudi Arabia has accomplished in decades the progress of centuries.

Nevertheless, the cynics remain undeterred. Undaunted by the Kingdom's success in facing the social strains of sudden affluence, the forecasters of doom now predict that the inevitable, eventual reduction in the Kingdom's oil revenues will be accompanied by a decline of the Kingdom itself. Having accustomed themselves to vast national wealth (so the argument runs), Saudi Arabia will be unable to adjust to more modest national life-style.

Again, such critics are mistaken. The oil revenues have financed and will continue to finance the Kingdom's development programs. But these development programs have been devised with the clear economic objective of reducing the Kingdom's dependence on oil. The Kingdom's industrial and agricultural goals, once met, will give Saudi Arabia as much self-sufficiency as can be attained in today's complex interdependent world.

Furthermore, the true strength of the Kingdom of Saudi Arabia is Islam; its true wealth is its people. Neither of these will diminish with the oil revenues. This is not mere rhetoric. Long before oil, the foundation of the culture of the Arabian peninsula was laid in Islam. Again before the oil, King Abdul Aziz Ibn Saud forged the Saudi nation. Both will, without any doubt, survive the exhaustion of the oil fields. The uses to which the oil revenues have been put bears witness to the enduring values of Saudi Arabian society. Unshaken in its faith in Islam, the Kingdom has used its revenues from oil to provide all Saudi Arabian citizens with the fullest opportunities for self-development and thence for making a positive contribution to the development of their own society.

The fourth Development Plan reflects the requirement for fiscal restraint and discretion in the immediate future. Such reductions in Government revenues would have totally disrupted most other economies. But the Kingdom of Saudi Arabia, despite budgetary constraints, looks forward to sustained and steady progress towards the attainment of its goals.

There will always be those who feel that they elevate themselves by denigrating others but the recent history of the Kingdom of Saudi Arabia makes the position of those who question the Kingdom's ability to respond to change less and less tenable.

The majority, who assess Saudi Arabia's policies and performance impartially, will conclude that the greatest achievement of Saudi Arabia is not the building of the Kingdom's infrastructure, nor the development of industrial and agricultural sectors of the economy, nor even its ability to adjust to extreme fluctuations in national revenues; rather it must be the steadfast purpose of the Government and people which, despite the inevitable social strains involved in the changes which Saudi Arabia has undergone, is creating a modern society with a developed economy which remains entirely consistent with the teachings of Islam.

---

[1] For further analysis of the nature of Islamic scholarship, see Marshall Hodgson, *The Venture of Islam* 1 (Chicago: The University of Chicago Press, 1974): 3–11. See also Ralph Braibanti, "Reflections on Bureaucratic Reform in India," in Ralph Braibanti and Joseph Spengler, eds., *Administration and Economic Development in India* (Durham, N.C.: Duke University Press, 1963), pp. 19–26; and Ralph Braibanti, "Environment of Research," in Ralph Braibanti, *Research on the Bureaucracy of Pakistan* (Durham, N.C.: Duke University Press, 1966), pp. 15–19. These two latter works deal with Islamic scholarship in India rather than the Arabic Middle East but some of the observations are, *mutatis mutandis*, pertinent.

Treatment of the Political Development of Saudi Arabia in Literature Available in the U.S.A.

The Arabs are heirs to a millennial culture which was born and nurtured in their rugged environment, and which offers its own values and self-sustained way of life. Chaucer reminds us of the great debt that Western Civilization owes to the Arabs for their contributions to mathematics and astronomy, medicine and literature, which stimulated Europe in its own emergent epoch.[1]

Introduction

This Appendix surveys published material on the Kingdom of Saudi Arabia available in English in the United States, up to the mid-1970s. It divides into five parts. The first, treating nine major journals, reveals the degree to which these leading journals, each within its own sphere of specialty, reported on Saudi Arabia. The second part looks at seventy-four books, the major theme of which is political and administrative developmental theory and practice. The third part of this survey examines the coverage of Saudi Arabia in the SAGE Series material. The fourth part deals with the Social Science Research Council–Committee on Comparative Politics (SSRC-CCP) (Princeton) Series on political development, and the fifth part examines the American Society for Public Administration – Comparative Administration Group (ASPA CAG) (Duke) Series; in both the objective is the same, to determine the extent of the treatment of Saudi Arabia.

Synopsis of Journal Content

The first part of this survey covers the following journals listed chronologically by the dates when they first appeared.

A: THE ECONOMIST

Published weekly by the Economist Newspaper, Limited, London. Currently active. The first issue appeared in September 1843, but our survey begins in 1950. *The Economist* devotes much attention to Saudi Arabia, and a brief analysis will be made here. How much attention is paid to Saudi Arabia in the remaining eight journals is shown by Table A.1. Table A.2 narrows the focus on subject matter concerning Saudi Arabia in each individual journal.

The articles indicated in the following tables are totally devoted to Saudi Arabia. The many other mentions of Saudi Arabia in the form of notes and minor reporting are not included.

We will begin with *The Economist*. From 1950 through the June issue of 1974 (volumes 158–251), it makes mention of Saudi Arabia in only 564 pages out of a total number of 117,347 pages (0.48 per cent). Of these 564 pages only 204 (0.1738 per cent) gave major emphasis to Saudi Arabia. All tables were compiled by the author.

A1 Percentage of Articles and Pages Dealing with the Kingdom of Saudi Arabia

Name of Journal	N=	Pages Percentage Mentioning Saudi Arabia	N=	Articles Percentage Mentioning Saudi Arabia
1 **The Economist** (1950–1974)	117,347	0.48	9,045	1.45
2 **American Political Science Review** (1950–1974)	16,329,703	0.0	1,050	0.0
3 **The Journal of Near Eastern Studies** (1950–1974)	4,357	0.0	670	0.0
4 **The Middle East Journal** (1950–1974)	13,244	0.68	394	2.03
5 **World Politics** (1950–1974)	15,582	0.0	842	0.0
6 **Middle Eastern Affairs** (1950–1963)	5,495	0.364	296	1.69
7 **Journal of Developing Areas** (1966–1974)	4,387	0.0	166	0.0
8 **Comparative Politics** (1968–1974)	3,420	0.0	165	0.0
9 **Comparative Political Studies** (1968–1974)	3,365	0.0	173	0.0

A2 Incidence of Articles on Specific Aspects of Saudi Arabian Affairs in Nine Journals (in which Saudi Arabia is a Dominant Theme)

Specific Aspects of Saudi Arabian Affairs

Name of Journal	Foreign Policy	International Islamic Relations	Petroleum Policy	Domestic Affairs	Saudi–American Relations	Arab Petroleum Affairs	OPEC Affairs	Development Affairs	Others
1 The Economist (1950–1974)	+	+	+	+	+	+	+	+	+
2 American Political Science Review (1950–1974)	0	+	0	0	0	0	0	0	0
3 The Journal of Near Eastern Studies (1950–1974)	0	0	0	0	0	0	0	0	+
4 The Middle East Journal (1950–1974)	0	+	0	0	0	+	+	0	+
5 World Politics (1950–1974)	0	0	0	0	0	0	0	0	0
6 Middle Eastern Affairs (1950–1963)	+	0	+	+	0	0	+	0	0
7 Journal of Developing Areas (1966–1974)	0	0	0	+	0	0	+	+	+
8 Comparative Politics (1968–1974)	0	0	0	0	0	0	0	0	0
9 Comparative Political Studies (1968–1974)	0	0	0	0	0	0	0	0	0

Key: + = articles appear; 0 = no articles

1 Foreign policy

The following major happenings and achievements were dealt with by *The Economist* in the twenty-four years of the survey.

In 1952, Saudi Arabia declared its adoption of the Truman Proclamation of September 28, 1945, by which the United States extended its jurisdiction over all deposits of petroleum lying off its coasts. This concept covers the area known as the Continental Shelf. On November 2,

1956, Saudi Arabia broke off diplomatic relations with Britain as a result of Britain's invasion of Egypt. In early 1957, King Saud visited Washington, D.C. and conferred with President Eisenhower. During the same year, the King made two foreign visits to Jordan and Iraq following his trip to the United States. In the first quarter of 1958, an agreement was reached between the governments of Saudi Arabia and Bahrain on the off-shore area separating them, and certain islands which were to be divided between them. In 1965, King Faisal met President Nasser of Egypt in Jiddah, Saudi Arabia, and signed the Jiddah Accord by which both agreed to put an end to the Yemen conflict.

On December 14, 1965, King Faisal visited the Shah of Iran and discussed two important issues. The first was the reaching of a formula to solve the problem of the continental shelf on the Gulf; the second issue was concern over the future of the Gulf after Britain's evacuation of the area. In 1966, King Faisal made an official visit to the United States, during which he declared that "Jews who support Israel [thus being Zionists] are enemies of Arabs".[2] Consequently, Mayor John Lindsey of New York City cancelled his planned banquet for King Faisal, and Governor Nelson Rockefeller of New York decided not to make the expected courtesy call on King Faisal. *The Economist* in its July 2 issue of 1966 indicated that it was an election year in New York, which has 2.2 million Jewish residents. During the same year, King Faisal made official visits to Turkey, Morocco, Guinea, Mali and Tunisia, which were judged by *The Economist* to be successful.

After the June 5th war of 1967, some Arab states, among them Saudi Arabia, imposed a selective petroleum embargo on certain Western nations. This embargo was lifted in July of the same year. In May 1967, Britain extended an official invitation to King Faisal to visit London. In 1968, the Shah of Iran made an official visit to Saudi Arabia. In the October 3 issue of 1970, *The Economist*, in an article on skyjacking, reported that "the failure to ratify the Tokyo Convention on sky hijacking seems to have been partly political and partly a matter of inertia. Among the holdouts are the Soviet Union, Cuba, and all the Arab countries except Saudi Arabia".[3] In 1971, United States Secretary of State William Rogers made a visit to four Arab capitals, Riyadh, Amman, Beirut and Cairo. In 1971, King Faisal accepted an invitation from President Sadat of Egypt to visit Egypt and during the same year King Hussein of Jordan met with King Faisal in Saudi Arabia.

In the June 8 issue of 1972, *The Economist* reported that diplomatic relations were restored between the government of Saudi Arabia and Sultan Qaboos of Oman. Within two weeks of the start of the Ramadan war of 1973 (the October war), the Arab nations, on October 17, 1973, had imposed a 5 per cent cutback in their petroleum production. This was followed by a total embargo after the massive United States military aid to Israel.

Saudi Arabia, in the January 12 issue of 1974, concluded an agreement with the Italian government on an exchange of petroleum for industrial goods.

Former President Richard Nixon visited Saudi Arabia in June of 1974.

On April 23, 1974, Cardinal Pignedoli, then Pope Paul's personal representative, visited Saudi Arabia and met King Faisal in Riyadh. Both sides agreed explicitly that "their holy places in Jerusalem cannot remain indefinitely under the exclusive sovereignty of the Jewish state".[4]

Sixty-two major articles on Saudi Arabia, concerning foreign policy, appeared in *The Economist* from 1950 to January 1974.

2 Saudi Arabian petroleum policy

During the suspension of petroleum operations in Iran from July 1951, *The Economist* issue of January 1952 reported that Saudi Arabia had achieved a remarkable expansion in petroleum output from 26 million tons to 38 million tons, and that in 1950 Saudi Arabian production of crude petroleum was 199.5 million barrels annually. Saudi Arabia's petroleum revenues in 1950 were $112.0 million, $155.0 million in 1951, and $170.0 million in 1952.

In the issue of January 13, 1951, it was reported that King Abdul Aziz Al Sa'ud had concluded a new agreement with the Arabian American Oil Company (Aramco) under which the latter waived the tax exemption clause included in the original concession. Also, the company offered to pay Saudi Arabia, in addition to royalties at the present rate of 34 cents a barrel, an income tax of up to 50 per cent on its net profits after the deduction of the United States income tax. In 1957 Saudi Arabia signed a petroleum agreement with Japan. The site of the new concession was the sea bed off the Saudi sector of the neutral zone between Saudi Arabia and Kuwait.

In March 1957 *The Economist* reported that the flow of Saudi Arabian petroleum to the West started the moment the news came that Israel had retreated from the Gaza and the Sinai Coast. Also during the same year, the Saudi Arabian Government made a proposal for an Arab pipeline system which would be financed by the World Bank at a cost of £300 million. For the first time since the establishment of Aramco, a Saudi Arabian was elected to its board of directors, in accordance with an agreement to allow the Saudi government representation on the board of directors.

Following the June 5th war of 1967, Saudi Arabia joined some Arab states in the imposition of a selective petroleum embargo on Western nations. But by July 1967, it had lifted its embargo on the United States and Britain.

During 1967, Saudi Arabia successfully broke the petroleum companies' front against higher prices for crude oil in a modest but highly significant way. "The Saudis invoked 'an extraordinary circumstance' clause in their agreement with Aramco to forego the normal 6.5 per cent discount, though only in respect of that part of Saudi Arabia's oil that comes out by pipeline to the Mediterranean port of Sidon (in Lebanon)." The agreement was to be enforced as long as the Suez Canal remained shut.[5]

In 1972, Saudi Arabia, represented by Sheikh Ahmad Zaki Yamani, the Saudi Petroleum Minister, concluded an agreement with the Western petroleum companies operating in Saudi Arabia on the participation question. The agreement, reached in New York City, stated the participation "at 25 per cent rising to 51 per cent in 1983. The 25 per cent will remain until 1978, climb to 30 per cent in 1979 with 5 per cent more each year until 1982, then a further 6 per cent to 51 per cent in 1982".[6]

In November of 1973 and during the sequence of events in the Middle East following the Ramadan War, Saudi Arabia declared that it wanted to take over 51 per cent of the Arabian American Oil Company as soon as possible rather than wait until 1982. During 1973, Saudi Arabia, along with all the Arab petroleum producing nations, suspended petroleum shipments to the Western world, specifically to the United States, as a result of its $2.8 billion military aid to Israel.

In March 1974, the Arab petroleum embargo came to an end and it was believed that "the ending of the Arab oil embargo against America has put even more power into the hands of Saudi Arabia".[7]

In early 1974, Sheikh Ahmad Zaki Yamani visited Japan to obtain industrial knowledge from Japan in exchange for petroleum supplies. Finally, in 1974, the Saudi government successfully concluded an agreement with Aramco on the participation issue, by which Saudi Arabia gained a 60 per cent share, retroactive to January 1, 1974, in the ownership of the Arabian American Oil Company.

Twenty-two major articles on petroleum policy appeared in *The Economist* from 1950 to 1974.

3 Saudi–American relations
Two major articles dealt with the conflicting interests of the United States in the Middle East – its vital strategic interest in Saudi Arabia on the one hand and its support for Israel on the other. In 1961 the Saudi government refused to renew the lease of the American air base at Dhahran, which was to expire in April 1962. King Faisal visited the United States during President Lyndon Johnson's administration.

In 1972, the Saudi government "proposed an oil deal to the United States last weekend whose reverberations are going to be felt for a long time. Saudi Arabia would guarantee a flow of oil to America in return for the lifting of duties on the oil and the right to invest its revenues in the American oil industry."[8]

On June 5, 1974, Prince Fahd Ibn Abdul Aziz Al Sa'ud, second deputy Premier and Minister of the Interior of Saudi Arabia, and U.S. Secretary of State Henry Kissinger signed, in Washington, D.C., a wide-ranging agreement on military and economic cooperation between their two countries.

Six major articles appeared on Saudi–American relations in *The Economist* from 1950 to 1974.

4 Internal affairs

In the issue of November 14, 1953 a lengthy article reported the death of King Abdul Aziz Al Sa'ud and dealt with various aspects of the King's life. It was reported that during 1959 a Saudi loan to Syria of $6 million was concluded. In March 1957 the Saudi Arabian currency, the Riyal, was devalued.

In March 1958 a change in Saudi leadership was reported – the transfer of legislative and executive authority from King Sa'ud ibn Abdul Aziz to Crown Prince Faisal by a Royal Decree on March 22, 1958. This marked the beginning of major internal changes in the Saudi government. In May 1958, it was reported that "the Royal decree of May 12, setting up a cabinet system[9] gives hope that the Saudi regime recognizes the dire necessity for doing something to strengthen its [home-front and to improve the worsening situation in the country]".[10]

Many articles reported the efforts of Crown Prince Faisal to reform the administration of Saudi Arabia and his insistence on strict observance of budget allocations. An issue in February 1959 indicated that Crown Prince Faisal's new programme, which he launched in 1958, on all fronts, was beginning to show positive results.

In an article entitled "Quick Recovery", in 1960, it was reported that

by using . . . its ample oil revenues sensibly (and under the able leadership of Crown Prince Faisal) for the first time, the Saudis have managed a complete financial recovery in barely eighteen months. The gold, silver and hard currency reserves rose from $24 million in the summer of 1958 to $186 million in February 1959.[11]

On December 21, 1960, King Saud reassumed his authority in Saudi Arabia and Crown Prince Faisal, who was also the Prime Minister, resigned. But in 1962, Crown Prince Faisal presided over a new cabinet as the Prime Minister of Saudi Arabia.

In 1964, Crown Prince Faisal was proclaimed King of Saudi Arabia, as a result of the consensus of the people of Saudi Arabia, the Royal Family, the *Ulama* and the Bedouin tribes of the Kingdom. The assumption of rule by King Faisal marked the beginning of a new era in Saudi Arabian history.

In 1965, an article, "Faisal the Fabian", reported that His Majesty King Faisal had just launched the biggest budget in Saudi Arabia's history. It disposed of some £330 million, representing a 27 per cent increase over the preceding year.[12]

Reporting on Saudi Arabia's annual resources, *The Economist* said that the Saudi annual revenue reached £360 million. It also mentioned

the King's personal commitment to developing his country [as] shown by the 43.7% of the 1968–1969 budget . . . devoted to development projects. [Furthermore] the King also does not want to involve the country in any external physical commitment as it would exhaust the country's resources originally allocated for the development projects.[13]

Twenty-six major articles on Saudi Arabia's domestic affairs appeared in *The Economist* from 1950 to 1974.

5 Islamic–Saudi Arabian international affairs

In the field of pan-Arab affairs, a royal federation between Jordan and Iraq on the one hand, and the federation among Egypt, Syria and Northern Yemen on the other, were among the principal events in 1958. On September 1, 1959, an Arab League summit conference took place at Casablanca, Morocco. The two major items on its agenda were the Algerian war and the Palestinian refugees. Of the ten member states then in the League, Iraq and Tunisia were absent. In January 1964, the first Arab League conference of heads of state, which instituted a tradition which is still continuing, convened in Cairo to discuss the important issue of the Israeli project to divert the Jordan River. All the Arab heads of state attended the conference, except for the President of Lebanon and the King of Saudi Arabia. The second Arab League summit conference met in Alexandria, Egypt, in September of 1964. It was attended by all member states in the league. The basic issue on the conference agenda was the Yemen war. The third summit conference of heads of state met in September 1965, again in Casablanca, Morocco. The fourth conference was held in Khartoum, Sudan, in August 1967, to discuss the aftermath of the June 1967 war with Israel. At that summit, three major policies were decided upon. The first was to lift the petroleum embargo on the West; the second was the agreement between the Kingdom of Saudi Arabia and Egypt to end the Yemen dispute, and finally that Saudi Arabia, Kuwait, and Libya would pay considerable subsidies to Egypt and Jordan until all the effects of the Israeli aggression were eliminated. The fifth in this sequence was the Arab League summit conference that convened in Rabat, Morocco, on December 20, 1969. It was a full scale conference of the member states, designed to discuss further the deadlock in the Middle East conflict and to study common strategy in the Arab–Israeli dispute. On November 27, 1973, the sixth summit conference was opened in Algeria. All Arab member states in the League attended the conference except Libya and Iraq. The meeting examined the effects and results of the 1973 Ramadan War with Israel as well as the Arab petroleum embargo. Between the sixth and the seventh Arab League summit conferences, a limited summit was held in Algeria and attended by King Faisal of Saudi Arabia, President Anwar Sadat of Egypt, President Hafez Assad of Syria and President Haouri Boumédienne of Algeria. This conference discussed the current situation of the Middle East conflict, the Arabian front in general, and Arab relations with the external world in general and the superpowers in particular. The seventh Arab league summit met in Rabat, Morocco in September of 1974. All Arab heads of state were present except that of Libya, which sent a representative in lieu of its President. The major resolution adopted by the meeting was the declaration that the Palestine Liberation Organization (PLO) was the sole legitimate representative of all the Palestinian people.

Islamic international affairs may be summarized as follows: In September 1969, a major international Islamic summit conference convened in Rabat, Morocco. The conference reflected the successful achievements of both King Faisal of Saudi Arabia and King Hassan of Morocco. The leaders of most of the Islamic world, represented by twenty-five delegations, attended the conference. The two major issues on its agenda were the fire that occurred at the Mosque of the Rock in Jerusalem and the question of the future of that city. In March of 1972, King Faisal was the host to the delegates of thirty Muslim nations in Jiddah, Saudi Arabia. On February 22, 1974, at Lahore, Pakistan, the Second International Islamic Conference opened its first session. The conference dealt with the Middle East conflict, the future of the city of Jerusalem, and the issue of Israeli withdrawal from occupied Arab lands held since 1967. The conference, embracing both Arab and non-Arab states, was attended by delegations of thirty-six Islamic nations. In June 1974, the Islamic Foreign Ministers' Conference convened at Kuala Lumpur, Malaysia. Thirty-eight Muslim nations were represented at this conference. In April 1974, King Faisal received Pope Paul's personal representative, Cardinal Pignedoli, in Riyadh. Both Islamic and Christian issues related to Jerusalem were discussed and an agreement on a statement was reached.

Since 1959 meetings of Arab and non-Arab Muslim nations have been held for purposes that serve both Arabs and Muslims. Participation of nations at these conferences has varied from conference to conference. It cannot be said in regard to Islamic conferences that these were a series of consecutive meetings under the same sponsorship. Nevertheless it is important to list them in chronological order because they show a cumulative expansion of the awareness of international responsibility on the part of the Muslim nations. The cumulative expansion of Islamic awareness was accompanied by an expansion of participation by the Muslim nations. The number of Islamic states attending these conferences grew from twenty-five at the Rabat Conference of 1969 to thirty-six at the second summit, at Lahore, in 1974. In June of the same year, just four months after the Lahore conference, the delegations attending the Kuala Lumpur conference had increased to thirty-eight. The next conference is expected to embrace over forty states.

Fourteen articles on Arab–Islamic affairs appeared in *The Economist* from 1950 to 1974.

6 Arab petroleum policy and related affairs

In 1957, the Arab League's committee of petroleum experts met in Baghdad, Iraq, with three main items on their agenda. In 1959, the first Arab Petroleum Congress (predecessor of the larger, more inclusive OPEC) was held in Cairo, and concluded its work by April 23. In that Congress, a proposal for an Arab petroleum pipeline company was discussed.

In November 1959, the Arab petroleum experts met in Jiddah, Saudı Arabia. They adopted three important resolutions, among which was the lowering of petroleum production which would mean higher prices of petroleum.

In 1960 another Arab Petroleum Congress meeting took place in Beirut, Lebanon. The Congress examined the second cut in posted prices of crude petroleum made by the Western petroleum companies operating in their countries – the first having been made in February 1959.

In November 1963, another Arab Petroleum Congress met in Beirut, Lebanon. It was followed in March 1965 by a similar Congress in Cairo.

A selective petroleum embargo was imposed on the United States and Britain by some Arab states following the June War of 1967. This was lifted in July 1967. On October 17, 1973, an Arab petroleum embargo was imposed on selected Western countries at the height of the Ramadan war of 1973. This embargo was lifted after the meeting of the Arab Petroleum Ministers in Tripoli, Libya, in March 1974.

Twenty articles on the affairs of the Arab world *vis-à-vis* their petroleum policies appeared in *The Economist* from 1950 to 1974.

7 OPEC affairs

One of the very early OPEC meetings was the conference held in Baghdad, Iraq, in September 1960. It was followed by another OPEC conference in Caracas, Venezuela, in January 1961. Another OPEC conference was held in Geneva in 1962, when Libya joined OPEC.

In March 1964, another OPEC meeting convened in Geneva. Later, at the then OPEC headquarters in Geneva, another OPEC meeting was held. Another conference was held before Christmas 1970 in Caracas. In Teheran, Iran, early in 1971 an OPEC conference was held with the international petroleum companies present to discuss vital issues with the OPEC members. In October 1971, a further OPEC conference met in Beirut, Lebanon, to discuss relations with and policies toward international petroleum companies operating in their area.

Following the devaluation of the U.S. dollar in 1972, OPEC members met with major international petroleum companies to reassess the out-flow of six petroleum producing states – Saudi Arabia, Iran, Iraq, Kuwait, Abu Dhabi and Qatar.

In June 1974 an OPEC meeting was held in Ecuador. All the OPEC members except Saudi Arabia expressed the desire to raise posted prices of crude petroleum by 10–12 per cent a barrel. But Saudi Arabia's strong opposition to such a rise prevented it from happening.

Ten articles on OPEC affairs appeared in *The Economist* from 1960 to 1974.

Tables A.1 and A.2 demonstrate the extent of coverage of Saudi Arabia in the nine major journals which are the focus of this survey, both by percentages and according to subject matter dealing with specific aspects of Saudi Arabian affairs. Table A.1 reveals the serious short-comings of the treatment of Saudi Arabia in these leading journals. As for Table A.2, this should be self-explanatory.

B: OTHER JOURNALS

1 American Political Science Review

Published quarterly by the American Political Science Association from 1906. The survey here begins with 1950. Marginal mention of Saudi Arabia was traced in some articles but without any major attention whatsoever.

2 The Journal of Near Eastern Studies

Published quarterly by the University of Chicago Press, Chicago, Illinois. Starting in January 1942, but survey here begins with 1950.

The Journal of Near Eastern Studies' treatment of Saudi Arabia con-sists of one article written by Bruce Howe, *Two Groups of Rock Engravings from the Hijaz* in Volume 9 of 1950.

3 The Middle East Journal

A quarterly publication of the Middle East Institute, Washington, D.C. The starting date of this journal was January 1947. Nonetheless, the beginning year of the survey is 1950.

The *Middle East Journal*'s treatment of Saudi Arabia does not exceed three or four articles, a book review on OPEC and the resolutions of the Islamic Conference in Pakistan in the document section.

4 World Politics

A quarterly journal of international relations published by the Center of International Studies, Princeton University Press. The journal first appeared in 1948. Again, the survey of this journal begins in 1950. There was nothing in it about Saudi Arabia.

5 Middle Eastern Affairs

Published monthly, except June–July and August–September when bimonthly, by the Council for Middle Eastern Affairs Press, Elmont, New York. The journal started in 1950, but was suspended in 1963. Its coverage of Saudi Arabian affairs is rather sparse.

6 The Journal of Developing Areas

Published quarterly in October, January, April and July by the Western Illinois University Press, Macomb, Illinois, from 1966. The survey begins in that year through 1974.

The *Journal of Development Areas*' treatment of Saudi Arabia consists of three major articles, along with no more than three other articles dealing with the Kingdom at a more cursory level.

7 Comparative Politics

Published quarterly by the City University of New York from 1968.

There is nothing of value to report on the treatment of Saudi Arabia by this journal.

8 Comparative Political Studies

Published quarterly by SAGE Publications, Beverley Hills, California, from 1968.

This journal too contained nothing at all of any significance on the Kingdom of Saudi Arabia through 1974.

SYNOPSIS OF BOOKS

The following pages survey seventy-four books dealing with what may be considered as major themes in political and administrative development. Table A.3 lists these books along with their authors or editors.

A3 Books Reflecting Major Themes in Political Developmental Thought*

Author or editor	Title	Remarks
1 Albinski, Henry	**Asian Political Processes: Essays and Reading**	No comment
2 Almond, Gabriel, Flanagan, Scott and Mundt, Robert, eds.	**Crisis, Choice and Historical Studies in Political Development**	No comment
3 Almond, Gabriel and Powell, G. B.	**Comparative Politics— A Developmental Approach**	No comment
4 Almond, Gabriel and Coleman, James	**The Politics of the Developing Areas**	See text
5 Almond, Gabriel and Verba, Sidney	**The Civic Culture**	No comment
6 Apter, David	**The Politics of Modernization**	No comment
7 Apter, David	**Political Change: Collected Essays**	No comment
8 Apter, David	**Some Conceptual Approaches to the Study of Modernization**	No comment
9 Asher, Robert, et al.	**Development of the Emerging Countries: An Agenda**	No comment
10 Barringer, Herbert Blanksten, George and Mack, Raymond, eds.	**Social Change in Developing Areas**	No comment
11 Basch, Antonin	**Pragmatic Approach to Economic Development**	No comment
12 Bauer, P. T.	**Dissent on Development**	No comment
13 Benjamin, Roger	**Patterns of Political Development**	No comment
14 Binder, Leonard, et al.	**Crises and Sequences in Political Development**	No comment
15 Black, Cyril	**Dynamics of Modernization**	See text
16 Brakensha, David, and Hodge, Peter	**Community Development**	No comment
17 Braibanti, Ralph ed.	**Tradition, Values and Socio-Economic Development**	No comment

Author or editor	Title	Remarks
18 Braibanti, Ralph, ed.	**Administration and Economic Development in India**	No comment
19 Braibanti, Ralph, ed.	**Political and Administrative Development**	No comment
20 Butwell, Richard, ed.	**Foreign Policy and the Developing Nations**	No comment
21 Caiden, Gerald	**Administrative Reform**	No comment
22 Clark, Robert, Jr.	**Development and Instability – Political Change in the Non-Western World**	See text
23 Cole, Taylor and Piper, Don, eds.	**Post-Primary Education and Political and Economic Development**	No comment
24 der Mehden, Fred von	**Politics of the Developing Nations**	See text
25 Duchacek, Ivo	**Comparative Federalism: The Territorial Dimension of Politics**	No comment
26 Eisenstadt, S. N., ed.	**Post-Traditional Societies**	No comment
27 Emerson, Rupert	**From Empire to Nation: The Rise of Self-Assertion of Asian and African Peoples**	See text
28 Enloe, Cynthia	**Ethnic Conflict and Political Development**	No comment
29 Fickett, Lewis, Jr., ed.	**Problems of the Developing Nations**	See text
30 Finkle, Jason and Gable, Richard, eds.	**Political Development and Social Change**	No comment
31 Friedmann, John	**Urbanization Planning and National Development**	No comment
32 Goulet, Denis	**The Cruel Choice: A New Concept in the Theory of Development**	No comment
33 Hartz, Louis, ed.	**The Founding of New Societies**	No comment
34 Heaphey, James, ed.	**Spatial Dimensions of Development Administration**	No comment

	Author or editor	Title	Remarks
35	Huntington, Samuel	Political Order in Changing Societies	See text
36	Ilchman, Warren, and Thomas, Norman	The Political Economy of Change	No comment
37	Jacobs, Norman	Modernization without Development	No comment
38	Kebschull, Harvey, ed.	Politics in Transitional Societies	See text
39	La Palombara, Joseph, ed.	Bureaucracy and Political Development	No comment
40	Lekachman, Robert and Novack, David	Development and Society, The Dynamics of Economic Change	See text
41	Lerner, Daniel	The Passing of Traditional Society	No comment
42	Leys, Colin, ed.	Politics and Change in Developing Countries: Studies in the Theory and Practice of Development	No comment
43	Levine, Robert	Public Planning: Failure and Redirection	No comment
44	Lipset, Seymour M.	The First New Nation: United States in Historical and Comparative Perspective	No comment
45	Meadows, Paul	The Many Faces of Change: Exploration in the Theory of Social Change	No comment
46	Meier, Richard	Developmental Planning	See text
47	Millikan, Max and Blackmer, Donald, eds.	The Emerging Nations	No comment
48	Mishan, Edward	Technology and Growth: The Price We Pay	No comment
49	Montgomery, John and Siffin, William, eds.	Approaches to Development: Politics, Administration and Change	No comment
50	Montgomery, John	Technology and Civic Life: Making and Implementing Decisions	No comment
51	Morse, Chandler and Ashford, Douglas, et al.	Modernization in Design: Social Changes in the Twentieth Century	No comment

	Author or editor	Title	Remarks
52	Myrdal, Gunnar	**Asian Drama** (three volumes)	See text
53	Nettl, J. P.	**Political Mobilization**	No comment
54	Nisbet, Robert, ed.	**Social Change and History: Aspects of the Western Theory of Development**	No comment
55	Organski, A. F. K.	**The Stages of Political Development**	No comment
56	Packenham, Robert	**Liberal American and the Third World: Political Development Ideas in Foreign Aid and Social Science**	No comment
57	Pearson, Lester, chairman	Commission on International Development of the International Bank for Reconstruction, **Partners in Development**, Report of the Commission	See text
58	Poats, Rutherford	**Technology for Developing Nations: New Directions for United States Technical Assistance**	No comment
59	Prybla, Jan and Shaffer, Harry, eds.	**From Underdevelopment to Affluence: Western, Soviet and Chinese Views**	No comment
60	Pye, Lucian and Verba, Sidney, eds.	**Political Culture and Political Development**	No comment
61	Pye, Lucian, ed.	**Aspects of Political Development**	No comment
62	Rabushka, Alvin and Shepsle, Kenneth	**Politics in Plural Societies: A Theory of Democratic Instability**	No comment
63	Riggs, Fred, ed.	**Frontiers of Development Administration**	No comment
64	Rostow, W. W.	**Politics and the States of Growth**	See text
65	Rustow, Dankwart	**A World of Nations: Problems of Political Modernization**	No comment

66	Said, Abdul A.	Protagonists of Change: Sub-cultures in Development and Revolution	No comment
67	Schaffer, Bernard	Administration Training and Development: A Comparative Study of East Africa, Zambia, Pakistan and India	No comment
68	Shils, Edward	Political Development in the New States	No comment
69	Silvert, K. H., ed.	Expectant Peoples Nationalism and Development	See text
70	Smith, Donald Eugene	Religion, Politics, and Social Change in the Third World: A Source Book	See text
71	Tachan, Frank, ed.	The Developing Nations: Path to Modernization	No comment
72	Tullis, F. La Mond	Politics and Social Change in Third World Countries	No comment
73	Waldo, Dwight, ed.	Temporal Dimensions of Development Administration	No comment
74	Welch, Claude, ed.	Political Modernization	No comment

*Complete bibliographical material can be found in the bibliography at the end of this work.

Among the authors of these books are prominent writers and scholars in the realm of political and administrative development, such as Leonard Binder, Ralph Braibanti, Gunnar Myrdal, Joseph La Palombara and Fred Riggs.

In the three-volume *Asian Drama* by Gunnar Myrdal, which amounts to 2,221 pages, no mention was made of Saudi Arabia. In Rupert Emerson's *From Empire to Nation: The Rise to Self-Assertion of Asian and African Peoples*, Saudi Arabia was mentioned cursorily three times.

Despite its recent date (1973), *Crisis, Choice, and Change: Historical Studies in Political Development*, edited by Almond, Flanagan and Mundt, does not deal with Saudi Arabia at all.

The report submitted by Lester B. Pearson to Robert S. McNamara, President of the International Bank for Reconstruction and Development, called *Partners in Development*, failed to include Saudi Arabia, although it made reference to studies of other Middle Eastern countries.

In Fred R. von der Mehden's *Politics of the Developing Nations*, all that was said on Saudi Arabia – in the appendix – is that it was never a colony of any major power, does not have political parties and has an élitist national ideology. Again, Donald Eugene Smith, in his *Religion, Politics, and Social Change in the Third World: A Source Book*, treated Islam, and major Islamic nations, *e.g.* Pakistan, Egypt and Jordan, without making any major reference to the Kingdom of Saudi Arabia, the religious center of the entire Islamic world. Lewis P. Fickett Jr.'s book, *Problems of the Developing Nations*, included case studies on Algeria (p. 141), Tunisia (p. 163), India (p. 172), Pakistan (p. 191), and Thailand (p. 201), but made no mention of Saudi Arabia. In a co-edited book, *Development and Society: The Dynamics of Economic Change*, Harry J. Benda said in a paper called "Non-Western Intelligentsias as Political Elites" that

> Non-Western societies can broadly be divided into two categories, those that have so far remained outside the orbit of Westernization or have, at least, barely or only superficially embarked upon it; and those that have travelled along the road of Westernization to a more or less marked and significant degree. The first group is fairly rapidly dwindling; its hallmarks are a combination of the old socio-political moulds and *mores*, with political authority continuing to be vested in traditional elite groups. Some Arab sheikhdoms, including (for the time being at least) Saudi Arabia, and the tribal societies in many parts of Negro Africa are the prototypes of this group.[14]

This is, to say the least, an ethnocentric statement which totally ignores the fact that the Kingdom of Saudi Arabia, characterized by Benda as an "Arab Sheikhdom", is about one-third the size of the continental United States, and as large as Britain, France and Italy combined.

In Cyril E. Black's *Dynamics of Modernization*, a single reference to the Kingdom of Saudi Arabia appeared on page 931, in a table, stating that the "consolidation of modernizing leadership" in the Kingdom started in 1964. Yet, in fact, ambitious and important developmental projects and the general modernization of Saudi Arabia began in 1958 when King Faisal, then the Crown Prince, assumed the office of the Prime Minister and began a comprehensive program for the development of Saudi Arabia.

For convenience, at this stage, a list of books that made marginal mention of Saudi Arabia will follow, without detail about their minor findings. These books are: W. W. Rostow, *Politics and the Stage of Growth* (Cambridge, England, 1971), Richard L. Meier, *Development Planning* (New York: McGraw-Hill, 1965), Harvey G. Kebschull, ed., *Politics in Transitional Societies* (New York, 1968), Robert P. Clark, Jr., *Development and Instability: Political Change in the Non-Western World* (Hillsdale, Illinois, 1974), Samuel P. Huntington, *Political Order in Changing*

Societies (New Haven, Conn., 1968), Gabriel A. Almond and James S. Coleman, eds., *The Politics of the Developing Areas* (Princeton, 1960). Of the seventy-four books surveyed, only one, *Expectant Peoples, Nationalism and Development*, edited by K. H. Silvert, devoted a whole chapter to Saudi Arabia – "From Nomad Society to New Nation: Saudi Arabia," by Richard H. Nolte.

SAGE Series

We shall now deal with the SAGE Series, Professional Papers published in the Comparative Politics Series by SAGE Publications, Beverley Hills, California.

A survey of volumes 1 to 5, covering 1970–1975, reveals that the authors range from established scholars to newcomers in the field of comparative politics, including a few doctoral candidates. An examination of fifty-six issues of this series, all of which are listed in the bibliography of this book, reveals that ten items out of the total fifty-six deal with topics which could reasonably include either mention or analysis of Saudi Arabia. The ten items are the following:

M. Eckstein, *The Evaluation of Political Performance: Problems and Dimensions* (1971), 88 pp.

T. Gurr and M. McClelland, *Political Performance: A Twelve-Nation Study* (1971), 88 pp.

M. C. Hudson, *Conditions of Political Violence and Instability: A Preliminary Test of Three Hypotheses* (1970), 56 pp.

R. F. Moy, *A Computer Simulation of Democratic Political Development: Tests of the Lipset and Moore Models* (1971), 72 pp.

R. Rogowski and L. Wasserspring, *Does Political Development Exist? Corporatism in Old and New Societies* (1971), 56 pp.

J. R. Scarritt, *Political Development and Culture Change Theory: A Propositional Synthesis with Application to Africa* (1972), 64 pp.

L. Sigelman, *Modernization and the Political System: A Critique and Preliminary Empirical Analysis* (1971), 64 pp.

A. J. Sofranko and R. C. Bealer, *Unbalanced Modernization and Domestic Instability: A Comparative Analysis* (1972), 88 pp.

R. B. Stauffer, *Nation-Building in a Global Economy: the Role of the Multinational Corporation* (1973), 48 pp.

S. Verba, *et al.*, *The Modes of Democratic Participation: A Cross-National Comparison* (1971), 80 pp.

Only two writers have made mention of Saudi Arabia and that quite marginal. These are Lee Sigelman – SERIES: 01–016, volume 2, 1971; and A. J. Sofranko and Robert C. Bealer – SERIES: 01–036, volume 3, 1972. Many of the SAGE writers have dealt with countries like Algeria, Syria, Iraq, Lebanon, Japan, Nigeria, various Latin

American nations and the United States. Nevertheless, the Kingdom of Saudi Arabia was not included.

Social Science Research Council – Committee on Comparative Politics (SSRC-CCP) (Princeton Series)

As this series embodies volumes edited by scholars in political and administrative development, a treatment of each relevant volume individually might be profitable.

Gabriel A. Almond and James S. Coleman, eds., *The Politics of the Developing Areas* (Princeton University Press, 1960).

It was stated in this volume that Saudi Arabia is a traditional oligarchy and does not have political parties. In this otherwise sophisticated analysis, the Kingdom of Saudi Arabia is treated rather naively and in a stereotyped way. Probably the most accurate statement on Saudi Arabia in this volume is that which says "few polities whose political culture even approximate to homogeneity are quite exceptional: Argentina, Chile, . . . in Latin America, and Turkey . . . [Japan], and, in a very special sense, Saudi Arabia." (p. 544).

Lucian Pye, ed., *Communications and Political Development* (Princeton University Press, 1963).

This volume dealt with studies on Turkey, Iran, Thailand, Communist China and Egypt. There is no mention of Saudi Arabia.

Joseph La Palombara, ed., *Bureaucracy and Political Development* (Princeton University Press, 1963).

Here, there were references to and examinations of bureaucracy and political development in Eastern Europe. Similar studies on Nigeria and Vietnam were also included. A study of the public bureaucracy and judiciary in Pakistan was made by Ralph Braibanti. There was nothing on the Kingdom of Saudi Arabia.

Dankwart Rustow and Robert Ward, eds., *Political Modernization in Japan and Turkey*, (Princeton University Press, 1964).

As the title suggests, this book deals basically with Japan and Turkey. There is no major reference to Saudi Arabia.

James S. Coleman, ed., *Education and Political Development* (Princeton University Press, 1965).

In Part One of Coleman's book, various authors, such as Malcolm H. Kerr and Leon Carl Brown, discussed education and its problems in French Africa, Indonesia, Tunisia, Nigeria, Egypt and Brazil. Saudi Arabia was not examined although its budget for education is second only to defense, and the advances made in education in recent years are among the most significant of any developing country in the world.

Leonard Binder, James S. Coleman, Joseph La Palombara, Lucian N. Pye, Sidney Verba and Myron Weiner, Contributors, *Crises and Se-*

quences in Political Development (Princeton University Press, 1971).

This volume made no reference to Saudi Arabia, marginally or otherwise.

Lucian Pye and Sidney Verba, eds., *Political Culture and Political Development* (Princeton University Press, 1965).

Pye and Verba's volume included studies on Japan, England, Germany, Turkey, Ethiopia, Italy, Mexico, Egypt and Soviet Russia. There is no mention of Saudi Arabia.

American Society for Public Administration–Comparative Administration Group (ASPA–CAG) (Duke Series)

Its general editor is Ralph Braibanti and the editorial board includes other prominent scholars such as Fred Riggs and John D. Montgomery. Dwight Waldo, ed., *Temporal Dimensions of Development Administration* (Durham, N.C.: Duke University Press, 1970).

This volume made no reference to Saudi Arabia.

Edward W. Weidner, ed., *Development Administration in Asia* (Durham: Duke University Press, 1970).

No mention of the Kingdom of Saudi Arabia is made. Pakistan and India were treated in a major fashion.

Allan Kornberg and Lloyd Musolf, eds., *Legislatures in Developmental Perspective* (Durham: Duke University Press, 1970).

The United States political system was discussed in Part Four of this volume, by Roger H. Davidson. The Indian political system was dealt with in Part Five by C. M. Singhvi. Included in this volume also were studies of the Chilean political system, the Lebanese political system, the politics of Kenya *vis-à-vis* its National Assembly and the Philippine political system.

James J. Heaphey, ed., *Spatial Dimensions of Development Administration* (Durham: Duke University Press, 1971).

This volume made no reference to, or study of, Saudi Arabia at all.

Fred Riggs, ed., *Frontiers of Development Administration* (Durham: Duke University Press, 1971).

In this volume, Saudi Arabia was mentioned five times in an article written by Alfred Diamant. First (p. 491), Diamant classified Saudi Arabia as being pre-developmental and said that the process of modernization had just started. Diamant's work was published in 1971. Yet modernization of the Kingdom of Saudi Arabia started in 1958 when Crown Prince Faisal assumed the office of Prime Minister.

In three other instances Diamant dealt with Saudi Arabia in a similarly cavalier manner.

[1] Brian G. Johnson, Editor's foreword, *Journal of International Affairs*, 19 (November 1, 1965): ix.

[2] *The Economist*, 220 (July 2, 1966): 39–40.

[3] *Ibid.*, 237 (October 3, 1970): 32.

[4] *Ibid.*, 251 (May 18, 1974): 36.

[5] *Ibid.*, 224 (September 23, 1967): 1125.

[6] *Ibid.*, 245 (October 14, 1972): 92.

[7] *Ibid.*, 250 (March 16, 1974): 74–76.

[8] *Ibid.*, 245 (October 7, 1972): 91.

[9] Author's note: The cabinet system originated in 1953. This statement refers to the new 1958 constitution of the Council of Ministers.

[10] *The Economist*, 187 (May 31, 1958): 774.

[11] *Ibid.*, 217 (January 10, 1960): 193.

[12] *Ibid.*, 217 (November 13, 1965): 712.

[13] *Ibid.*, 231 (April 5, 1969): 24.

[14] Harry Benda, "Non-Western Intelligentsias as Political Elites," in David E. Novack and Robert Lekachman, eds., *Development and Society: The Dynamics of Economic Change* (New York: St. Martin's Press, 1964), p. 406.

Glossary

Abdul Aziz Al Sa'ud (also known as Ibn Saud)	(b. 1880 – d. 1953). Founder of the Kingdom of Saudi Arabia; he reigned from 1902–1953.
Abdul Aziz ibn Sa'ud	(b. ? – d. 1803). Of the first House of Al-Sa'ud whose rule extended over an area embracing the cities of Riyadh and Dir'iyah from 1765 to 1803.
Abdallah ibn Abdul Aziz	(b. 1921–). Crown Prince; President of the National Guard; Deputy Prime Minister.
Abd Allah ibn Abdul Rahman	(b. ? – d. 1977). Brother of King Abdul Aziz al Sa'ud.
Abd Allah ibn Sa'ud	(b. ? – d. 1818). Of the first House of Al Sa'ud who ruled over the same area as Abdul Aziz ibn Sa'ud (1814–1818).
Abdul Rahman ibn Faisal	(b. ? – d. ?). Father of the founder of the Kingdom, King Abdul Aziz; reigned from 1889–1891.
Abha	Capital of the highland province of Asir, about 8,000 feet above sea level.
Abu Dhabi	One of the United Arab Emirates jutting from the coast of the Arabian Peninsula.
Ad-Dir'iyah	The original town, near Riyadh, of the House of Sa'ud.
Ahmad ibn Hanbal	(b. 780 – d. 855). Founder of Hanbalite school of jurisprudence.
Al-Baha	A town in the Hijaz province.
Al-Hasa	The region along the Arabian Gulf where the petroleum fields are located, and, more specifically, the vicinity of Hofuf.
Al-Khobar	City east of Dhahran in the Eastern province.
Allah	Muslim word for God.
Al-Mantika al-Gharbia	Western province of Saudi Arabia.
Al-Mantika al-Shamaliya	Northern frontier province.
Al-Mantika al-Janubiya	Southern province.
Al-Mantika al-Sharkiya	Eastern province of Saudi Arabia.
Al-Mantika al-Wosta	Central province of Saudi Arabia.
Al-Mohayda	The Neutral Zone between Kuwait and Saudi Arabia.
Al-Qatif	An agricultural town (oasis) in Al-Hasa region.
Al-Salah	Prayer; one of the Five Pillars of Islam.
Al Sa'ud	Founding dynastic name: The House of Al-Sa'ud.

Al-Shahadah	The testimony of oneness of God, and Muhammad is His Prophet. First of the Five Pillars of Islam.
Al-Siyam	Compulsory fasting during Ramadan; one of the Five Pillars of Islam.
Alayhi as-Salah wa Salam	"Peace and prayer be upon him" (that is, the Prophet Muhammad). Always appears in print in Saudi Arabia after the name of the Prophet.
Arafat	A plain about twelve miles east of Makkah where pilgrims gather on the ninth day of Dhu al-Hijjah at the Hajj.
Asir	One of the Kingdom's five geographical districts in the southern part of the country, bordering Yemen.
Awqaf	Religious endowment; commonly associated with mosques or other religious establishments.
Ayaina	Birthplace of Sheikh Muhammad ibn Abdul Wahhab, the eminent religious leader and founder of the Wahhabi movement. See Muhammad ibn Abdul Wahhab below.

B

Batin	Group: subdivision of a Bedouin tribe. A typical Bedouin tribe (*kabila*) is divided first into *batin* (groups) which are subdivided into *fakhed* (divisions), which are also subdivided into *fasila* (clan). Finally, *fasila* are divided into *rahat* (family).
Buraimi Oasis	Located near Oman.
Buraydah	An important town in the heart of the Najd.

D

Dahna	One of the distinctive geographical features of Saudi Arabia is the Dahna. These sands extend about 800 miles in a huge arc from the Great Nafud in the north to the Rub' al-Khali in the south.
Dammam	Commercial seaport on the Arabian Gulf in the Eastern province.
Dhahran	A city in the Eastern province of the Kingdom comprised of the site of the Arabian American Oil Company and the University of Petroleum and Minerals.
Dhu al-Hijjah	The twelfth month of the Islamic calendar.
Dhu al-Qa'adah	The eleventh month of the Islamic calendar.

Dubai   A coastal emirate on the Arabian Gulf; one of the United Arab Emirates.

F

Fahd ibn Abdul Aziz   (b. 1919–   ). The present king of Saudi Arabia (1982).

Faisal ibn Abdul Aziz   (b. 1905 – d. 1975). King of Saudi Arabia (1964–1975).

Faisal ibn Sa'ud   (b. ? – d. 1865). Of the Second House of Sa'ud; ruled over Najd (1834–1865).

Fakhed   Subdivision of a Bedouin tribe. See *Batin* above.

Fasila   Smallest subdivision of a Bedouin tribe consisting of several families. See *Batin* above.

H

Hadith, The   Sayings of the Holy Prophet, Muhammad.

Hanbali School   One of the four schools of jurisprudence in Islam.

Hanifa   (b. 700 – d. 767). Founder of Hanifite school of jurisprudence.

Hijaz   The Kingdom's Western province.

Hijrah   The year marking the beginning of the Arabian calendar, Anno Hegirae (AH), in which the Prophet Muhammad emigrated from Mecca to Medina.

I

Ikhwan   Literally, "Brothers", a movement established by King Abdul Aziz Al Sa'ud (1902–1953) for political and religious purposes.

Islam   To more than 700 million Muslims in the world, Islam is the religion of God.

J

Jawf   An ancient oasis in the northern part of Saudi Arabia.

Jiddah   Saudi Arabia's major port on the Red Sea, the diplomatic capital of the country, a center for banking and commerce, located in the Western province.

Jizan   A Saudi Arabian town on the Red Sea north of the Arab Republic of Yemen.

Jubail   A town on the Arabian Gulf with a seaport outlet.

Jumada al-Ula   The fifth month of the Islamic calendar.

Jumada ath-Thaniyah   The sixth month of the Islamic calendar.

K

Kabila	Tribe; usually nomadic or Bedouin. See *Batin* above.
Ka'bah	The House of God in Mecca, to Muslims all over the world. Muslims, at prayer, face toward this *Ka'bah*, which is shrouded in black silk and into which is set, in one corner, the sacred Black Stone.
Khafji	A major petroleum field in the Saudi–Kuwaiti Neutral Zone.
Khalid ibn Abdul Aziz	(b. 1912 – d. 1982). King of Saudi Arabia (1975–1982).
Khamis Mushayt	A city in the Asir province.
Khartoum	The capital of Sudan, a Muslim nation in sub-Saharan Africa.

M

Ma'Had Al-Idara Al-Ama	Institute of Public Administration in Riyadh, Saudi Arabia.
Madinah (Medina)	The Muslim's second Holy City and site of the tomb of the Prophet Muhammad.
Majlis al-Shura	The Consultative Council, advisory to the king of Saudi Arabia.
Majlis al-Wukala	Council of Deputies organized in the 1930s by King Abdul Aziz and replaced in 1953 by the Council of Ministers. See below.
Majlis al-Wuzara	Council of Ministers; the first central administrative apparatus in Saudi Arabia.
Malike	(b. 715 – d. 795). Founder of the school of Malikite jurisprudence in Islam.
Makkah	The premier Holy City of Islam, a visit to which is the object of the Hajj.
Mina	Religious site near Makkah.
Muhammad	(b. 570 – d. 632). The Prophet of Islam.
Muhammad Ali	(b. 1769 – d. 1852). Viceroy of Egypt (1805–1849).
Muhammad ibn Abdul Wahhab	(b. 1703 – d. 1792). The eminent religious leader who founded the Wahhabi movement in Saudi Arabia. See *Ayaina* above.
Muhammad ibn Sa'ud	(b. ? – d. 1765). Of the first House of Sa'ud; ruled the town of Ad-Dir'iyah (1744–1765).
Muharram	First month of the Islamic calendar.
Muslim	Follower of Islam (plural, Muslims).
Muzdalfah	Religious site near Makkah.

N

Najd	The heart land of the Kingdom of Saudi Arabia.

Q

Qasim	A district southeast of the Jabal Shammar in Najd.
Qatar	An independent Emirate jutting from the east coast of the Arabian Peninsula.
Qatif	An oasis in the Eastern province; also the name of a petroleum field in the same province.
Quran	Sacred book of Islam, to Muslims it is God's revelation.
Quraysh Tribe	Tribe of the Prophet Muhammad.

R

Rabi' al-Awwal	The third month of the Islamic calendar.
Rabi' ath-Thani	The second month of the Islamic calendar.
Rabig	A town with an outlet on the Red Sea between Jiddah and Medina.
Rahat	Family. See *Batin* above.
Rajab	The seventh month of the Islamic calendar (beginning of each fiscal year in the budget of Saudi Arabia).
Ramadan	The ninth month of the Islamic calendar during which the Fast (*Al-Siyam*) is to be observed. See *Al-Siyam* above.
Riyadh	The Royal capital of Saudi Arabia.
Riyal	Unit of Saudi monetary currency.
Rub' al-Khali	The Empty Quarter, located in the southern part of the Kingdom. An immense sand body approximately 750 miles long with a maximum width of nearly 400 miles. It covers an area of about 250,000 square miles, nearly the size of Texas, and is the largest continuous body of sand in the world.

S

Safar	The second month of the Islamic calendar.
Sa'ud ibn Abdul Aziz	(b. 1900 – d. 1969). The second king of modern Saudi Arabia (1953–1964).
Sa'ud ibn Muhammad ibn Mugrin	(b. ? – d. ?). 18th century; of the first House of Sa'ud and the founder of the Saudi dynasty as the Royal Family's name was derived from his name back in the 18th century. He was the first ruler of the House of Sa'ud.
Sa'ud ibn Sa'ud	(b. ? – d. 1814). Of the first House of Sa'ud who ruled over the same area as Abdul Aziz Ibn Sa'ud (1803–1814).
Sha'ban	Eighth month of the Islamic calendar.

Shafi'	(b. 767 – 820). Founder of the Shafi'ite school of jurisprudence.
Shari'ah	Laws of Islam.
Shawwal	The tenth month of the Islamic calendar.
Sheikh	A title of considerable social and/or religious status. Usually accorded tribal chiefs and eminent religious leaders of Islam.
Sultan Ibn Abdul Aziz	(b. 1920–). Second Deputy Prime Minister; Defense Minister of Saudi Arabia (1978)
Sunnah	The Prophet's tradition.

T

Tabuk	Growing major city in the Northern province of the Kingdom.
Tahara	Total cleanliness; a necessary ritualistic prelude to Muslim prayer.
Ta'if	The government's summer site and a major city in the Western province of the Kingdom.
Turki ibn Sa'ud	(b. ? – d. 1834). Of the second House of Sa'ud, ruled over Najd (1824–1934).

U

Ulama	The Islamic religious scholars and leaders.
Ummah	The whole Islamic community in the world.
Unayza	A famous town in Najd.

W

Wadi ad-Dawasir	A long valley neighboring the Riyadh area.
Wahhabi	An adjective describing a religious movement and derived from the name of its founder, Muhammad ibn Abdul Wahhab.
Wakfa	The Arafat standing during the Hajj, on the morning of the ninth day of Dhu al-Hijjah during the Hajj. The pilgrims move *en masse* to the plain of Arafat for the Wakfa, the culmination, yet not the end, of the Hajj.

Y

Yanbu	A modern seaport in Saudi Arabia north of Jiddah, on the Red Sea between Jiddah and Medina.
Yemen, Arab Republic of	A state bordering Saudi Arabia on the south.

Z

Zakat or *Zaka* (also *al-Zakat* or *al-Zaka*)	Almsgiving; one of the Five Pillars of Islam.

Selected Bibliography

Books and Pamphlets

ALBINSKI, Henry, ed. *Asian Political Processes. Essays and Reading*. Boston: Allyn and Bacon, 1971

ALMOND, Gabriel and COLEMAN, James, eds. *The Politics of the Developing Areas*. Princeton, NJ: Princeton University Press, 1960

ALMOND, Gabriel; FLANAGAN, Scott; and MUNDT, Robert, eds. *Crisis, Choice and Chance: Historical Studies in Political Development*. Boston: Little, Brown, 1973

ALMOND, Gabriel and POWELL, G. B. *Comparative Politics: A Developmental Approach*. Boston: Little, Brown, 1966

ALMOND, Gabriel and VERBA, Sidney, *Civic Culture: Political Attitudes and Democracy in Five Nations*. Princeton, NJ: Princeton University Press, 1963

American Association of Collegiate Registrars and Admissions Officers, Foreign Students Committee, Prepared by Alfred Thomas, Jr. *Saudi Arabia; a Study of the Educational System of the Kingdom of Saudi Arabia and Guide to the Academic Placement of Students from the Kingdom of Saudi Arabia in the United States*. Saudi Arabia: Educational Institutions, 1968

APTER, David. *Political Change: Collected Essays*. London: Cass, 1973

APTER, David. *The Politics of Modernization*. Chicago: University of Chicago Press, 1965

APTER, David. *Some Conceptual Approaches to the Study of Modernization*. Englewood Cliffs, NJ: Prentice-Hall, 1968

ARMSTRONG, H. C. *Lord of Arabia: Ibn Saud, An Intimate Study of a King*. London: Arthur Barker, Ltd, 1934

ASHER, Robert, *et al. Development of the Emerging Countries: An Agenda for Research*. Washington, DC: Brookings Institution, 1962

BAKER, Muhammed; KETTANI, M. Ali; and SEIFERT, William, eds. *Energy and Development: Case Study*. Cambridge, Mass.: Massachusetts Institute of Technology Press, 1973

BARRINGER, Herbert; BLANKSTEN, George; and MACK, Raymond, eds. *Social Change in Developing Areas: A Reinterpretation of Evolutionary Theory*. Cambridge, Mass.: Schenkman, 1965

BASCH, Antonin. *Pragmatic Approach to Economic Development*. New York: Vantage Press, 1970

BAUER, P. T. *Dissent on Development: Studies and Debates in Development Economics*. Cambridge, Mass.: Harvard University Press, 1972

BENJAMIN, Roger. *Political Development*. Boston: Little, Brown, 1972

BINDER, Leonard, *et al. Crises and Sequences in Political Development*. Princeton: Princeton University Press, 1971

BLACK, Cyril. *The Dynamics of Modernization: A Study in Comparative History*. New York: Harper & Row, 1966

BLACKMER, Donald and MILLIKAN, Max, eds. *The Emerging Nations*. New York: 1961

BRAIBANTI, Ralph, ed. *Administration and Economic Development in India*. Durham, NC: Duke University Press, 1963

BRAIBANTI, Ralph. *Political and Administrative Development*. Durham, NC: Duke University Press, 1969

BRAIBANTI, Ralph. and SPENGLER, Joseph, eds. *Tradition, Values, and Socio-Economic Development*. Durham, NC: Duke University Press, 1961

BRAKENSHA, David and HODGE, Peter. *Community Development*. San Francisco: Chandler Publishing Co, 1969

BUTWELL, Richard, ed. *Foreign Policy and the Developing Nations*. Lexington, Ky.: University of Kentucky Press, 1969

CAIDEN, Gerald. *Administrative Reform*. Chicago: Aldine Publishing Co, 1969

CLARK, Robert, Jr. *Development and Instability: Political Change in the Non-Western World*. Hinsdale: Dryden Press, 1974

COLE, Taylor and PIPER, Don, eds. *Post-Primary Education and Political Economic Development*. Cambridge: Cambridge University Press, 1964

COLEMAN, James. *Education and Political Development*. Princeton, NJ: Princeton University Press, 1965

CONRAD, Edward Smith, ed. *The Constitution of the United States*. New York: Barnes and Noble, 1972

DUCHACEK, Ivo. *Comparative Federalism: The Territorial Dimensions of Politics*. New York: Holt, Rinehart and Winston, 1970

EISENHOWER, Dwight D. *Waging Peace, 1956–1961*. New York: Doubleday and Company, Inc., 1965

EISENSTADT, S. N., ed. *Post-Tradition Societies*. New York: W. W. Norton & Company, 1972

EMERSON, Rupert. *From Empire to Nation: The Rise of Self-Assertion of Asian and African Peoples*. Cambridge, Mass.: Harvard University Press, 1960

ENLOE, Cynthia. *Ethnic Conflict and Political Development*. Boston: Little, Brown, 1973

FICKETT, Lewis, Jr., ed. *Problems of the Developing Nations*. New York: Thomas Y. Crowell Company, 1966

FINKLE, Jason and GABLE, Richard, eds. *Political Development and Social Change*. New York: John Wiley and Sons, 1966

FRIEDMAN, John. *Urbanization, Planning, and National Development*. Beverly Hills, Ca.: Sage Publications, 1973

AL GHONAMI, Muhammad. *Al-Ahkam Al-'Aama Fe Kanun Al-Umam (General Rules in the Law of Nations)*. Alexandria, Egypt: Al Ma'arif Publishing House, n.d

GOULET, Denis. *The Cruel Choice: A New Concept in the Theory of Development*. New York: Atheneum, 1971

HAMZA, Fouad. *Al-Bilad al-Arabiyyah al-Sa'udiyyah (The Country of Saudi Arabia)*. Riyadh: Maktabat al-Nasr al-Hadithah, 1968

HAMZA, Fouad. *Qalb Al-Jazira Al-Arabia (The Heart of the Arabs' Peninsula)*. Riyadh: Maktabat al-Nasr al-Hadithah, 1968

HARTZ, Louis, ed. *The Founding of New Societies*. New York: Harcourt, Brace and World, 1964

HEAPHY, James, ed. *Spatial Dimensions of Development Administration*. Durham, NC: Duke University Press, 1971

HITTI, Philip. *A Short History of Near East*. Princeton, NJ: D. Van Nostrand Company, Inc, 1966

HODGSON, Marshall. *The Venture of Islam*. 3 volumes. Chicago: The University of Chicago Press, 1974

HOWARTH, David. *The Desert King: A Life of Ibn Saud*. London: Collins, 1964

HUNTINGTON, Samuel. *Political Order in Changing Societies*. New Haven: Yale University Press, 1968

ILCHMAN, Warren and UPHOFF, Norman Thomas. *The Political Economy of Change*. Berkeley and Los Angeles: University of California Press, 1969

JACOBS, Norman. *Modernization without Development*. New York: Praeger Publishers, 1971

KEBSCHULL, Harvey, ed. *Politics in Transitional Societies*. New York: Appleton-Century-Crofts, 1968

KUBBAH, Abdulamir, *OPEC: Past and Present*. Vienna: Petro-Economic Research Center, 1974

LA PALOMBARA, Joseph, ed. *Bureaucracy and Political Development*. Princeton, NJ: Princeton University Press, 1963

LEKACHMAN, Robert and NOVACK, David. *Development and Society, The Dynamics of Economic Change*. New York: St. Martin's Press, 1964

LENCZOWSKI, George. *The Middle East in World Affairs*. 3rd ed. New York: Cornell University Press, 1962

LERNER, Daniel. *The Passing of Traditional Society*. New York: Free Press, 1958

LEVINE, Robert, ed. *Public Planning: Failure and Re-direction*. New York: Basic Books, 1972

LEWIS, Bernard. *Islam in History: Ideas, Men and Events in the Middle East*. London: Alcone Press, 1973

LEYS, Colin, ed. *Politics and Change in Developing Countries: Studies in the Theory and Practice of Development.* Cambridge, London: Cambridge University Press, 1969

LIPSET, Seymour M. *The First New Nation: The United States in Historical and Comparative Perspective.* New York: Basic Books, 1963

LIPSKY, George. *Saudi Arabia: Its People, Its Society, Its Culture.* New Haven: Hraf Press, 1959

LUFTI, Ashraf. *OPEC Oil.* Beirut: Middle East Research and Publishing Center, 1968. Arabic edition

LUFTI, Ashraf. *OPEC Oil.* Beirut: Middle East Research and Publishing Center, 1968

MEADOWS, Paul. *The Many Faces of Change: Exploration in the Theory of Social Change.* Cambridge, Mass.: Schenkman, 1971

MEHDEN, Fred von der. *Politics of the Developing Nations.* Englewood Cliffs, NJ: Prentice-Hall, 1964

MEIER, Richard. *Developmental Planning.* New York: McGraw-Hill, 1965

METCALF, John E. *Saudi Arabia: a New Economic Survey.* Riyadh: First National City Bank, n.d

MEULEN, Daniel van der. *The Wells of Ibn Sa'ud.* New York: Praeger, 1957

MILLIKAN, Max and BLACKMER, Donald, eds. *The Emerging Nations: Their Growth and United States Policy.* Boston: Little, Brown, 1961

MISHAN, Edward. *Technology and Growth: The Price We Pay.* New York: Praeger, 1969

MONROE, Elizabeth. *Philby of Arabia.* London: Faber, 1973

MONTGOMERY, John. *Technology and Civic Life: Making and Implementing Decisions.* Cambridge, Mass.: Massachusetts Institute of Technology Press, 1974

MONTGOMERY, John and SIFFIN, William, eds. *Approaches to Development, Politics, Administration and Change.* New York: McGraw-Hill, 1966

MORSE, Chandler; DOUBLAS, E.; BENT, Frederick T.; FRIEDLAND, William H.; LEWIS, John W.; and MACKLIN, David B. *Modernization by Design: Social Change in the Twentieth Century.* Ithaca, NY: Cornell University Press, 1969

MYRDAL, Gunnar. *Asian Drama: An Inquiry into the Poverty of Nations.* 3 volumes. New York: Pantheon Books, 1968

NETTL, J. P. *Political Mobilization: A Sociological Analysis of Method and Concepts.* New York: Basic Books, 1967

NISBET, Robert, ed. *Social Change and History: Aspects of the Western Theory of Development.* New York: Oxford University Press, 1969

NOLTE, Richard, ed. *The Modern Middle East.* New York: Atherton Press, 1963

NUTTING, Anthony. *The Arabs.* London: Hollis and Carter, 1964

ORGANSKI, A. F. K. *The Stages of Political Development*. New York: Alfred A. Knopf, 1967

PACKENHAM, Robert. *Liberal American and the Third World: Political Development Ideas in Foreign Aid and Social Science*. Princeton, NJ: Princeton University Press, 1973

PEARSON, Lester, *et al. Partners in Development: Report of the Commission on International Development*. New York: Praeger, 1969

PHILBY, H. St. John. *Arabia of the Wahhabis*. London: Constable and Company, Ltd, 1928

PHILBY, H. St. John. *The Heart of Arabia: A Record of Travel and Exploration*. 2 volumes. London: G. P. Putnam's Sons, 1923

PHILBY, H. St. John. *Saudi Arabia*. New York: Praeger, 1955

POATS, Rutherford. *Technology for Developing Nations: New Directions for United States Technical Assistance*. Washington, DC: Brookings Institution, 1972

PRYBLA, Jan and SHAFFER, Harry, eds. *From Underdevelopment to Affluence: Western, Soviet and Chinese Views*. New York: Appleton-Century-Crofts, 1968

PYE, Lucian, ed. *Aspects of Political Development*. Boston: Little, Brown, 1966

PYE, Lucian and VERBA, Sidney, eds. *Political Culture and Political Development*. Princeton, NJ: Princeton University Press, 1965

AL QAISSY, Mohyeidin. *Al' Mo'ushaf W'a Al Sa'yf (The Quran and the Sword)*. Riyadh: National Press, n.d

QUTB, Muhammed. *Islam the Misunderstood Religion*. Kuwait: Ministry of Awqaf and Islamic Affairs, 1964

RABUSHKA, Alvin and SHEPSLE, Kenneth. *Politics in Plural Societies: A Theory of Democratic Instability*. Columbus, Ohio: Merrill, 1972

RIGGS, Fred, ed. *Frontiers of Development Administration*. Durham, NC: Duke University Press, 1970

RIYHANI, Ameen. *Ibn Sa'oud of Arabia: His People and His Land*. London: Constable and Company, Ltd, 1928

ROSTOW, W. W. *Politics and the Stages of Growth*. London: Cambridge University Press, 1971

RUSTOW, Dankwart. *A World of Nations: Problems of Political Modernization*. Washington, DC: Brookings Institution, 1967

SAID, Abdul Aziz, ed. *Protagonists of Change: Subcultures in Development and Revolution*. Englewood Cliffs: Prentice-Hall, 1971

SAUNDERS, J. *A History of Medieval Islam*. New York: Barnes and Noble, 1965

SAYEGH, Kamal. *Oil and Arab Regional Development*. New York: Praeger,

SCHAFFER, Bernard. *Administration Training and Development: A Comparative Study of East Africa, Zambia, Pakistan and India.* New York: Praeger, 1974

SERJEANT, R. B., and BIDWELL, R. L., eds. *Arabian Studies.* 2 volumes. London: Hurst and Company, for the Middle East Centre, University of Cambridge

SHILS, Edward. *Political Development in the New States.* The Hague: Mouton, 1962

SILVERT, K. H., eds. *Expectant Peoples: Nationalism and Development.* New York: Random House, 1963

SMITH, Donald Eugene, ed. *Religion, Politics, and Social Change in the Third World: A Source Book.* New York: Free Press, 1971

STACEY, T. C. G., and others, ed. *The Kingdom of Saudi Arabia.* London: Stacey International, 1977

TACHAU, Frank, ed. *The Developing Nations: What Path to Modernization?* New York: Dodd, Mead, 1972

TULLIS, F. Lamond. *Politics and Social Change in Third World Countries.* New York: John Wiley and Sons, Inc, 1973

TWITCHELL, K. S. *Saudi Arabia, with an Account of the Development of Its Natural Resources.* Princeton, NJ: Princeton University Press, 1958

WALDO, Dwight, ed. *Temporal Dimensions of Development Administration.* Durham, NC: Duke University Press, 1970

WELCH, Claude, ed. *Political Modernization: A Reader in Comparative Political Change.* Belmont, Ca.: Wadsworth, 1967

The fifty-six issues, all published by SAGE Publications, Beverly Hills, California, in Volumes 1 to 5 covering 1970–1975, are as follows (listed serially rather than alphabetically):

NAMENWIRTH, J. Zvi and LASSWELL, Harold D. *The Changing Language of American Values: A Computer Study of Selected Party Platforms.* Vol. 1. 1970

JANDA, Kenneth. *A Conceptual Framework for the Comparative Analysis of Political Parties.* Vol. 1. 1970

THOMPSON, Kenneth. *Cross-National Voting Behavior Research: An Example of Computer-Assisted Multivariate Analysis of Attribute Data.* Vol. 1. 1970

QUANDT, William B. *The Comparative Study of Political Elites.* Vol. 1. 1970

HUDSON, Michael C. *Conditions of Political Violence and Instability: A Preliminary Test of Three Hypotheses.* Vol. 1. 1970

OZBUDUN, Ergun. *Party Cohesion in Western Democracies: A Causal Analysis.* Vol. 1. 1970

NELLIS, John R. *A Model of Development Ideology in Africa: Structure and Implications.* Vol. 1. 1970

KORNBERG, Allan; SMITH, Joel; and CLARKE, Harold F. *Semi-Careers in Political Work: The Dilemma of Party Organizations.* Vol. 1. 1970

GREENSTEIN, Fred I. and TARROW, Sidney. *Political Orientations of Children: The Use of a Semi-Projective Technique in Three Nations.* Vol. 1. 1970

RIGGS, Fred W. *Administrative Reform and Political Responsiveness: A Theory of Dynamic Balance.* Vol. 1. 1970

DONALDSON, Robert H. and WALLER, Derek J. *Stasis and Change in Revolutionary Elites: A Comparative Analysis of the 1956 Party Central Committees in China and the USSR.* Vol. 1. 1970

PRIDE, Richard A. *Origins of Democracy: A Cross-National Study of Mobilization, Party Systems, and Democratic Stability.* Vol. 1. 1970

VERBA, Sidney; NIE, Norman H.; and KIM, Jae-On. *The Modes of Democratic Participation: A Cross-National Comparison.* Vol. 2. 1971

SCHONFELD, William R. *Youth and Authority in France: A Study of Secondary Schools.* Vol. 2. 1971

BODENHEIMER, Susanne J. *The Ideology of Developmentalism: The American Paradigm-Surrogate for Latin American Studies.* Vol. 2. 1971

SIGELMAN, Lee. *Modernization and the Political System: A Critique and Preliminary Empirical Analysis.* Vol. 2. 1971

ECKSTEIN, Harry. *The Evaluation of Political Performance: Problems and Dimensions.* Vol. 2. 1971

GURR, Ted Robert and MCCLELLAND, Muriel. *Political Performance: A Twelve-Nation Study.* Vol. 2. 1971

MOY, Roland F. *A Comparative Simulation of Democratic Political Development: Tests of the Lipset and Moore Models.* Vol. 2. 1971

NARDIN, Terry. *Violence and the State: A Critique of Empirical Political Theory.* Vol. 2. 1971

ILCHMAN, Warren. *Comparative Public Administration and "Conventional Wisdom."* Vol. 2. 1971

BERTSCH, Gary K. *Nation-Building in Yugoslavia: A Study of Political Integration and Attitudinal Consensus.* Vol. 2. 1971

WILLEY, Richard J. *Democracy in the West German Trade Unions: A Reappraisal of the "Iron Law."* Vol. 2. 1971

ROGOWSKI, Ronald L. and WASSERSPRING, Lois. *Does Political Development Exist? Corporatism in Old and New Societies.* Vol. 2. 1971

DALY, William. *The Revolutionary: A Review and Synthesis.* Vol. 3. 1972

STONE, Carl. *Stratification and Political Change in Trinidad and Jamaica.* Vol. 3. 1972

GITELMAN, Zvi. *The Diffusion of Political Innovation: From Eastern Europe to the Soviet Union.* Vol. 3. 1972

CONRADT, David. *The West German Party System: An Ecological Analysis of Structure and Voting Behavior, 1961–1969.* Vol. 3. 1972

SCARRITT, James. *Political Development and Culture Change Theory: A Propositional Synthesis with Application to Africa.* Vol. 3. 1972

DALY HAYES, Margaret. *Policy Outputs in the Brazilian States 1940–1960: Political and Economic Correlates.* Vol. 3. 1972

STALLINGS, Barbara. *Economic Dependency in Africa and Latin America.* Vol. 3. 1972

MCCAMANT, John and TALBOT CAMPOS, Judith. *Cleavage Shift in Colombia: Analysis of the 1970 Elections.* Vol. 3. 1972

FIELD, G. Lowell and HIGLEY, John. *Elites in Developed Societies: Theoretical Reflections on an Initial Stage in Norway.* Vol. 3. 1972

SZYLIOWICZ, Joseph. *A Political Analysis of Student Activism: The Turkish Case.* Vol. 3. 1972

HARGROVE, Erwin. *Professional Roles in Society and Government: The English Case.* Vol. 3. 1972

BEALER, Robert and SUFRANKO, Andrew. *Unbalanced Modernization and Domestic Instability: A Comparative Analysis.* Vol. 3. 1972

CORNELIUS, Wayne. *Political Learning Among the Migrant Poor: The Impact of Residential Context.* Vol. 4. 1973

WHITE, James. *Political Implications of Cityward Migration: Japan as an Exploratory Test Case.* Vol. 4. 1973

STAUFFER, Robert. *Nation-Building in a Global Economy: The Role of the Multinational Corporation.* Vol. 4. 1973

MARTIN, Andrew. *The Politics of Economic Policy in the United States: A Tentative View from a Comparative Perspective.* Vol. 4. 1973

WELFLING, Mary B. *Political Institutionalization: Comparative Analyses of African Party System.* Vol. 4. 1973

AMES, Barry. *Rhetoric and Reality in a Militarized Regime: Brazil Since 1964.* Vol. 4. 1973

BROWNE, Eric. *Coalition Theories: A Logical and Empirical Critique.* Vol. 4. 1973

BARRERA, Mario. *Information and Ideology: A Case Study of Arturo Frandizi.* Vol. 4. 1973

KASTNER, Daniel; MURPHY, Walter; and TANENHAUS, Joseph. *Public Evaluations of Constitutional Courts: Alternative Explanations.* Vol. 4. 1973

LANE, Ruth. *Political Man: Toward a Conceptual Base.* Vol. 4. 1973

THOMPSON, William. *The Grievances of Military Coup-Makers.* Vol. 4. 1973

WEISSTAGEN, Patricia. *Chilean Universities: Problems of Autonomy and Dependence.* Vol. 4. 1973

KESSELMAN, Mark and ROSENTHAL, Donald. *Local Power and Comparative Politics*. Vol. 5. 1974

BERTSCH, Gary. *Value Change and Political Community: The Multinational Czechoslovak, Soviet, and Yugoslav Cases*. Vol. 5. 1974

SCHWEITZER, David. *Status Frustration and Conservatism in Comparative Perspective: The Swiss Case*. Vol. 5. 1974

HOLM, John. *Dimensions of Mass Involvement in Botswana Politics: A Test of Alternative Theories*. Vol. 5. 1974

GRAHAM, Lawrence. *Portugal: The Decline and Collapse of an Authoritarian Order*. Vol. 5. 1975

MIDDLEBANK, Kevin and SCOTT PALMER, David. *Military Government and Political Development: Lessons from Peru*. Vol. 5. 1975

ZUCKERMAN, Alan. *Political Clienteles in Power: Party Factions and Cabinet Coalitions in Italy*. Vol. 5. 1975

KAUTSKY, John. *Patterns of Modernizing Revolutions: Mexico and Soviet Union*. Vol. 5. 1975

Documents

Area Handbook for Saudi Arabia. 2nd ed. Washington, DC: US Government Printing Office, 1971

United States Government Printing Office. *The Budget of the United States Government*. Fiscal year 1973

Commission on Human Resources, National Research Council. *Summary Report 1974 Doctorate Recipients from United States Universities*. Washington, DC: National Academy of Science, 1975

Arabian American Oil Company. *Aramco Handbook: Oil and the Middle East*. Dhahran: Arabian American Oil Company, 1969

The Statute of the Organization of the Petroleum Exporting Countries. Vienna: Organization of Petroleum Exporting Countries, 1971

It' Fakiyat Mu' Nazimat Al' Aktar Al' Arabia Al Musadera Lil Petrol (Agreement: Organization of Arab Petroleum Exporting Countries). Kuwait: OAPEC, n.d

Munazimat Al' Aktar Al' Arabia Al Musadera Lil Petrol (Organization of Arab Petroleum Exporting Countries: A Brief Report on Its Activities, 1968–1973). Kuwait: Fahd Al Marzok Printing Press, 1974

Munazimat Al' Aktar Al' Arabia Al Musadera Lil Petrol (Organization of Arab Petroleum Exporting Countries). General Secretary First Annual Report. Kuwait: Dar Al' Ka'bass Printing, 1974

Ta'Krer A'n A'Zmat Al Ta'ka Wa Ta'wfer Ba'daiel Al N'aft (Report on Energy Crisis and Development of Alternative Sources of Petroleum). Kuwait: Dar Al' Ka'bass Printing, 1974

Agreement between the Saudi Arab Government and the Arabian American Oil Company. 2nd ed., Makkah: Government Press, 1384 AH/1964 AD

Agreement between the Saudi Arab Government and the Japan Petroleum Trading Company. Ltd. 2nd ed., Makkah: Government Press, 1384 AH/1964 AD

Constitution of the Council of Ministers and Constitution of the Division of the Council of Ministers. (Published in *Umm al-Qura* [*Government Official Gazette*]. No. 1508, 26 March 1954/21 Rajab 1373 AH) Dammam, Saudi Arabia, Language Services Section, Local Government Relations Department, Arabian American Oil Company, May 1954

Dalil Ma'had Al-Idara Al-Amah (Guide to the Institute of Public Administration). IPA Publication No. 22. Riyadh: Al-Ga'Zira Printing Corporation, 1975

General Agreement on Participation between the Government of Abu Dhabi-Saudi Arabia and Major Oil Companies. (Copy obtained from Saudi Ministry of Petroleum and Mineral Resources, Legal Department.) Riyadh: June 1975

Kingdom of Saudi Arabia. Central Planning Organization. *Development Plan, 1390 AH (1970).* Dammam: Al-Mutawa Press Co, 1970

Kingdom of Saudi Arabia. Central Planning Organization. *Report of the Central Planning Organization 1394 AH–1974 AD.* Jiddah: Banani Printers, 1974

Kingdom of Saudi Arabia. Central Planning Organizaticn. *General Personnel Bureau. Dalil Diwan Al-Muwazafen Al-A'am (Guide to General Personnel Bureau).* Riyadh: Al-Jazira Printing, 1975

Kingdom of Saudi Arabia. Central Planning Organization. Industrial Studies and Development Center. *Guide to Industrial Investment in Saudi Arabia.* 4th ed. Jiddah: Daral Asfahan & Co (Al Asfahani Publishing Co), 1974 AD/1394 AH

Kingdom of Saudi Arabia. Central Planning Organization. Ministry of Defense. *Al-Ta'liem Fe al-Kowat Al Arabia Al Saudia (Education in the Saudi Arabian Armed Forces),* 1st ed. Riyadh: The Army Press, 1974 AD/ 1394 AH

Kingdom of Saudi Arabia. Central Planning Organization. Ministry of Education. Center of Documentary Education and Statistics (Statistical Section). *Dalil Rasael Al-Doctora Wa Al-Majestar Lil Mowatinin Al-Saudien, 1348–1394 AH (Guide to Doctoral and Master's Degrees of Saudi Citizens. 1927–1974).* Riyadh: May 1975

Kingdom of Saudi Arabia. Central Planning Organization. Ministry of Education. Statistics, Research and Educational Documents Unit (Statistical) Unit). 6th issue. *Educational Statistics Yearbook 1971–1972.* Riyadh: National Offset Printing Press, 1972

Kingdom of Saudi Arabia. Central Planning Organization. Ministry of Finance and National Economy. Central Department of Statistics. *Statistical Yearbook, 1393 AH/1973 AD.* 9th issue. Riyadh: National Offset Printing Press, 1973

Kingdom of Saudi Arabia. Central Planning Organization. Ministry of the Interior. General Directorate of Passport and Nationality. *Pilgrims' Statistics for 1384 AH/1964 AD* Riyadh: 1964

Kingdom of Saudi Arabia. Central Planning Organization. *Pilgrims' Statistics for 1385 AH/1965 AD* Riyadh: 1965

Kingdom of Saudi Arabia. Central Planning Organization. *Pilgrims' Statistics for 1386 AH/1966 AD* Riyadh: 1966

Kingdom of Saudi Arabia. Central Planning Organization. *Pilgrims' Statistics for 1387 AH/1967 AD* Riyadh: 1967

Kingdom of Saudi Arabia. Central Planning Organization. *Pilgrims' Statistics for 1388 AH/1968 AD* Riyadh: 1968

Kingdom of Saudi Arabia. Central Planning Organization. *Pilgrims' Statistics for 1389 AH/1969 AD* Riyadh: 1969

Kingdom of Saudi Arabia. Central Planning Organization. *Pilgrims' Statistics for 1390 AH/1970 AD* Riyadh: 1970

Kingdom of Saudi Arabia. Central Planning Organization. *Pilgrims' Statistics for 1391 AH/1971 AD* Riyadh: 1971

Kingdom of Saudi Arabia. Central Planning Organization. *Pilgrims' Statistics for 1392 AH/1972 AD* Riyadh: 1972

Kingdom of Saudi Arabia. Central Planning Organization. *Pilgrims' Statistics for 1393 AH/1973 AD* Riyadh: 1973

Kingdom of Saudi Arabia. Central Planning Organization. *Pilgrims' Statistics for 1394 AH/1974 AD* Riyadh: 1974

Kingdom of Saudi Arabia. Ministry of Labor and Social Affairs. *Center for Training and Applied Research in Community Development.* Riyadh: Publication of Ministry of Labor and Social Affairs and the UNDP Office, May, 1973

Kingdom of Saudi Arabia. Ministry of Labor and Social Affairs. Ministry of Petroleum and Mineral Resources. Economics Department. *Petroleum Statistical Bulletin,* No. 2. Riyadh: 1971

Kingdom of Saudi Arabia. Ministry of Labor and Social Affairs. *Petroleum Statistical Bulletin,* No. 5. Riyadh: 1974

Kingdom of Saudi Arabia. Ministry of Labor and Social Affairs. *Petroleum Statistical Bulletin,* No. 6. Riyadh: 1975

University of Riyadh. Studies and Information Department. *Al-Ke'tab Al-E'Hssaie (Statistical Book).* 1974 AD/1394 AH Riyadh: National Offset Printing Press, 1974

University of Riyadh. Studies and Information Department. *A Statistical Handbook: A Self-Study Special Document, April, 1975-Rabiel, 1395*. Riyadh: University of Riyadh Press, 1975

The Holy Qu'ran. Text, translation and commentary A. Yusuf Ali. Beirut: Dar Al'Arabia, 1968. Copy approved by the Muslim World League, Secretariat General, Makkah, Mukarramah

Articles

ANDERSON, Arnold C. "Economic Development and Post-Primary Education," in Don C. Piper and Taylor Cole, eds., *Post-Primary Education and Economic Development* (Durham, NC: Duke University Press, 1964), pp.3–26

BENDA, Harry. "Non-Western Intelligentsias as Political Elites," in David E. Novack and Robert Lekachman, eds., *Development and Society: The Dynamics of Economic Change* (New York: St. Martin's Press, 1964), pp. 406–421

BRAIBANTI, Ralph. "External Inducement of Political-Administrative Development: An Institutional Study," in Ralph Braibanti, ed., *Political and Administrative Development* (Durham, NC: Duke University Press, 1969), pp. 3–106

COLEMAN, James S. "Introduction to Part III," in James S. Coleman, ed., *Education and Political Development* (Princeton, NJ: Princeton University Press, 1965), pp. 225–233

ENDERS, Thomas O., "OPEC and the Industrial Countries," *Foreign Affairs* 53 (July 1975): 605–624

FARMAIAN, Khodadad Farman; GUTOWSKI, Armin; OKITA, Saburo; ROOSA, Robert V., and WILSON, Carroll L., "How Can the World Afford OPEC Oil?" *Foreign Affairs* 53 (January 1975): 201–222

"The Gazelles and the Lions," *The Economist* 249 (November 17, 1973): 14

HARRINGTON, Charles W., "The Saudi Arabian Council of Ministers," *The Middle East Journal* 12 (1958): 1–19

JOHNSON, Brian G., "Editor's Foreword," *Journal of International Affairs* 19 (1965): ix–x

NAWWAB, Ibrahim Ismail, "The Hajj; An Appreciation," *Aramco World Magazine* 25 (1974): 12–13

NOLTE, Richard H., "From Nomad Society to New Nation: Saudi Arabia," in K. H. Silvert, ed., *Expectant Peoples* (New York: Random House, 1963), pp. 77–88

SANGE, Richard H., "Ibn Saud's Program for Arabia," *The Middle East Journal* 1 (1947): 180–190

SOLAIM, Soliman A., "Saudi Arabia's Judicial System," *Middle East Journal* 25 (1971): 403–407

"Saudi Arabia: Kingdom's Foreign Policy Remains Unchanged," *The Link*. Americans for Middle East Understanding, 1975 (Summer)

Unpublished Material

BEAN, Lee L. "Demographic Changes in Iran, Pakistan and the Gulf Area with Particular Emphasis on the Developing Labor Force Need." Paper submitted to the International Conference on Islam, Pakistan, Iran and the Gulf States, Bellagio Conference and Study Center, Lake Como, Italy, August 13–18, 1975, pp. 1–38

BRAIBANTI, Ralph. "Recovery of Islamic Identity in Global Perspective." Paper presented to International Conference on Islam, Pakistan, Iran and the Gulf States, Bellagio Conference and Study Center, Lake Como, Italy, August 13–18, 1975, pp. 1–48

BRAIBANTI, Ralph. "Saudi Arabia: Contextual Considerations." Report submitted to the Ford Foundation, Beirut, Lebanon, August, 1972 (typewritten), pp. 1–21

KUTBI, Al-Sayed Hassan (former Minister of Pilgrimage and Endowment), "How the Free World Should Look at the Religion of Islam." Paper delivered in South Korea in his official capacity (copy obtained by author in May, 1975, from the former Minister), pp. 1–16

SOLAIM, Soliman A., "Constitutional and Judicial Organization in Saudi Arabia." Unpublished Ph.D. dissertation. The John Hopkins University, 1970

Periodicals

Al-Hawadith. Beirut. 1975
American Political Science Review. Menasha, Wisconsin. 1950–June, 1974
Aramco World Magazine. New York, New York. 1974
Comparative Political Studies. Beverly Hills, California. 1968–1974
Comparative Politics. New York, New York. 1968–1974
The Economist. London. 1950–1974
The Journal of Developing Areas. Carbondale, Illinois. 1950–1974
The Journal of Near Eastern Studies. Chicago, Illinois. 1950–1975
The Middle East Journal. Washington, District of Columbia. 1950–1974
Middle Eastern Affairs. New York, New York. 1950–1974
World Politics. Princeton, New Jersey. 1950–1974

Newspapers

Al-Ahram. Cairo
Al-Riyadh. Riyadh
Okaz. Jiddah
The Wall Street Journal. New York

Interviews

SHEIKH ABD AL-RAHMAN ABA AL-KHAIL, Former Minister of Labor and Social Affairs. Riyadh: May 1975

DR. ABDUL RAHMAN AL-SHEIKH, Saudi Minister of Agriculture. Riyadh: June 1975

MR. MOSTAFA BADAW, Programs Assistant, United Nations Development Program, Riyadh Office. Riyadh: May 1975

DR. FAYZ BADR, Saudi Vice-President of Central Planning Organization. Riyadh: May 1975

SHEIKH MUHAMMAD AL-HARAKAN, Former Saudi Minister of Justice. Riyadh: May 1975 (currently, Head of Saudi Port Authority)

DR. SALAH HOUTAR, Supervisor of Department of Studies and Information, Riyadh University. Riyadh: May 1975

MR. SOLIMAN AL JA'BHAN, Director of Agency of Social Affairs, Saudi Ministry of Labor and Social Affairs. Riyadh: June 1975

SHEIKH ABDULLAH KAMEL, Former Director General of De'wan of the Saudi Council of Ministers. Riyadh: May 1975

AL SA'YED HASSAN KUTBI, Former Saudi Minister of Pilgrimage and Endowment. Riyadh: May 1975

DR. ALI MAHJOUB, Chief Adviser and Superviser of the Training Center in Al-Dir'iyah. Riyadh: June 1975

AL-SAYED HASHIM MATTOUK, Saudi Deputy Minister of Interior for Passports and Nationality. Riyadh: June 1975

MR. MUHAMMAD MUFTI, Director of the General Administration of Saudi Central Planning Organization. Riyadh: May 1975

DR. IBRAHIM OBAIED, Director of the Office of Saudi Minister of Petroleum and Mineral Resources. Riyadh: June 1975

DR. ABD AL-'AZIZ AL O'HAL, Director of the Department of Planning and Budgeting, Saudi Ministry of Defense. Riyadh: June 1975

MR. MUSTAFA QASSTY, Director of Employees' Affairs, Saudi Ministry of Communications. Riyadh: June 1975

AKEL FADL'ALLAH AL Q'UWAIYI, Director of Public Relations Department, Saudi Ministry of Defense. Riyadh: June 1975

DR. SOLIMAN A. SOLAIM, Saudi Minister of Commerce. Riyadh: May 1975

MR. OSAMA TARABOULSI, Economics Department, Saudi Ministry of Petroleum and Mineral Resources. Riyadh: May 1975

DR. FREDERICK THOMAS, Deputy Regional Representative of United Nations Development Program for Saudi Arabia and the Gulf Area, Riyadh Office. Riyadh: June 1975

Index

Page numbers in *italics* refer to charts or tables, those in **bold** refer to illustrations or maps. **Bold** roman numerals refer to plates facing p. 160 f.f.
Dates in brackets are years AD, 'r' before this date means 'ruled'